Getting Started in
Options

The *Getting Started In* Series

Getting Started in
Options
THIRD EDITION

Michael C. Thomsett

John Wiley & Sons, Inc.

New York • Chichester • Weinheim • Brisbane • Singapore • Toronto

Copyright © 1997 by Michael C. Thomsett
Published by John Wiley & Sons, Inc.

Library of Congress Cataloging-in-Publication Data:
Thomsett, Michael C.
    Getting started in options / Michael C. Thomsett — 3rd ed.
        p.   cm.—(Getting started in)
    Includes index.
    ISBN 0–471–17758–X (pbk. : alk. paper)
    1. Stock options.   2. Options (Finance).   I. Title.   II. Series.
    HG6042.T46   1997
    332.63˙228—dc21   96–49244

Printed in the United States of America

10 9 8 7 6 5 4 3 2

Contents

Acknowledgments

I want to thank the many readers of previous editions who took the time to write and offer suggestions for improving this book. Their letters have helped add to the clarity of examples, definitions, and explanations, which ultimately helps all other readers.

Getting Started in
Options

An Investment with Many Faces

Most people recognize and understand some types of investments: Stocks, mutual funds, and real estate, for example, are widely popular forms of investment, and so many people take part in them in one form or another that a common knowledge exists that is easily available. These investments are generally accepted as good investments engendering a sense of legitimacy among investors. When first thinking about investing, people usually turn to the stock market and consider buying stocks directly or through mutual funds. Some new investors are so comfortable with what they believe about the stock market that they are unaware of its risks. Those risks can be learned and managed, however, by using the services of a stockbroker or financial advisor.

When we buy our own homes, we buy security and long-term appreciation. That is also a form of investment. Because home buyers are so directly involved in the process—looking at open houses, studying listings, talking to agents—the risks are better understood and appreciated by the homeowner/investor. Like new stock market investors, new real estate investors can educate themselves by asking questions, reading a broad range of books and articles on the topic, and working with an agent.

Learning about markets and risks makes new investors smarter and improves their chances for success. In those broadly popular markets of stocks and real estate, a lot of help is available, so the newcomer who wants to learn has little trouble finding information. The investor who develops understanding can enter specific markets with relative ease. The popularity of well understood markets has led to the availability of information; and the availability of information makes it easier for more new investors to enter the market. This is a healthy process that leads to a robust, broadly represented market. The more the public knows, the better it is for everyone who places money at risk.

Just as well-informed investors make markets healthier and better for everyone involved, poorly-informed investors make markets unhealthy and dangerous. When investors do not understand markets, those markets cannot thrive. Successful markets depend more than anything else on informed, educated investors who know the risks they face and who understand not only the potential for profit but also the potential for loss. For example, smart investors in the stock market have profit goals *and* bail-out points (the point at which they will cut their losses). They know realistically that they stand to win or to lose, and they approach risk with a complete understanding of how much they can afford. They diversify among several investments rather than risking everything in one place. And they educate themselves by reading and keeping up to date with changing trends.

Some markets are too exotic for mainstream tastes. They may contain risks that are too high, require too much capital, or depend on too much technical knowledge for the average investor. Only a small number of knowledgeable specialists can participate successfully in such markets.

Certain markets fall somewhere in between these extremes. They are not broadly understood like stocks or real estate. Yet, with knowledge, many investors can find ways to participate profitably and manage risks. Typically, such markets are poorly understood by the investing public. From a lack of understanding, the risks in a market may be exaggerated or overstated; the complexity may be emphasized, when in fact it is only a matter of terminology that confuses or frightens would-be investors.

The options market is one such market. It is not broadly understood, and most investors who have heard about options see this market as highly risky and dangerous. Lack of understanding creates fear and apprehension, and appropriately so. As a premise to this book, the following general rule for investing is stated:

No one should ever invest in *any* market without first becoming educated as to that market's risks, opportunities, rules of trading, and terminology.

One of the guidelines of investment advisors is called the "know your customer" rule. Stockbrokers and other advisors are supposed to know the customer's level of sophistication, what that person can afford, and what risks he or she is willing and able to accept. The same approach should be taken by the customer. Use the "know your investment" rule *before* you invest. And if you use the services of a stockbroker or other financial advisor, you should also apply the "know your advisor" rule. Make sure your advisor knows a market before giving you advice.

The "know your investment" rule is a good place to start. When you hear the word *options*, what is your reaction? Some people equate options with complexity and risk, and reject the whole market because they believe it is only appropriate for speculators willing to take very high risks. This is not necessarily true. Options might be highly speculative or very conservative, depending on the strategy employed. The options market can be used in many ways, and includes many different strategies. Options can be used to hedge other investment positions, or as insurance to reduce possible losses. You will be able to overcome apprehension about options by gaining knowledge about the range of investment possibilities. Learning about a market leads to informed judgments.

If, upon learning about options, you decide this market is not right for you, that will be an informed judgment rather than just an opinion. Rejecting an investment market without first learning what risks and ranges of possibilities are involved could be a lost opportunity. Any market could be beneficial to you; how will you know unless you investigate it?

Options were first traded publicly in 1973. The stock market has been around for centuries in one form or another, so that the rules of trading have been refined and fine-tuned over a great many years. However, the options market has had a relatively short trading and performance history. This disparity makes it difficult to compare options with the stock market. You might ask, "If options are not as risky as I've heard, why don't more people take part in options trading?" The answer is twofold. First, the relatively brief existence of the market itself has kept it out of the public eye. Second, while the various strategies involved in options trading are not as technically complicated as many people think, the language of options is highly specialized. When language is overly technical, the average person feels alienated and intimidated by it. Unfortunately, the terminology in the options market is not user-friendly at all. One of the main features of this book is that it carefully attempts to make clear the *ideas* behind the terminology through examples and explanations.

Because options are relatively new, we cannot see what would have happened to options investments in the crash of 1929, nor how options investors would have fared in the bull market of the 1950s. We can only apply an understanding of options to the market as we see it today. Most investors can relate to this. If your parents invested in stocks, you probably have a well developed knowledge about that market and an opinion about risks that is based on your parents' experience in that market. But it is less likely that your parents invested in the options market over many years.

Options today serve a number of different purposes. This book is concerned with the strategic uses of stock options that are traded publicly (i.e., on the public exchanges), either for speculation or for one of the more conservative and less risky purposes many people have learned. On the speculative side, options are pure risks, a form of betting on a stock's future movement. On the conservative extreme of the spectrum, options can be employed to insure against losses in a stock investment, by hedging a position. In between these two extremes, a broad range of possible strategies and combinations of strategies can be employed. To decide how you might best use options in your investment portfolio—or to determine first whether options are even appropriate in your situation—you need to go through a four-step process of evaluation:

1. Master the terminology of this highly specialized market. Recognize that it is not the complexity of the investment, but rather the complexity of its language, that makes it difficult for new investors to understand what is going on. The language of options is foreign even to seasoned stock market investors, because many ideas utilized in the options market are not common to the stock market. Options traders and experts have developed a shorthand language of their own in order to quickly communicate with one another.

2. Study the options market in terms of risk. Break down each proposed idea and strategy (or combination of strategies) in terms of the risk level you are willing and able to assume for yourself. Don't expect one profile to fit everyone. Your situation is unlike anyone else's, so a proposed strategy that is right for one investor is not necessarily right for you. Many investors and speculators use a broad range of strategies in their portfolios that involve options, and not always in the same way. Because of the wide range of possible uses for options, it's likely that one investor will find dissimilar uses for options, often opposing strategies at the same time. Because it's possible to take opposing positions in stocks, for example, it is just as realistic to run into a situation in which opposing option strategies will be required.

This means that a broad range of risk is sometimes necessary as well, as you might imagine. The traditional investor in the stock market buys shares, holds them, and eventually sells them. However, some investors "go short," meaning they *sell* shares of stock that they have not yet purchased. In that situation, a different risk profile is undertaken. Certain option strategies apply and can be helpful to short sellers in the market. The broader a stock investment strategy, the broader the likely and corresponding option strategy will be as well. The same argument goes for risk. If you expand your range of stock market strategies, you broaden your risks.

You will need to determine whether you are a high-rolling speculator willing to take high risks or a very conservative investor who wants to insure against every possible unanticipated event. Chances are you're somewhere in between. Just as you carefully decide how to buy and sell stocks as defined by acceptable risks, you will need to use the same range of risk identification for options.

3. Observe the market. Learn how to read option listings as well as the stock listings in the newspapers. Track the way options rise or fall over time, and note how option pricing reacts to price and volume changes in the broader market. What factors besides stock prices affect option values? When does time work for you and when does it work against you? By identifying the important factors influencing option values, you will be equipped to evaluate each option strategy and select the one that best suits you.

4. Set a risk standard for yourself. This is the most critical step in any form of investing. You should have specific goals, because without goals you cannot know when to buy or sell, why you're investing in the first place, or even whether a particular strategy is appropriate. Everything is defined by goals, and goals dictate appropriate timing and use of strategies. The decisions you make and how well they are clarified by standards and goals ultimately determine your success as an investor.

This four-part process should apply to all forms of investing, not just to the options market. Even when you buy shares of stock, the same four steps are useful and important. Successful investing depends on developing a thorough knowledge of how the market works and what levels of risk are involved. After identifying risks, the important step of tracking the market and matching changing circumstances to personal goals defines the difference between successful investors and those who are sometimes just lucky.

You have a tremendous advantage over the option investor and speculator of the mid-1970s. Today, relatively inexpensive computer programs and wide use of on-line modem access to the floor of an exchange have made option investing instantaneous, simple, and affordable. With access to information once available only to stockbrokers, you can place orders 24 hours a day, track your option investment by the minute if you want to, and enjoy the same advantages previously available to only a few people on the trading floor in a major exchange.

Not very many years ago, all forms of stock market investing were inconvenient and remote, meaning that a delay of from 15 minutes up to an hour or more was not uncommon between the time of decision and execution of an order. Investment volume depended upon the limited ability of a finite number of brokers to react to orders. Today, though, you have computerized power and access unimagined 20 years ago. In addition, until recently only a few specialists even remotely understood the options market. Today, this market is growing in popularity as automation makes it available and practical for ever-growing numbers of investors. As the popularity and applications grow, so do the opportunities.

The technical convenience is not enough. Your broker should be expert in options trading, and should be able to steer you to the right strategies in line with your goals. If you get to the point of being proficient enough to make your own decisions without help from a stockbroker, you will save a lot of expense by trading through a discount broker. Be sure to comparison shop so that you will get the best possible rates for the type of trading and the frequency of transactions you are undertaking. When working with a broker, remember that the broker's livelihood is based on commissions. A broker might not be as competent in the options market as you would hope. If you trade often, you might become more knowledgeable than the broker, and it will be time to move on. In this highly specialized market, you should be willing to take responsibility for making your own decisions. Even when working directly with a broker, it is your money and ultimately your decision how to invest.

This book is designed to introduce you to this highly specialized market, to show how the opportunities can be best put to use, and to help you define your personal investment goals. The book does not recommend any one course of action, nor even that you should become an options investor. Everyone is different. To make a broad assumption and a single recommendation would violate the very principle upon which this book is designed and presented. The book does attempt to carefully and completely define terminology, to explain options investing in an order that makes sense, and to present strategies that you might be able to put to work for yourself. Each chapter takes a step-by-step approach to its topic, combining terminology with practical examples, and, when helpful, by presenting likely outcomes on a graph. The purpose in this approach is to help you to comprehend in real terms exactly what a particular strategy achieves, and how much risk—or what range of risk—is involved. The risk profiles show maximum potential profit and loss in each strategy through identification of "profit zones" and "loss zones."

In many cases, the discussion involves the cost of an option, sale price, and profit, but excludes calculation of brokerage and trading commissions. Every time you buy or sell options, you are charged a transaction fee, just as you are charged for buying and selling shares of stock. This factor is left out of the examples for two practical reasons. First, every brokerage rate differs, so an example won't be representative in every case. Second, commission rates vary by the volume involved. For example, the per-option commission will normally be higher for a single option trade than it would be for a set of 5, 10, or 20 options. As a general rule, the rate decreases as more units and more dollars are involved. As you compare the examples in this book to your own case, be sure to modify the assumed ranges of profit or loss to allow for brokerage commissions as they will be applied to you.

In order for any strategy to work, it must be appropriate, comfortable, and affordable. No one idea works for every investor, and options are no exception to this rule. No matter how easy, practical, or foolproof an idea seems in print, and no matter how well it works out on paper, remember that any investment should feel right. It should be both profitable *and* enjoyable for you. Too many would-be investors make their decisions on the basis of advice from others—friends, family members, brokers, or books—without really researching on their own. They forget the importance of research and practical application of information in a *real* situation, using *real* money and taking *real* risks. Analysis by itself is not enough, while action by itself is poor planning.

You will have the best chance of success by first gathering the facts and information you need to make an intelligent decision. Mere profit is not worth the effort if it is obtained at the expense of your peace of mind and personal satisfaction. Success in the market is a combination of personal accomplishment and financial gain. Part of the accomplishment is the satisfaction of mastering a difficult and complex market to the extent that you are in control. By applying information to your own situation, you will have mastered one of the many possible avenues to becoming a successful and knowledgeable investor.

Chapter

Calls and Puts

There are only two overall methods of investing—equity and debt. An *equity investment* is purchase of part ownership in a company. The best-known example of this is the purchase of stock through the stock market. Each *share* of stock represents part of the capital, or ownership in the company. The second broad form is a *debt investment,* also called a debt "instrument." A debt investment is a loan to the company, and the best-known example is the bond. Corporations, cities and states, and the federal government finance their operations through bond issues, and investors in bonds are lending money to the issuer.

When you buy 100 shares of stock, you are in complete control of that investment. You decide how long to hold the shares, and when to sell. Stocks give you a tangible value, because they represent part ownership in the company. Owning stock entitles you to dividends and gives you the right to vote in matters before the board of directors. If the stock rises in value, you will gain a profit. If you wish, you can hold that stock for many years, even for your whole life. Stocks, because they have tangible value, can be traded to other people or used as collateral to borrow money.

When you own a bond, you also have tangible value because you are a lender. You have a contract with the issuer, who promises to pay you interest and to repay

equity investment
an investment in the form of part ownership, such as the purchase of shares of stock in a corporation

share
a unit of ownership in the capital of a corporation

debt investment
an investment in the form of loan made to earn interest, such as the purchase of a bond

that loan by a specific due date. Like stocks, bonds can be transferred or used as collateral. They also rise and fall in value based on their interest rate in comparison to changed rates in today's market.

The purpose of this very brief rundown is to introduce you to a *third* method of investing. Most investors take comfort in the fact that stocks and bonds are tangible and contain tangible features. They earn dividends or interest and they don't expire when a deadline is passed. For most investors, the idea of putting money in an intangible investment that literally evaporates upon the passing of a deadline is beyond consideration. Imagine an intangible investment that is guaranteed to be worthless—in fact, nonexistent—in less than one year. To make it even more interesting, imagine that the value of this intangible investment will decline just because time goes by.

These are some of the features of options, the subject of this book. And although at first glance it seems that intangible investments like options are too risky and of questionable value, you should read on. This book shows you a variety of very interesting uses to which options can be put. Not all methods of investing in options are as risky as you might think. Some are quite conservative. However you might use options in the future, the many strategies available certainly make them one of the more interesting ways to invest.

An *option* is a contract providing you with the right to execute a stock transaction, that is, to buy or to sell 100 shares of stock at a specified, fixed price and by a specified date in the future. When you own an option, you do not own any equity in the stock, and you don't have a debt position either; you only have the contractual right to buy or to sell 100 shares of a company's stock. Since you can always buy or sell 100 shares anyway, you might ask, "Why do I need to purchase an option to gain that right?" The answer is that the option fixes the price of the 100 shares. That is the key to everything. Prices are dynamic; they rise and they fall, sometimes substantially. The option freezes the price as far as you are concerned, so that no matter how much movement occurs in the stock's

option
the right to buy or to sell 100 shares of stock at a specified, fixed price and by a specified date in the future

value, you as an option owner have fixed the price of your purchase (or sale), and that fixed price determines the option's value as time goes by.

Some restrictions come with the option. Such a right is not offered indefinitely, but only exists for a few months. When the deadline has passed, the option is worthless. So the value of the option tends to decrease as the deadline approaches. In addition, each option applies only to 100 shares of stock, no more and no less. Stock transactions normally occur in blocks divisible by 100, and that has become the standard, acceptable trading unit of publicly traded shares of stock. You have the right in the market to buy any number of shares you want, but you are charged a higher commission when you buy fewer than 100 shares (called an "odd lot").

There are two types of options. First is the *call* option, which grants its owner the right to buy 100 shares of stock in a company on which the option is given. Every option is related specifically to the stock of one company specifically, and to its per-share price. When you buy an option, it is as though someone is saying to you, "I will allow you to buy 100 shares of this company's stock, at a specified price per share, at any time between now and a date in the future. For that privilege, I expect you to pay me a price."

That price is determined by how attractive an offer is being made. If the price per share of stock specified in the option is attractive based on the current price of the stock, the cost will be higher. The more attractive the fixed option price per share, the higher the cost of the option. Each option's value changes according to the changes in the price of the stock. If a stock's value goes up, the value of a call option will go up as well. And if the stock's market price falls, the call option's value will fall as well. When an investor buys a call, and the stock's market value rises after the purchase, the investor profits because that call becomes more valuable. The value of the option is directly related to the value of the stock.

The second type is the *put* option. This contract grants its owner the right to sell 100 shares of a specified company's stock in the future. When you buy a put, it is

call
an option acquired by a buyer or granted by a seller, to buy 100 shares of stock at a fixed price

put
an option acquired by a buyer or granted by a seller, to sell 100 shares of stock at a fixed price

as though someone said to you, "I will allow you to sell 100 shares of this company's stock, at a specified price per share, at any time between now and a date in the future. For that privilege, I expect you to pay me a price."

Remember, the buyer of a call option hopes the stock's value will rise. If that happens, the call becomes more valuable. The put buyer hopes the opposite, believing that the value of the stock will fall. If that happens, the put becomes more valuable. Calls and puts are opposites, and investors in each have opposite beliefs in the stock's future price movement.

If an option buyer—dealing either in calls or in puts—is correct about the future movement in a stock's *market value*, then that investor earns a profit. When it comes to options, an additional factor has to be remembered: the movement in the stock's market value has to occur by the deadline attached to every option. In other words, you might be right about a stock's prospects in the long term, but options relate only to the stock's short-term value. This is a critical point: Options are finite. Unlike stocks, which you can hold as long as you want, or bonds, which are paid by a due date, options cease to exist and they lose all value by a short-term deadline. Because the option ceases to exist altogether within a few months, time is a determining factor in whether or not a buyer will have a profit or a loss.

Why does the option's market value change when the stock's price moves up or down? First of all, the option is only a right, and has no tangible value of its own. That right is related to a specific stock *and* to a specified price, but only for a limited amount of time. Consequently, if the timing of the purchase is poor—meaning the stock's movement doesn't happen by the deadline—then the buyer of a call or a put will not be able to earn a profit.

When you buy a call, it is as though you are saying, "I am willing to pay the price being asked to acquire a contractual right. That right enables me to buy 100 shares of stock at the specified fixed price per share, and I can buy those shares at that price at any time between now and the specified deadline." If the stock's market price

---

market value

the value of an investment at any given time or date; the amount a buyer is willing to pay to acquire an investment, and that a seller is also willing to receive to transfer the same investment rises above the fixed price indicated in the option contract, the call becomes more valuable. Imagine that you buy a call option giving you the right to buy 100 shares at the price of $80 per share. Before the deadline, though, the stock's market price rises to $95 per share. As the owner of the call option, you have the right to buy those 100 shares at $15 lower than current market value.

The same scenario can be applied to put buying, but with the stock moving in the opposite direction. When you buy a put, it is as though you are saying, "I am willing to pay the asked price to buy a contractual right. That right enables me to sell 100 shares of stock at the indicated price per share, at any time between now and the specified deadline." If the stock's price falls below that level, you will be able to sell 100 shares *above* current market value. Using the same example as before, let's say you buy a put option giving you the right to sell 100 shares at $80 per share. Before the deadline, the stock's market value falls to $70 per share. As the owner of the put option, you have the right to sell 100 shares at $10 per share higher than current market value. As you can see, the potential value of options is in the contractual right they provide. This contract right is so important that each option is referred to as a *contract*.

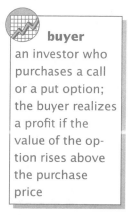

contract
a single option, the agreement providing a buyer with the rights the option grants (Those rights include identification of the stock, the cost of the option, the date the option will expire, and the fixed price per share of the stock to be bought or sold under the right of the option.)

THE CALL OPTION

A call is the right to buy 100 shares of stock at a fixed price per share, any time between purchase of the call and the specified deadline in the future. The time is limited. As a call *buyer* you acquire the right and as a call *seller* you grant the rights in the option to someone else. (See Figure 1.1.)

Let's walk through the illustration and apply both buying and selling to call options:

1. *Buyer of a call:* When you buy a call, you hope the stock will rise in value, because that will cause the call's value to rise as well. As a result, it can be sold for more money than the original purchase price.

buyer
an investor who purchases a call or a put option; the buyer realizes a profit if the value of the option rises above the purchase price

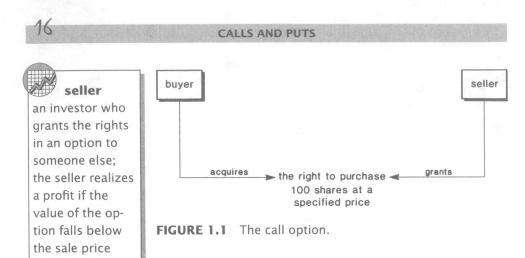

seller
an investor who grants the rights in an option to someone else; the seller realizes a profit if the value of the option falls below the sale price

FIGURE 1.1   The call option.

2. *Seller of a call:* When you sell a call, you hope the stock will fall in value, because that will cause the call to fall in value as well. As a result, it can be repurchased for less money than the original sale price.

In the stock market, you can sell options (and stocks) before you buy. This idea—being a seller *before* buying, is difficult to grasp at first. However, it is not unique to the options market. In fact, calls are used in many ways, but are not always referred to as calls.

Example: You own a house and use it as a rental property. You lease it to a tenant who expresses an interest in buying it, but who does not have enough for a down payment. So you enter into a contract called a lease with an option to buy (or, "lease option"). The contract breaks down a monthly payment into two parts. First is the monthly rent, and second is a partial payment toward the down payment to purchase the house. The future price of the house is fixed at $125,000, but the tenant agrees to close the deal within three years. If the tenant decides not to buy the house within that term, the accumulated deposit will be returned. However, as long as the lease option contract is in effect, you agree that you will not sell the house to anyone else.

Three years later, real estate prices have risen dramatically and that house is now worth $150,000, or $25,000 more than the agreed lease option price. The tenant has the right to buy the house for $125,000. You might approach the tenant and say, "I would like to cancel your option to buy my house. I will give you back the accumulated deposit, plus an additional $10,000, if you will agree to cancel." The tenant might respond, "I am still interested in buying the house at the agreed-upon price. If I go elsewhere, I will have to pay $150,000 for a comparable house. So I will agree to cancel our agreement, but instead of $10,000, I want $15,000."

This is exactly the same as a call option. Because the market value of the house grew beyond the agreed-upon price, the owner had an incentive to pay in order to cancel the agreement. The tenant was in the position of knowing that values had risen, so that his lease option appreciated in value. In this example, the option is negotiated between the landlord (seller of the option) and tenant (buyer of the option). Because the property increased in value, the option became a valuable asset. As long as both sides are able to agree on a price to cancel the option, the contract can be nullified. If not, then the tenant would have the right to buy the house at the agreed price.

　　　The arguments might be different if the house fell in value. For example, let's say the lease option specified a price of $125,000, but the market value of the house had fallen to $110,000. The tenant would have no incentive to buy that house for $125,000, so the option would have no market value.

　　　Listed options—those traded publicly through exchanges like the New York, Chicago, and Philadelphia Stock Exchanges—are not negotiated in the same way. Due to a high volume of trading every business day, listed option prices are established strictly through the *auction market* under the same principles that govern the buying and selling of stocks. An increase in demand for a particular stock or option drives up its price, while a decrease in demand leads to more availability and lower prices. Market value is the current price in the auction market that buyers are willing to pay and that sellers are willing to receive. Under this system, call buyers and sellers always have a ready market, and will always be able to cancel an option contract at the current market price.

auction market
the public exchanges, in which options, as well as stocks, bonds, and other publicly traded issues, are valued according to supply and demand (Demand drives up prices, while excess of supply softens the market and forces prices down. Those prices are bid upon by buyers and sellers.)

This feature is of critical importance. If, for example, there were always many more buyers than sellers of options, the market value would be vastly distorted. If buyers had to scramble to find unwilling sellers for their options, the market would not be efficient. The demand between buyers and sellers is rarely equal, so the public exchanges place themselves in a position to make the market operate efficiently. They "facilitate" the market by acting as seller to every buyer, and as buyer to every seller.

How Call Buying Works

When you buy a call, you are not obligated to buy the 100 shares of stock. In fact, it's reasonable to say that the vast majority of call buyers do *not* actually buy 100 shares of stock. You have until the *expiration date* to decide what action to take. There are several choices, and the best one to make depends entirely on what happens to the market price of the *underlying stock*, and on how much time remains in the option period.

1. If the market value of the underlying stock rises, you can do one of two things. First, you can *exercise* the option and buy the stock below current market value. Or if you don't really want to own 100 shares of stock, you can sell the option for a higher premium than you paid, and realize a profit in the difference. Remember, every option fixed the price of the 100 shares of stock. That fixed price is called the *striking price* of the option. Striking price is expressed as a number equivalent to the dollar price per share, without dollar signs. Striking price is always divisible by 5.

Example: You decided two months ago to buy a call. You paid the price of $200, which entitled you to buy 100 shares of a particular stock at $55 per share. The striking price is therefore 55. The option will expire later this month. The stock is currently selling at $60 per share, and the option's current market value is $600. You have a choice: Either exercise the call and buy 100 shares at the

expiration date
the date on which an option becomes worthless, which is specified in the option contract

underlying stock
the stock that the option grants the right to buy or sell, which is specified in every option contract

exercise
the act of buying stock under the terms of the call option or selling stock under the terms of the put option, at the specified price per share in the option contract

agreed price of $55 per share, which is $5 per share below current market value, or sell the call for $600, realizing a profit of $400 on the investment (current option value of $600, less original price of $200).

> **striking price**
> the fixed price to be paid for 100 shares of stock specified in the option contract, which will be paid or received by the owner of the option contract upon exercise, regardless of the current market value of the stock

2. If the market value of the stock does not change after a call has been purchased, the purchaser has three alternatives: sell that call before its expiration date (after which the option will be worthless); hold onto the option, in the hope that the stock will rise before expiration, resulting in a rise in the call's value as well; or sell the call now and take a loss. The last choice is sometimes advisable, because a limited loss may be better than a total loss later on. An option is a *wasting asset*. If the market value of the stock does not rise above the striking price before its expiration date, it will eventually lose its value. The *premium* value—the current market value of the option—will be less near expiration than it was at the time you purchased it. The difference reflects the value of time itself. The longer the time until expiration, the more opportunity there is for the stock (and the option) to change in value.

> **wasting asset**
> any asset that declines in value over time (An option is an example of a wasting asset because it only exists until expiration, after which it becomes worthless.)

Example: You purchased a call a few months ago "at 5." (This means you paid $500.) You hoped that the underlying stock would increase in value, causing the option to also rise in value. The call will expire later this month but, contrary to your expectations, the stock's price fell. Your call is now worth only $100. You may sell and accept a loss of $400 or you can hold, hoping for a last-minute rise in the stock's price. Either way, you need to take action before the expiration date, when the call will become worthless.

3. If the market value of a stock falls, calls written on that stock will fall as well. The value of the call is directly tied to the value of the stock. If the stock's price drop is substantial, your call will be worth much less than you paid. You may sell and accept a limited loss or, if the option is worth nearly nothing, you also have the option of letting it simply expire.

premium
the current price of an option, which a buyer pays and a seller receives at the time of the transaction (The amount of premium is expressed as the price per share, without dollar signs; for example, stating that an option is "at 3" means its current market value is $300.)

Example: You bought a call four months ago and paid 3 (a premium of $300). You expected the stock's value to rise, resulting in a rise in the call's value as well. But the stock's market value fell instead, and the option's premium value followed suit. It is now worth 1 ($100). You have a choice: Either sell the call for 1 and accept a $200 loss, or hold onto the call until just before expiration. It can happen that a stock will rise in value at the last minute, for any number of reasons. However, by holding you risk further deterioration in the call's premium value. Of course, if you wait until expiration, the call will be worthless. Buying options is risky. Because they have a limited life, time works against the call buyer; you could lose the entire investment. However, one advantage of investing in calls is that the risk is limited. Rather than investing a large sum in the stock itself, you expose yourself to a limited risk of loss *and* to the potential for substantial gain.

Example: You bought a call last month for 1 (premium of $100). The current price of the stock is $80 per share. For your $100 investment, you have a form of control over 100 shares with a market value of $8000. (Of course, that control does not include voting rights or dividend income, only price control.) Even if the stock's value falls far below the current market price per share of $80, your risk is limited. The most you can ever lose is $100, the premium you paid to buy the option. In comparison, if you put $8000 in the stock, all of that money is at risk, and it is all tied up and unavailable for other investments. Pricing of options depends on the current market value of the stock, in comparison to the striking price of the call *and* the time remaining until expiration. The pricing of calls is explained later in this chapter.

Example: You gain control over 100 shares of stock at $80 per share by purchasing a single call option at 1 ($100). Your potential loss is limited to $100; your potential gain is limited only by time. By using this tactic and accepting the limitation of time, you do not need to tie up $8000. For the benefit of limited time control, you are required to commit much less capital.

In some respects, this comparison defines the difference between "investment" and "speculation." Investment usually indicates a longer-term mentality. Because stock doesn't expire, investors have the luxury of being able to wait out short-term market movement, hoping that over several years that company's fortunes will lead to profits— not to mention dividends in the meantime. It cannot be denied that investors have advantages in actually owning shares of stock. Speculators, in comparison, risk losing all of their investment or realizing spectacular gains. However, when it comes to options, exposure to this potential risk/reward scenario is severely limited by the ever-looming expiration date. To truly understand how the speculative nature of call buying affects you, consider the two following examples.

Example when the stock price rises: You buy a call for 2 ($200), giving you the right to buy 100 shares of a specific stock for $80 per share. If the stock's value rises above $80, your call will rise in value nearly dollar for dollar with the stock. So if the stock goes up four dollars per share (to $84), the option will also rise four points, or $400. You will earn a profit of $400—*if* you sell the call at that point. That would be the same profit you would realize by investing $8000 and buying 100 shares. (This comparison also ignores the brokerage commission, which would be much greater to transact 100 shares than it would be for a single call option.)

Example when the stock price falls: You buy a call for 2 ($200), giving you the right to buy 100 shares of a particular stock at $80 per share. By expiration date of the call option, the stock has fallen in value to $68 per share. You lose the entire $200 investment. However, if you had purchased 100 shares and paid $8000, your loss at this point would be $1200 ($80 per share previously, less current market value of $68 per share). Compared to buying the stock directly, your option risks are smaller. Stockholders have the right to wait out a temporary drop in price, even indefinitely. But remember, in the stockholder's situation, $8000 is tied up and there is no way to tell how long it might take to realize a profit. As an option buyer, you are at risk for only a few months. Stockholders often suffer the opportunity cost of holding stocks—their capital is committed and meanwhile other opportunities come and go.

In situations where an investment in stock falls, stockholders can wait until the stock rebounds. During that time, they are entitled to dividends, so their investment is not completely in limbo. If an investor is interested in long-term gains, a temporary drop is not catastrophic. That individual should not be working with options, which are short-term in nature. Another feature of owning stock is that the investment can be pledged as collateral, which is not the case for option buyers. The option itself has no tangible value, so its value cannot be pledged like stock.

The real advantage in buying calls is that you are not required to tie up a large sum of money and keep it at risk; yet, you control the same 100 shares as though you had bought them outright. Losses are limited to the amount of the premium you pay, and only during the life of that option.

Investment Standards for Call Buyers

People who work in the stock market—including brokers who work with investors and help them buy and sell—regularly offer advice on stocks. If a stockbroker or financial planner is qualified, he or she may also offer advice on buying options. Several critical points should be kept in mind when working with a broker, especially for calls:

1. The broker might not know as much about the market as you do. Just because a person has a license does not mean he or she is an expert on all types of investments. Even brokers with expertise in the stock market might be completely ignorant about options. One rule for all options investors is: Be your own expert and don't depend on others to give you working strategies.

2. Don't expect a broker to train you. Remember, the broker earns a living by earning commissions on orders. That means the primary motive is to get investors to buy and sell. The broker is not a teacher, and, although many talented and caring brokers will give you guidance about the market, that should not be expected as part of the service.

3. There are no guarantees. Risk is everywhere and in all markets. While it's true that buying calls contains specific risks, that doesn't mean that stock investing is always safe in comparison. It all depends on timing, on the market, and on what changes in investment value happen in the future. But if you invest money in the market, you will be taking some form of risk.

4. Options are highly specialized and every individual should design a program and a series of strategies to suit his or her own requirements. For that reason, it might not make sense to work with a broker at all. You might consider investing through a discount broker who offers only a transaction service and no advice. A broker is paid, theoretically, for giving advice. But in the options market, changes happen too rapidly and strategies must be individualized, so that a broker's advice is not always helpful and in fact may be contrary to your best interests.

Brokers are required by law to ensure that you are qualified to invest in options. That means you should have at least a minimal understanding of the risks in the market, the procedures, and the terminology, and that you understand what you're doing. Brokers are required to apply a rule called "know your customer." Most brokerage firms ask options investors to complete a short form explaining their knowledge or experience with options, and they also give out an options prospectus, which is a disclosure report explaining the risks in the market, along with the advice to read the prospectus before investing.

The investment standard for buying calls is that you understand how the market works, and that you invest only money that you can afford to have at risk. Beyond that, you have every right to decide for yourself how much risk you are willing to take. Ultimately, you are responsible for your own profit and loss in the market. The role of the broker is to document the fact that the right questions were asked before your money was taken and put into the investment.

How Call Selling Works

Buying calls is similar to buying stocks. You invest money and after some time has passed you decide whether or not to sell. The transactions occur in a predictable order. First you buy, then you sell. Call selling doesn't work that way. A seller starts by selling a call and later buys the same call to close out the transaction.

Many people have trouble grasping the idea of selling *before* buying. A common reaction is, "Are you sure? Is that legal?" or "How can you sell something you don't own?" It is legal, and it is possible to sell something before you buy it. This is done all the time in the stock market through a device known as "short selling." An investor sells short, meaning stock is sold that is not owned by the investor. Later, a separate "buy" order is entered to close out the position.

The same technique is used in the options market, and is far less complicated. Because options have no tangible value, becoming an option seller is relatively easy. Instead of buying a right, option sellers sell the right granted in the option. A call seller grants the right to someone else to buy 100 shares of a specified stock, at a fixed price per share by a specified expiration date. In return, the call seller is paid a premium. As a call seller, you are paid but you must also be willing to deliver the 100 shares if the call buyer exercises the option. This strategy has greater risks than buying calls, because you could end up having to furnish 100 shares of stock.

When you are an option buyer, the decision to exercise or not is entirely up to you. But as a seller, that decision belongs to someone else. As an option seller, you can make or lose money in one of three ways:

1. If the market value of the underlying stock rises, the value of the call rises as well. For a buyer, this is good news. But for the seller, the opposite is true. If the buyer exercises the option, referred to as "calling" the 100 shares of stock, you will be required to deliver those shares to the buyer. That doesn't literally mean you have to buy them yourself and then sell them; you merely pay the difference when the call is exercised. However, that means you will lose money. Remember, an option will be exercised only if the stock's current market value is higher than the striking price. So that would mean you will have to pay the difference.

Example: You sell a call on a stock which specifies a striking price of $40 per share. You happen to own 100 shares of the stock, so you consider your risks minimal in selling a call. In addition, the call is worth $200, and that is paid to you in exchange for selling the call. One month later, the stock's market value rises to $46 per share. The buyer exercises the call, and you are obligated to deliver your 100 shares at $40 per share. That is $6 per share below current market value. Although you received a $200 premium for selling the call, you lose the market value of $600 because the stock is $6 per share higher than the striking price of your call. Your net loss is $400 (market value loss of $600, less premium you received of $200).

Example: Given the same circumstances as above, but assuming you do not own 100 shares, what happens if the option is exercised? In this case, you are still required to deliver 100 shares at $40 per share. You will be required to pay the difference of $600 (market value of $46 less striking price of $40 per share) to satisfy the contract.

    2. If the market value of the stock remains at or near the level when you sell a call, the value of the call declines over time. Remember, the call is a wasting asset. While that fact is a problem for the call buyer, it is a great advantage for the call seller. While time is working against buyers, it works for sellers. You have the right to cancel your position at any time. So if you sell a call and it falls in value, you have the right to buy it at a lower premium and realize a profit.

Example: You sell a call for a premium of 4 ($400). Two months later, the stock's market value is about the same as it was when you sold the call. The option has fallen in value to 1 ($100). You cancel your position by buying the option at 1, realizing a profit of $300.

Example: Given the same situation as above, you have a second choice. Instead of buying the reduced-value option and closing the position, you can simply hold onto it, hoping the stock does not recover its value before expiration. If the stock remains at the current level and the option expires, then the entire $400 premium will be profit to you.

3. If the market value of the stock falls, the option will also decline in value. This gives you an advantage as a call seller. Remember, you were paid a premium for selling the call, and you want to buy it for less at a later date, or allow it to expire worthless. You have a choice: Buy the option and cancel the position at any time, or wait for it to expire.

Example: You sell a call and receive a premium of 5 ($500). The stock's market value later falls far below the striking price of the option and, in your opinion, a recovery is not likely. If the market value of the stock is at or below the striking price of the option as of expiration, the option will not be exercised. By allowing the option to expire in this situation, the entire $500 is a profit for you.

Example: Given the same circumstances as above, you are not certain whether the stock will recover. In the past, the stock's market value has tended to have sudden fluctuations up or down, and the option has more than three months to go until expiration. The call's value is now at $200. Rather than risk exercise in the future, you decide to buy, closing the position and taking your profit of $300 (original sales premium of $500, less current premium of $200).

You need to remember three important points as a call seller. First, the transaction is backwards, with a sale occurring before a purchase. Second, when you sell a call, you are paid the premium, compared to buying a call and paying the same premium. And third, what is good news to a buyer is bad news for you, and vice versa. A call seller wants the stock's value to fall, not rise. A rise in market value is bad news, because that means the option is worth more than it was when you sold it. You may better understand how call selling works by reviewing some similar transactions in other markets:

✔ An art dealer sells limited edition prints, but has only one print to show each customer. After the sale is made, she orders and pays for the prints needed to deliver to purchasers. The art dealer has completed a sale in advance of the purchase.

✔ A car dealer fixes the price of a car with special features, and sells it to a customer. Only after the sale is the car ordered from the factory. The car dealer has sold the car before paying the factory to build it.

✔ A contractor sells hundreds of tract homes by showing models before the homes themselves have been built. The contractor sells the homes and uses the down payments to obtain financing to build the homes.

When you sell a call option, you assume what is called a *short position*. The sale opens the position and it can be closed in one of two ways. First, a buy order can be entered, which closes the position. Or second, you can wait until expiration, at which point the short position ceases to exist and the entire premium becomes a profit. In comparison, the more commonly understood "buy first and then sell" approach is called a *long position*. A long position is closed in one of two ways. First, you may sell the investment, closing the position. Or second, in the case of an option, you can allow it to expire worthless, meaning the entire investment is a loss.

Investment Standards for Call Selling

The standards for investing as a call seller are vastly different than those for call buying. It is still true that you should understand the markets, the procedures, and the

short position
the status assumed by investors when they enter a sell order in advance of entering a buy order (The short position is closed by later entering a buy order, or through expiration.)

long position
the status assumed by investors when they enter a buy order in advance of entering a sell order (The long position is closed by later entering a sell order, or through expiration.)

terminology of the options market; however, the risk levels are substantially different, and that means a different investment standard has to be applied to sellers.

As a call buyer, you have limited risk. You stand to lose only the amount of the premium you have paid. However, as a seller you are granting a right to someone else and you receive a premium for granting that right. As a consequence, your risk is virtually unlimited. As a practical matter, risk is limited by the time element and time is on your side in most cases. However, stocks have been known to take phenomenal leaps and if you're in a short position when that happens, it could be costly.

Example: You sell a call on a specified stock and you are paid a premium of 7 ($700). The striking price is $35 per share. Two months later, an announcement is made that the company has been sold to another corporation for $60 per share. Your option is exercised two days later and you lose $1800. You are required to deliver 100 shares at $35 per share. However, the current market value of that stock is now $60 per share. The difference translates to $2500. You received an original premium of $700, so to meet the call, you lose the difference of $1800.

From the point of view of the broker who allows you to sell calls, the standards have to be higher than for call buyers. For a buyer, the question of affordability relates only to the level of premiums being paid. But for the call seller, the question is whether you can afford to pay potentially higher losses in the event of a large movement in the value of the underlying stock.

The risk applies when you sell calls without already owning the stock. Obviously, if you already own 100 shares of stock, you still suffer the losses but you already have the stock on hand, so from the broker's point of view, the risk is minimal.

Example: Given the same circumstances as above, the one difference is that you own 100 shares of the stock. From your point of view, the $700 you receive for selling the call would justify exercise because the stock is in your portfolio and is available. When the announcement is made that the stock is being sold for $60 per share, you are still required to deliver the 100 shares, and you lose the *potential* gain you would have made if you had not sold the option. However, you do not have to come up with an additional $1800 to meet the call. You lose only the stock and the potential gain.

Such losses as the one described above are not necessarily bad news. Some stock investors intentionally sell calls against stock they own as a means of gaining profits. They know that eventually their stock will be called away, but they have already profited enough that the strategy is worthwhile.

Example: Given the same circumstances as above, let's add a few other assumptions. The striking price is $35 per share, but years ago, when you bought the stock, it cost you only $20 per share. No matter what, your stock is worth $15 per share more than when you bought it. So selling a call for 7 ($700) simply increases your profit to $2200 ($1500 in stock appreciation plus $700 for option premium). When the stock is called away because its market value is $60, you are aware that the value went from $35 per share to $60 per share overnight. So ask yourself this question: Have you lost $25 per share, or have you gained $22 per share?

The answer depends on your point of view. In real terms, you have gained $22 per share because you paid $15 less than the striking price, in addition to 7 ($700) paid for the call. So you close out the entire transaction with a $2200 profit. Some people see it in a different way, however. They argue that *if* they had not sold the call, they would have made an additional $2500 ($60 per share less $35 per share) and, in fact, that is a "loss." But the truth is, that's only a paper loss, an unrealized profit from an unexpected turn of events. It is one of the risks you take when you sell a call and accept money for it.

THE PUT OPTION

A put is the opposite of a call. It is a contract granting the right to sell 100 shares of stock at a fixed price per share and by a specified expiration date in the future. As a put buyer, you acquire the right to sell the stock and as a put seller, you grant that right to someone else. (See Figure 1.2.)

Buying and Selling Puts

As a buyer of a put, you expect the underlying stock's value to fall. A put is the opposite of a call so, as a put buyer, you want the stock's value to fall rather than to rise. If the stock's market value does fall, the put's value rises; and if the stock's market value rises, then the put's value will fall. There are three possible outcomes when you buy puts:

1. If the market value of the stock rises, the put's value falls in response. In that case, you can sell the put for a price below what you paid, and take a loss; or you can hold onto the put, hoping that the stock will fall before expiration date.

Example: You bought a put two months ago and paid a premium of 2 ($200). You expected the stock price to fall, in which case the value of the put would have risen. Instead, the stock's market value rose, meaning the put's value fell. It is now worth only $25. You have a choice: Sell the put and take the $175 loss, or hold onto the put,

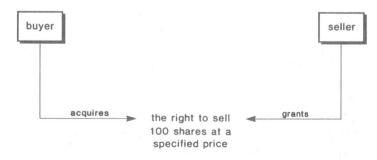

FIGURE 1.2 The put option.

hoping the stock will fall before expiration. If you hold the put beyond expiration, it will become worthless.

This example shows how you need to assess risk. For instance, with the put currently worth only $25—nearly worthless—there is very little value left, so it might be considered too late to cut your losses. Considering that only $25 is at stake, it might be worth the long shot of holding onto the put. If the stock's price does fall before expiration, you have a chance of making back the original investment and possibly even a profit.

2. If the market value of the stock stays at about the same value as when the put is bought, the value of that put will still fall over time, because the put, like the call, is a wasting asset. Some of its value is related to the amount of time remaining between now and expiration. The closer to expiration, the lower the value. In this situation, you can either sell the put and accept the partial loss, or hold onto it, hoping that the stock's market price will fall before expiration of the put.

Example: You bought a put three months ago and paid a premium of 4 ($400). You had expected the stock's market value to fall, in which case the put's value would have risen. Expiration comes up later this month. Unfortunately, the stock's market price is about the same as it was when you bought the put, and the put has declined in value to $100. Your choices: Sell the put for $100 and accept the $300 loss, or hold onto the put on the chance the stock's value will fall before expiration.

The choice and assessment often comes down to a matter of timing with options. The more time you have, the easier the choice. For example, if there remain two months until expiration, it is easier to adopt a wait-and-see attitude. If the option expires next week, there is little hope that a loss will reverse itself. Time is constrained at that point and your decision is forced as a consequence.

3. If the market value of the stock falls, the put's value will increase. You have three alternatives in this outcome. First, hold onto the put in the hope that the stock's value will decline further and increase your profit; second, sell the put and take your profit now; and third, exercise the option and sell 100 shares of the stock at the fixed price, which is higher than current market value. The decision has to be made before expiration.

Example: You bought a put last month and paid a premium of $50. Meanwhile, the stock's market price has fallen $7 below the exercise price specified in the put contract, so the put is now valued at $750. There are three choices here. First, you can sell the option and take a $700 profit on your $50 investment. Second, you can hold onto the put and hope for further decline in the stock's market value, meaning more profit in the put (and the risk that the stock's price will rise, meaning less profit in the put). Third, you can exercise the option and sell 100 shares of stock for $7 per share more than current market value.

Example: You own 100 shares of stock that you bought last year for $38 per share. You are worried about the threat of a falling market; however, you also would like to hold onto the stock as a long-term investment. To protect yourself against the threat of a falling market, you recently bought a put option, paying a premium of $1/2$ ($50). This guarantees you the right to sell your 100 shares for $40 per share. Recently, the price of your stock did fall to $33 per share. The value of the put increased to $750, offsetting your loss in the stock.

You have a choice to make. You can sell the option and realize the $700 profit, which also offsets the loss in the stock. This choice is appealing because you take a profit now on the option, but you still own the stock. So if the stock's price rebounds, you will benefit twice.

A second alternative is to exercise the option and sell the 100 shares for $40 per share, which is $7 per share above current market value (but only $2 per share above the price you originally paid for the stock). This choice may appeal to you if you believe that it was a mistake to buy the stock in the first place. By bailing out now, you recover your full investment even though the stock's value has fallen significantly.

Third, you can hold off taking any action at the moment. You have no real risk in taking no action, because the option acts as insurance against further declines in the stock's value. For every dollar the stock value declines, the option value will increase. And if the stock's value increases, the option's value can be expected to decline to the same degree. As long as the put is exercised or sold before expiration, doing nothing now has no risk to you.

While some investors buy puts in the belief that a stock's market value will fall, or to protect their own investment in the stock, other investors sell puts. As a put seller, you grant someone else the right to sell 100 shares of stock to you at a fixed price. If that put option is exercised, you will be required to buy 100 shares at a price above the current market value. For taking this risk, you are paid a premium for selling the put. Like the call seller, put sellers do not have as much control over the outcome of their investment as do buyers, since it is the buyer's right to exercise.

Example: Last month, you sold a put with a striking price of 50 ($50 per share). The premium was $2^1/_2$ ($250), which was paid to you at the time of the sale. Since that time, the stock's market value has remained in a narrow range between $48 and $53 per share. Currently, the price is at $51. You don't expect the stock's price to fall below the striking price of 50. As long as market value of the stock remains at or above that level, which is the striking price of your put, that put will not be exercised. (The buyer will not exercise, meaning you will not be required to buy 100 shares of the stock at $50 per share.) If your speculation is correct and the stock's price remains at or above $50 per share, you will make a profit on your put.

Your risk is that the stock's price will decline below $50 per share before expiration, meaning you would be required to buy 100 shares at $50 per share. To avoid that risk, you have the right to get out of the put at any time by buying it at current market value. The closer to expiration (and as long as the stock's market value is greater than the striking price), the lower the market price of the put will be.

The risk in selling puts is less than that of selling calls. The strategy makes sense if you believe the price of $50 per share is reasonable for the stock. In the "worst case," you will be required to buy those shares. Your ultimate price in that case would be discounted, because you were paid a premium for selling the put.

Example: You sold a put with a striking price of 50 and received a premium of $2^1/_2$ ($250). Immediately before expiration, the stock's market value is only $44 per share, and the value of the put is 6 ($600). The buyer has the right to exercise the put, requiring you to buy 100 shares of the stock at $50 per share—$6 per share above current market value. You have two alternatives: First, let the buyer exercise the put, since you believe that $50 per share is a reasonable and fair price. (Besides, your *real* cost is only $47.50 per share, because you also received $250 for selling the put.) Second, you could buy the put to close the position, and pay $600, accepting a loss of $350.

Selling puts is a vastly different strategy than buying puts. From one point of view, it contains higher risks because you could be exercised and required to buy 100 shares. In response to this, set a logical standard for yourself: Never sell puts unless you would be willing to acquire 100 shares of that stock at the striking price. An advantage of selling puts, like that of selling calls, is that time works for you. As expiration date approaches, the put loses value. However, if movement in the underlying stock is opposite the movement you expected, you could end up with a loss, or buying stock for a higher price per share than the current market value. Sudden and unexpected changes in a stock's value can happen at any time, and the more inclined a particular stock is to sudden movements, the greater your risks as a seller. You may also notice as you observe the pricing of options that due to the greater risks, options on such stocks tend to have higher premium value than options on more dependable stocks.

As a put seller, your risk is limited to the striking price of the stock. In comparison, a call seller's risks are unlimited, since a stock's value can rise indefinitely, at least in theory. Because a stock cannot fall below zero, a put seller can theoretically identify the absolute worst case. But in fact, the stock's book value is the *actual* worst case. That's because book value represents the *real*, tangible value of the company: assets less liabilities. The maximum decline is restricted to book value.

Example: A stock is currently selling for $53 per share and its book value is $35 per share. You are considering selling a put with a striking price of 50, and you want to analyze your worst-case risk. At first, you might reason that if a stock's value falls all the way to zero, your maximum risk is $5000 (if the stock lost all its value and you were required to buy 100 shares, you would own worthless stock, but would be required to pay $50 per share). In reality, however, your real worst-case risk is only $1500, the difference between the striking price and book value.

Investment Standards for Buying and Selling Puts

Every investor has to decide whether a particular investment or strategy is appropriate for him or her. This decision is not simple and it cannot be done by formula. For example, what is right for you in one situation might not work at all in another.

Example: You own 100 shares of stock that slowly but steadily grows in value over time, and that pays a healthy, consistent dividend. You also own 100 shares of stock that tends to bounce up and down in a wide range, and for which price movement is impossible to anticipate and predict. Given these differences, it might make sense to sell a put against the second issue as a means of insuring against the possibility of loss. But the first 100 shares are more stable, so writing puts against those might not make as much sense.

Consider applying the following rules for buying or for selling puts, remembering that the rules should be flexible since different situations require different analysis.

1. Buy puts with money available for speculation. Never buy puts with money you cannot afford to lose.

2. Buy puts only if you understand the risks involved, with enough time until expiration so that there is a reasonable opportunity for the stock's market value to fall.

3. Sell puts only if you are willing to buy 100 shares of that stock at the striking price.

4. Trade in puts only if you are able to keep an eye on the market, so that you will be able to react to movement in the stock's market value.

5. Plan ahead. Before you trade, establish what actions you will take if the stock's price rises, if it falls, or if it remains within a narrow range and expiration is approaching. Only by knowing ahead of time how to react can you ensure that your strategies will make sense.

THE UNDERLYING STOCK

Option values change in direct proportion to the market value of the underlying stock. Every option is married to the stock of a specific corporation, and how you will fare as an options investor depends on how that stock's value changes in the immediate future.

This is critical to your success as an options investor. The selection of the option cannot be made in isolation. Whether you consider options as only side bets or use them in conjunction with buying and selling stock, you should always use your best judgment in the selection itself—both of the stock and of the option. Criteria for selection of stocks are at the center of smart stock market investing. The need for careful, thorough, and ongoing analysis cannot be emphasized too much. You will succeed in trading options only when you are first aware of the attributes of the underlying stock—financial strength, price stability, even quality of the organization's management. These are important fundamental considerations for buyers of stocks, and they are equally important to traders of options.

Selection of stock, by itself, is a complex topic involving variables and degrees of judgment that every investor has to sort through individually. This analysis is made more complex when options are involved. Even limiting the analysis to only price movement is not a simple task. As shown in Table 1.1, you will consider price movement in the underlying stock as either positive or negative, depending on whether you are a buyer or a seller, and on whether you are involved with calls or with puts.

Example: Two months ago, you bought a call and paid a premium of 3 ($300). The striking price was 40 ($40 per share). At that time, the underlying stock's price was $40 per share. In this condition—when the option's striking price is identical to the current price of the stock—the option is said to be *at the money*. If the market value per share of the stock increases so that the per-share value is above the option's striking price, an option is said to be *in the money*. And if the price of the stock decreases so that the per-share value is below the option's striking price, an option is said to be *out of the money*.

Figure 1.3 shows the in the money, at the money, and out of the money ranges in comparison with striking price of a call. For a put, the terms are reversed. When the market value of an underlying stock is lower than the striking price of a put, it is in the money, and when the market value is higher than the striking price of the put, it is out of the money.

at the money
the status of an option when the underlying stock's market value is identical to the option's striking price

in the money
the status of a call option when the underlying stock's market value is higher than the option's striking price, or of a put option when the underlying stock's market value is lower than the option's striking price

TABLE 1.1 Price Movement in the Underlying Security		
	Increase in Price	*Decrease in Price*
Call buyer	Positive	Negative
Call seller	Negative	Positive
Put buyer	Negative	Positive
Put seller	Positive	Negative

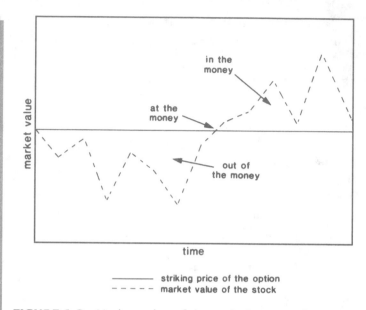

> **out of the money**
> the status of a call option when the underlying stock's market value is lower than the option's striking price, or of a put option when the underlying stock's market value is higher than the option's striking price

FIGURE 1.3 Market value of the underlying stock.

The approximate dollar-for-dollar movement of an option's value occurs whenever an option is in the money. At those times, the tendency is for option values to change one dollar for each corresponding change in the stock's per-share value. When the option is out of the money, changes in value are not as directly affected by changes in the stock's market value.

Example: You bought a put last month with a striking price of 30 ($30 per share) and paid 2 ($200). At that time, the stock's market value was $34 per share, so the option is $4 out of the money. (Remember, for puts, when the stock's value is higher than the striking price, it is out of the money, the reverse rule than that for calls.) More recently, the stock's price fell to $31, a downward movement of 3 points. However, your put has increased in value only 1½ points. Because the option is out of the money, its value does not react as directly to changes in the stock's pricing as it will when in the money.

Now the stock's market value continues to fall, going into the money by declining to less than the striking price of 30. Once in the money, the option's price will change dollar for dollar with changes in the underlying stock. For every dollar the stock falls, the option will increase in value by a dollar.

Example: You bought a call with a striking price of 45 ($45 per share) and paid a premium of 3 ($300). At the time you bought the call, the stock's price was $44 per share. About two weeks later, the stock's price rose to $45. The option is now at the money. However, you observe that your option's value has not changed at all. The next day, the stock's market price rose $1/2$ point, and the option also rose by $1/2$ ($50). The following week, the stock's price went up 7 points, and the option's premium value also rose 7 points, for a current value of $1050 (original cost $300 plus $7\frac{1}{2}$ points, $750 = $1050). If you were to sell the option at this point, you would earn a profit of $750. Note that when the option was in the money, price movement corresponded to price movement in the underlying stock. But when the option was out of the money, the option's premium value was not directly responsive to those movements.

volatility
a measure of the degree of change in a stock's market value, measured over a 12-month period and stated as a percentage (To measure volatility, subtract the lowest 12-month price from the highest 12-month price, and divide the answer by the 12-month lowest price.)

The value of options in the money is inescapably related directly to the underlying stock. But "value" in the market also depends on two additional factors. First is *volatility*—the degree of change in value of both the option and the underlying stock. Second is the time remaining until expiration. Also, changes in value often are accompanied by changes in *volume*, the level of trading activity in a stock, an option, or the market as a whole, at any given time. The level of volume in trading on an underlying stock also tends to affect the value of an option written on that stock.

volume
the level of trading activity in a stock, an option, or the market as a whole

How to Pick a Stock

The question of selecting stocks is more involved and complex than picking options. For options, the decision has to do with risk assessment, current value, and your own tolerance for risk. For stocks, there is no dependable way to know with certainty how a particular stock will act in the market of the future.

The selection of a stock is the critical decision point in determining whether or not you will succeed in options investing. You cannot just pick options based on current value and hope to succeed without also considering the prospects for the stock itself. Because option valuation is a factor of stock price and movement, time, volatility, volume, and quality of the company, its product, its markets, competition, and a broad range of other factors, you need to develop a means for evaluating stocks themselves.

Some investors select stocks strictly on the basis of *fundamental analysis.* This includes comparisons of financial statements, dividends paid by the company, its management, position within its industry, debt and capital financing, product or service, and a wide range of other strictly factual information. Other investors depend on *technical analysis,* the study of price trends in the stock. Both fundamental and technical approaches offer techniques that every investor can use.

Many investors use subscription services to analyze stocks. One broadly used industry standard for the study and comparison of stocks is Value Line, a service that constantly studies major stock issues for fundamental and technical changes, and ranks them into comparative level of recommendation. The same company also offers similar services for options investors. Numerous other subscription services are available, as well as newsletters, financial newspapers, and reports issued by brokerage houses. For the investor interested in research, there is no shortage of information.

No investor should select a stock or options related to a stock without a thorough investigation—not only of the issue itself, but of the various methods used for analysis of those stocks and options. You should not depend on the advice of a broker, a friend, or anyone else as to which investments or strategies should be used. You need to perform your own research and find your own method for selection.

fundamental analysis
a study of financial information and attributes of a company's management and competitive position, as a means for selecting stocks

technical analysis
a study of trends and patterns of price movement in a stock, including price per share, the shape of price movements on charts, high and low ranges, and trends in pricing over time

Why can't you depend on advice provided by those experts and professionals in the business? The answer is simple: Brokers are in the business of making money on commissions paid for transactions, and they often are instructed as to which issues to promote on any given day—not necessarily because of investment opportunities, but because the firm is a dealer in that stock. A study released in 1996 by Columbia University confirmed that taking a broker's advice is not always best for the investor. That university's business school analyzed more than 8000 stock evaluations made by brokerage companies. The study concluded that brokers are often pressured to give their clients overly optimistic reports on securities sold by client companies of the brokerage firm. While this fact has long been known in general, the Columbia University study is the first extensive analysis that proves that the problem exists.

So to the question every investor faces—How do I pick a stock?—the answer is: Read and research. Ask brokers their opinions on specific issues, rather than asking them to tell you which stocks to buy. Read industry reports, study Value Line and other subscription services, and read the financial press. Become familiar with the various methods in the broad classifications of fundamental and technical analysis, and learn how to pick stocks on a consistent basis that you believe points the way to future market performance.

Intrinsic Value and Time Value

Once you are comfortable with the methods of selecting stocks, you will be ready to comfortably and confidently approach the options market. For purposes of understanding the market, we assume that this discussion involves only the *listed option* market, or those options publicly traded on a stock exchange. It might be true that an option will be offered or traded privately, but that is not the subject of this book. A listed option and its pricing structure is best understood by breaking its value down into two parts. First is its *intrinsic value*, which is the portion of option premium equal to the degree that it is in the

listed option
an option traded on a public exchange and listed in the published reports in the financial press

intrinsic value
that portion of an option's current value equal to the number of points that it is in the money ("Points" equals the number of dollars of value per share; so 35 points equals $35 per share.)

> **time value**
> that portion of an option's current value above intrinsic value

money. Any additional value is known as *time value*, which predictably declines over the life of the option. With many months to go, time value can be a substantial portion of the option's total value, but as it approaches expiration, time value evaporates to nothing. In addition, the farther away from at the money, the less time value an option has. The relative degree of intrinsic value and time value is determined by the distance between striking price and current market value of the stock, adjusted for the amount of time remaining until expiration of the option.

Example: A call has a current premium of 3 ($300) and a striking price of 45 ($45 per share). At the time you buy the call, the underlying stock's market value is $45 per share. Because the option is at the money, there is no intrinsic value in this option. The entire premium represents time value. Time value will decrease over time so that, by expiration, there will be no time value remaining in this option. If the stock's market value remains at or below the striking price, there will be no intrinsic value by expiration. If the stock's market value rises above striking price, for each dollar it rises, the option will gain one point in intrinsic value. If at some point the stock is worth $46 per share, the option with a striking price of 45 will have one point of intrinsic value; any additional premium will be time value.

A comparison of option premium and the underlying stock is presented in Table 1.2. This reveals the direct relationship between intrinsic value of the option, market value in the underlying stock, and the declining nature of time value. Figure 1.4 shows how movement in the underlying stock (top graph) is identical to the option's intrinsic value (bottom graph). The underlying stock's pattern is identical to intrinsic value movements (darker portion) when in the money. Note how time value moves independently but declines as expiration approaches. When the option is at the money or out of the money, it has no intrinsic value. And when the option is in the money, the intrinsic value matches the number of points that the stock's value exceeds striking price of the op-

TABLE 1.2 The Declining Time Value of an Option				
		Option Premium (Striking Price of $45)		
Month	Stock Price	Total Value	Intrinsic Value[1]	Time Value[2]
1	$45	$3	$0	$3
2	47	5	2	3
3	46	4	1	3
4	46	3	1	2
5	47	4	2	2
6	44	2	0	2
7	46	2	1	1
8	45	1	0	1
9	46	1	1	0

[1]Intrinsic value reflects the price difference between the stock's current market value and the option's striking price.
[2]Time value is greatest when the expiration date is furthest away and declines as expiration approaches.

tion—exactly. You can also see how time value predictably dissolves over the life of the option.

The total amount of option premium might vary greatly between two stocks at the same price and with identical options, due to outside influences. These include the perception of value by other investors, as well as a stock's price history, the company's fundamental and technical indicators, the industry of the company, and a broad range of other influences. For example, two companies have stock with current options, both with striking prices of 55, and both stocks currently valued at $58 per share, and with identical time until expiration. Yet, the option premium for one is 5 and for the other at 7.

The variable is always in the time value, and that is where market factors come into play. In addition, time value will not always change in the same manner. The pattern and trend is predictable, but those outside variables will influence time value in different ways for different stocks, and at different market conditions. For

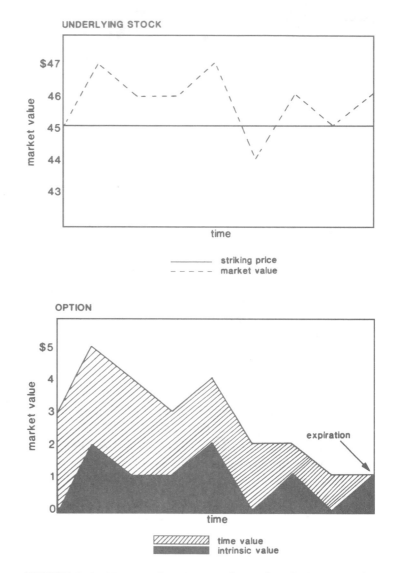

FIGURE 1.4   Time and intrinsic values of underlying stock and options.

example, one company might be rumored as a candidate for a pending takeover. That news, true or false, affects the market value of the stock, volume, and time value of all related options. The stock's volume may be much higher than normal, and its price movements more volatile than their historical trends. The *potential* for price movement in the stock's value may be perceived to be greater than normal, creating more interest in the stock— and of course, in all options related to that stock. Option buyers are willing to pay more in terms of time value when they perceive greater potential for price movement (upward movement for calls, downward movement for puts); and when a stock is perceived to be relatively lack-luster, the time value is lower due to less interest. Also, because of uncertainty pertaining to a particular stock, risks are higher for sellers and higher time value premiums will be demanded to justify those higher risks.

Making sound judgments about an option's time value is one important way to find bargains in the options market, whether as a buyer or a seller, or as both. To gain some insight takes experience and practice. Suppose, for instance, that an option with many months until expiration has an exceptionally low time value today; but it is close to the money. As a buyer, you might recognize that the option's price is almost all intrinsic value. Or suppose that an option with a striking price close to the current value of the stock has an unusually high time value and relatively short time until expiration. That could be an opportunity to sell the option and earn a profit based on changes you anticipate in the near future, in time value of that option. You know that as expiration approaches, the time value will disappear quickly. Such opportunities are rare, but can be caused by outside influences, such as market rumors.

You can easily recognize the time value in any option by comparing the stock's current value and the option's premium. For example, a stock currently priced at $47 per share and an option with a premium of 3 and with a striking price of 45, and how the premium for that option breaks down between intrinsic value and time value:

Stock Price

Current market value	$47
Less striking price	−45
Intrinsic value	$ 2

Option Premium

Premium	$ 3
Less intrinsic value	−2
Time value	$ 1

In the next chapter, several important features of options—striking price, expiration date, and exercise—will be more fully explored, especially in light of how these features affect your personal options strategy.

Chapter 2

Opening, Closing, and Tracking the Option

E very option is distinguished by four major attributes, collectively called the *terms* of the option. These are the striking price, expiration month, type of option (call or put), and the underlying security. These are also called *standardized terms*.

These are the four essential bits of information needed to tell which option is being discussed and how it differs from every other option. In making evaluations of risk and potential profit, every buyer and seller needs to have these four pieces of information. Of course, because the point of view is opposite, advantages to one may be disadvantages to the other. That is the nature of option investing: You have the choice of taking a position on either side, depending on where you think the advantage can be found.

1. *Striking price.* The striking price is the fixed price at which the option can be exercised. It is the price for which the underlying security will be traded if and when that option is exercised. The striking price is always divisible by 5 (except for some stocks with very low share prices, for which striking prices may be divided into $2\frac{1}{2}$-point intervals, and higher-priced stocks, which have intervals divisible by 10 points). The striking price is the set, unchanging price at which 100 shares of stock can be bought or sold, no matter how much change occurs in the market value of that stock.

terms
the attributes that describe an option, including the striking price, expiration month, type of option (call or put), and the underlying security

standardized terms
same as "terms"

47

class
all options traded on a single underlying security, including different striking prices and expiration dates

series
a group of options sharing identical terms

cycle
the pattern of expiration dates of options for a particular underlying stock (The three cycles occur in four-month intervals and are described by month abbreviations. They are (1) January, April, July, and October, or JAJO; (2) February, May, August, and November, or FMAN; and (3) March, June, September, and December, or MJSD.)

For the buyer, the striking price identifies the price at which 100 shares can be bought (for a call option) or sold (for a put option) if that buyer decides to exercise that option. For a seller, the striking price is the opposite: It is the price at which 100 shares of stock can be sold (for a call option) or bought (for a put option), in the event the *buyer* exercises the option and imposes the transaction on the seller.

2. *Expiration date.* Every option exists for only a limited number of months. That is the problem or the opportunity, depending on your point of view and on the strategies you employ. Every option is eventually canceled out, exercised, or allowed to expire, but it will not just go on forever. Because it is not tangible, the number of potential options is unlimited except by market demand. These factors increase risks, since buyers are not always able to make a profit by expiration date, and demand for the stock (and for options) will be reflected in pricing. At the same time, these factors work to the advantage of all sellers, since pending expiration eliminates time value, often quickly in the final weeks of an option's life. So while the buyer stands to lose money due to falling premium value, the seller depends on that for his or her profit. The buyer's greatest enemy is time, which is the seller's greatest advantage.

3. *Type of option.* The distinction between calls and puts is essential to success in the options market; even so, many first-time investors are confused by this distinction. The identical strategies cannot be used for calls and puts, as they are opposites. The call gives its buyer the right to purchase 100 shares; the put gives the buyer the right to sell the same 100 shares. If you believe the underlying stock will increase in value, you will want to buy calls (or sell puts). If you believe the underlying stock will go down in value, you will want to buy puts (or sell calls). This is only the most obvious of possible strategies, however. As we will see in later chapters, calls and puts can be used for many reasons and in many different strategies, including the use of both calls and puts at the same time.

4. *Underlying stock.* Every option is identified with a specific company's common stock. Listed options are offered on a limited number of stocks, and are traded only on certain exchanges (some options trade on more than one exchange). Options can exist only when a specific underlying stock is identified, since it is the stock's market value that determines the option's value in the market. All of the options traded for a specific underlying stock are referred to as a single *class* of options. Thus, a single stock might have a number of calls and puts with various expiration prices and dates, and all belong to the same class. In comparison, all of those options with the same combination of terms—identical striking prices, expiration month, type (call or put), and underlying stock—are considered a single *series* of options.

A Note on the Expiration Cycle

Expiration dates for options of a single underlying stock come up on a predictable expiration *cycle*. Every stock with listed options can be further broken down by the cycle in which its options expire. These cycles are:

✔ January, April, July, and October
✔ February, May, August, and November
✔ March, June, September, and December

In addition to these fixed expiration cycle dates, active options might also be available at any time for expiration in the next month and in the month following, regardless of the cycle in which that stock's options operate. For example, on issues with options expiring in the cycle month of April, contracts might also be available on a short-term basis, so that in February, you will be able to trade in options expiring in March, April, July, and October.

An option's expiration occurs on the third Saturday of the expiration month. An order for closing a position or for expiration must occur on the *last trading day* and before the indicated *expiration time* for the option. As a general rule, that means before close of business on the last trading day; however, not all brokerage firms enforce the same rules, so investors should ensure that they know

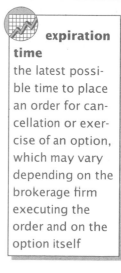

last trading day
the Friday preceding the third Saturday of the expiration month of an option

expiration time
the latest possible time to place an order for cancellation or exercise of an option, which may vary depending on the brokerage firm executing the order and on the option itself

their brokerage firm's rules for expiration cutoff time. Another point to remember: Some firms enforce automatic exercise rules for all options in the money as of expiration time. Every options investor should find out the rules and be sure he or she knows what will occur (or will not occur without special instructions) when their options are scheduled to expire.

Example: You bought a call scheduled to expire in the month of July. Its expiration date is the third Saturday in that month. You must place a sell order before expiration time on the preceding Friday, which is the last trading day before expiration. If you do not place your sell order by that time, the option will expire worthless and you will receive nothing.

OPENING AND CLOSING OPTION TRADES

Every option trade you make must specify all four of the terms: striking price, expiration month, call or put, and the underlying stock. If any one of these terms changes, it represents an entirely different option.

Whenever you make a trade, the terms must be described fully. Later in this chapter, you will learn the details of how trades are made by way of coded abbreviations. That makes it easier for brokers and customers to communicate. For now, it is only important to understand that there are two ways to open an option position: by buying and by selling. And there are three ways to close an option position: by cancellation (selling a previous "buy" or buying a previous "sell"), exercise, or expiration.

Whenever you buy an option and are holding it, or sell an option and it is being held, that is an *open position*. If you buy an option to open a position, it is called an *opening purchase transaction*. And if you start out by selling an option, that is called an *opening sale transaction*.

Example: You bought a call two months ago. When you entered your order, it was an opening purchase transac-

open position
the status of a transaction when a purchase (a long position) or a sale (a short position) has been made, and before cancellation, exercise, or expiration

opening purchase transaction
an initial transaction to buy, also known as the action of "going long"

opening sale transaction
an initial transaction to sell, also known as the action of "going short"

tion. That status remains the same as long as you take no further action. The position is closed upon entering a *closing sale transaction*, or upon exercise or expiration.

Example: You sold a call last month, putting yourself in a short position. As long as you take no further action, you are at risk of exercise. The buyer on the other end of the transaction can exercise at any time before expiration. You have choices. You can wait out the period between now and expiration, hoping the option does not go in the money (which would probably lead to exercise, requiring that you sell 100 shares at the striking price). Or you may choose to execute a *closing purchase transaction*, and end the option before expiration.

> **closing sale transaction**
> a transaction to close a long position, executed by selling an option previously bought, closing it out

DEFINING POSSIBLE OUTCOMES OF CLOSING OPTIONS

Every option will be canceled by an offsetting closing transaction, exercise, or expiration. The results of each affect buyers and sellers in different manners.

> **closing purchase transaction**
> a transaction to close a short position, executed by buying an option previously sold, canceling it out

Results for the Buyer

1. If you cancel your open long position with a closing sale transaction, you will receive payment. If that price is higher than the original purchase amount, you realize a profit; if lower, you suffer a loss.

2. If you exercise the option, you will receive (for a call) or sell (for a put) 100 shares of stock at its striking price. You will exercise only if this action is advantageous, based on the current market value of the underlying stock. That means market value will be higher than the striking price (of a call) or lower than the striking price (of a put).

3. If you allow the option to expire, you will lose the entire premium amount you paid for the original purchase. It is a complete loss.

Results for the Seller

1. If you cancel your open position with a closing purchase transaction, you will pay a premium, which is due on the following business day. If the price is lower than the price you received for the original opening sale transaction, you realize a profit; if higher, you suffer a loss.

2. If your option is exercised by the buyer, you are required to deliver 100 shares of the underlying stock at the striking price (for a call), or to purchase 100 shares of the stock at the striking price (for a put).

3. If the option expires worthless, you earn a profit. Your open position is canceled by the expiration, and the premium you received at the time you originally sold the option is yours to keep. It is all profit.

These outcomes are summarized in Figure 2.1. Notice that buyers and sellers have opposite results for each option upon close. The buyer receives cash, while the seller pays. The buyer chooses to exercise, while the seller has no choice in the decision. And upon expiration, the buyer has a total loss, while the seller has a total profit.

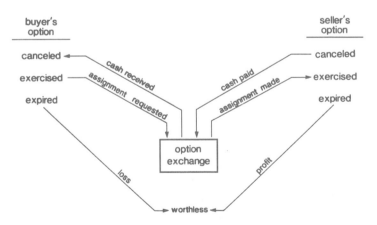

FIGURE 2.1 Outcomes of closing the position.

EXERCISING THE OPTION

Option transactions occur through the exchange on which that option is listed. While several different exchanges handle trading of options and the trend today is toward automated trading throughout the country, the Options Clearing Corporation (OCC) is the registered clearing agency for all stock options traded in the United States. The broad function of the OCC is to provide for orderly settlement of all listed option contracts, which occurs through contact between brokers and customers. When a option investor notifies a broker of the desire to execute a transaction, the OCC ensures that the terms of the contract will be honored. In this way, the seller and buyer do not have to depend on one another; the transaction is facilitated through the OCC, which depends on its member brokers to enforce *assignment*. Since there is no specific matching of open positions between buyers and sellers, the question arises: How does a seller know whether his or her option will be exercised? You cannot know. This is a risk, but it won't necessarily happen. When exercise occurs long before expiration date, the order can be assigned to any of the sellers with open positions in that option. This takes place either on a random basis or on the basis of first-in, first-out (the earliest sellers are the first ones exercised). Upon exercise of an option, 100 shares *must* be delivered. *Delivery* is the movement of stock ownership from the seller to the buyer. The buyer exchanges payment and receives registration of the shares, and the seller receives payment and relinquishes ownership of the same shares.

When a buyer decides to exercise an option, 100 shares of stock are either purchased ("called from") or sold ("put to") the seller. When you have sold a call, exercise by the buyer means 100 shares are called from you and transferred to the buyer; and when you sell a put, exercise requires you to buy 100 shares. The process of calling and putting stock upon exercise is called *conversion*. Stock is assigned at the time of exercise, a necessity since the number of buyers and sellers will rarely, if ever, match; so exercise is assigned at the time the election is

assignment
the act of exercise against a seller, done on a random basis or in accordance with orderly procedures developed by the Options Clearing Corporation and brokerage firms

delivery
the movement of stock ownership from one owner to another (In the case of exercised stock, shares are registered to the new owner upon payment by the seller.)

conversion
the process of moving assigned stock from the seller of a call option or to the seller of a put option

called away
the result of having stock assigned (Upon exercise, 100 shares of the seller's stock are called away at the striking price.)

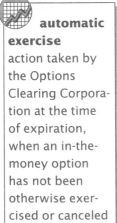

early exercise
the act of exercising an option prior to expiration date

automatic exercise
action taken by the Options Clearing Corporation at the time of expiration, when an in-the-money option has not been otherwise exercised or canceled

made. When a call is assigned, the stock is said to be *called away*.

Is exercise always a negative to the seller? At first glance, it would seem that exercise is most likely to occur at a bad time, considering the relative market value of the stock and the striking price of the option. However, the answer to this question really depends on the original purpose in going short by selling options. Most option sellers want to avoid exercise either by closing the position when the option is in the money or by initially selecting options considered most likely to expire worthless. Sellers have to be aware that exercise is a likely risk for any option, and they have to prepare for that outcome. Exercise can occur at any time, although the real risk exists only when those options are in the money. It is generally assumed that the majority of exercises occur at or shortly before expiration date; but remember, the buyer does have the right to exercise at any time (*early exercise*).

Exercise is not always generated by the buyer's action. *Automatic exercise* can occur due to action by the Options Clearing Corporation. Remember that the OCC, acting through the exchanges, acts as buyer to every seller, and as seller to every buyer. It will match up exercise for buyers against open positions held by sellers whenever possible. But if, at the time of expiration, there exists an excess of sellers, options in the money will be automatically exercised.

The decision to avoid exercise is made on the basis of current market value. As long as options are out of the money, there is no point in exercise and thus no danger of its occurring on the other side of the transaction. But once the option goes in the money, sellers must decide whether to risk exercise or to cancel the position with an offsetting transaction.

Example: You bought 100 shares of stock two months ago, paying $57 per share. You invested $5700 plus brokerage fees. Last month, the stock's market value was $62 per share. At that time, you decided to sell a call with a striking price of 60 ($60 per share). As the seller, you were paid a premium for that call of 7 ($700). You were willing to be placed in this short position. Your reasoning: If the call is exercised, your total profit will be $1000 before brokerage fees. That consists of 3 points per share (market value of $60, less your original cost of $57) plus $700 you were paid for selling the call:

Striking price	$60
Less: your cost per share	–57
Stock profit	$ 3
Plus: option premium	7
Total profit per share	$10

This example shows that it is possible for an investor to sell a call that is in the money, hoping for exercise. In the event of exercise, you stand to profit, both from the option premium and from a gain on the stock itself. At the same time, you protect profits already earned. That's because you receive money for selling the option. In the above example, the premium was $700. You could look at that as a discount on your original stock investment of $5700, or an adjusted basis of $5000. So even if the stock were to fall seven points, your original investment would still be intact.

Example: You recently sold a put and were paid a premium of 3 ($300). The striking price was 35. At the time of your transaction, the stock's market value was $33 per share, and today it continues to trade at about the same level. Even though the put is two points in the money, you are not concerned. If the put is exercised, you will be required to buy 100 shares at $35, two points above current market value. However, keep three things in mind: First, you received a premium of $300, so that in the event of exercise, your real cost is still one point lower than current market value. Second, whenever you sell a put, you should consider the striking price as a reasonable amount to pay for the stock. In the event of exercise at $35 per share, you would not mind owning 100 shares of stock. And third, if the stock's value rises above the striking price and remains there until expiration, it will not be exercised.

Example: You have owned 100 shares of stock for several years. You purchased the stock at $48 per share, and current market value is $59 per share. You want to sell a call against this stock. Recognizing that you are $11 per share ahead of your original cost, you are willing to risk part of your profit to earn a higher premium for selling a call. You decide to sell a call with a striking price of 55, which is 4 points in the money. For selling this call, you receive a premium of 6 ($600). In the event of exercise, you will not only gain $700 on the stock, you will also keep your option premium of $600, for a total profit of $1300. The $600 you were paid for the call consists of four points of intrinsic value (striking price, minus current market value) and two points of time value. As a seller, time is on your side, so, unless the option is exercised, the time value will come out of the premium by expiration date.

The decision to act or wait often is determined by the amount of time value in the option premium. As a general rule, the longer until expiration, the higher the time value will be; and the closer the gap between striking price and market value, the more important the time value level is, both to buyer and to seller. For the buyer, time value is a negative, so the higher the time value, the more risk. The opposite is true for the seller. Buyers pay an amount above intrinsic value—the difference between the stock's *current market value* and the option's striking price—knowing that the time value will disappear by the time of expiration. But as a seller, that same time value represents a potential profit. So the greater the time value when you sell an option, the greater your chance for profit, for the same reason: Time value will disappear between now and expiration date.

current market value
the market value of stock at any given time

Example: You have decided to buy a call with a striking price of 30. The underlying stock's current market value is $32 per share, and the option premium is 5 ($500). Your premium will include 2 points of intrinsic value (the difference between current market value of the stock and striking price of the option). The balance, 3 points, represents time value. If the stock's market value does not increase by expiration, all of the time value will evaporate. The stock's market value must increase by 3 points in order for you to break even, and by more to produce a profit.

This demonstrates the risk evaluation option buyers need to perform. In this example, time value represents three-fifths of the premium. If expiration comes up quickly, the stock will have to increase very dramatically in a short period of time if you hope to profit.

Example: Consider the same facts as in the previous example, but from the seller's point of view. You sell the option instead of buying it. That means you *receive* $500 instead of paying it. Of that, $300 is time value—a benefit rather than a problem. And the question of time until expiration is opposite as well. The sooner the option expires, the better. Now, the point of view is changed. As long as the stock's market value does not increase by more than 3 points between now and expiration, your transaction will be profitable. The premium you received will more than offset any difference of 3 points or less in a change in the stock's market value.

By the time of expiration, all of the time value will have disappeared from the option's premium value, and all remaining premium will consist entirely of intrinsic value. This condition is known as *parity*.

parity
the condition of an option at expiration, when the total premium consists of intrinsic value and no time value

Using the Daily Options Listings

When you invest in shares of stock, a lot of emphasis is placed on research and tracking *before* the investment is made. Once you have the stock, in most situations, you can afford to let matters take their own course. With options, however, you need to be able to keep an eye on a quickly changing market on an almost daily basis. Both buyers and sellers have to watch the stock's price movement as well as the option, so that they can take advantage of momentary opportunities, or take quick action to avoid suddenly evolving dangers. Open positions on both sides must be monitored.

With the widespread use of home computers and modem systems for investments, you can easily monitor your options values on an almost instantaneous basis. In the past, it was necessary to call a broker to check prices, or to wait until the following day and read listings in the paper. If you did not subscribe to a specialized financial publication, chances were quite high that your daily paper was inadequate. Detailed options listings, being of interest to only a small number of investors and taking up a lot of room, are simply not printed in broadly circulated daily newspapers. Options investors today have a great advantage over their counterparts one decade ago.

Example: You bought a call for 3 ($300) and a striking price of 50. Your goal is to sell when the stock's market value rises by 5 points or more. But you also know that time is working against you. With that in mind, you would like to anticipate trends in the underlying stock. So you track two things: the stock's price movement and the daily changes in the option's premium value. You plot these trends on a scaled chart.

Whether you use an automated system or published options listings, you need to learn how to read the listings. A typical daily options listing is shown in Figure 2.2. The first column identifies the underlying stock and the current price. In this example Delta closed at $37 per share. The second column shows the striking price for

		CALLS			PUTS		
		JAN	APR	JUL	JAN	APR	JUL
Delta	25	12	14	17 ½	¹⁄₁₆	s	s
37	30	7 ½	8 ⅜	9	r	⅛	r
37	35	2 ⅝	5 ⅛	7	⅜	2	3 ½
37	40	⅛	1 ½	r	3 ¼	5	r
37	45	r	r	s	8 ½	11	14 ⅛

r – no trades this date
s – not offered

FIGURE 2.2   Example of daily option listing.

each available option. As a general rule, stocks valued at $100 or less have options in 5-point intervals; above $100, in 10-point intervals. It is possible that options will be open above or below the ranges shown in the listings, but volume may be so small that they are not reported.

Columns three through five show current premiums for calls, and columns six through eight are the put premiums. Delta reports options on the January, April, July, and October (JAJO) cycle, so three different expiration dates are shown. Since options only exist for nine months or so, the farthest month in the cycle is not shown. In this illustration, no listing is provided for October calls or puts. That will appear only after the January options have expired. Notice that those options with the greater amount of time remaining until expiration tend to have greater time values than those nearer to expiration.

In this example, Delta's current market value is $37 per share. So the 35 calls are 2 points in the money and the 30 calls are 7 points in the money. The January 35 calls include 2 points of intrinsic value and only $5/8$th of a point of time value; for the longer-term 35 calls, time value is greater. The 30 calls include 7 points of intrinsic value. On the put side, the 40 contract is 3 points in the money, and current premium values reflect intrinsic value of at least that much.

Making an Evaluation

As an option investor, you need to make several judgment calls concerning the option and the underlying stock, including:

✔ Recent volatility and volume in stock trading.
✔ Time until expiration of specific options contracts.
✔ Relative levels of time and intrinsic value.
✔ Current premium levels.

Example: You are interested in buying calls on a particular stock you have been following. You recognize that certain stocks experience price movements desirable for particular option strategies. This stock is at present selling for $47 per share. You eliminate as possibilities those calls with striking prices of 35 and 40 as being too expensive. And the 55 striking price is 8 points out of the money. Considering the time problem, your most likely prospects are calls with striking prices of 45 and 50.

In this example, the 45 option is 2 points in the money, so you know that the value of the call will change almost dollar for dollar with the underlying stock. If the stock rises $2 per share, the 45 call will increase in value by 2 ($200) as well. But if the stock falls to $45 per share, the option will lose 2 points.

Also in this example, the January option will expire in the very near future. If you buy that option, you will be paying almost nothing for time value. From that point alone—and for the moment, ignoring the time factor—the January option represents the best bargain.

However, the time factor cannot ever be ignored in the options market. Because of the short time until expiration, you have greater risks that the option will expire before there is an opportunity for the underlying stock's value to increase. The pricing of options is invariably a balance between time value and expiration. In the above example, you might buy the option and the stock could go up 1 point the following day, creating a $100 profit immediately. It could also fall 1 point. Or, because time is short, the stock might not move at all between now and expiration.

The transaction cost is always a factor. Although that is not included in any of the examples in this book, you need to conduct your own analysis on a net basis. So in order to net a $100 profit, a change of $1^1/_2 points might be required; if a stock transaction is involved as well, you might require an even larger gap.

These are the points of evaluation and analysis to keep in mind when considering an option investment, either as buyer or as seller. The same processes should be applied to puts. In order to profit from investing in puts, you depend on changes in the underlying stock's value before expiration. For buyers, the desirable direction is downward. As a buyer of puts, you hope a decline in value is sufficient to:

✔ Offset time value premium.
✔ Cover brokerage transaction fees of buying *and* selling.
✔ Yield a reasonable profit net of costs.

For sellers, time is on your side. You hope that time value comes out of the premium without excessive movement in the underlying stock. With puts, you want the underlying stock to move in the opposite direction than with calls, but the motives and strategies are identical.

Opening and Closing Stock Trades

Many option investors are first attracted to the market because they already invest in common stocks. In fact, a significant number of option investors use options in conjunction with stocks they own and trade. As you will see in coming chapters, the speculation in short-term price movement is only the most obvious reason for buying or selling options.

With the connection between stocks and options, you should know how to trade in stocks as an essential part of your option strategy. The stock market is operated by a number of dealers and brokers. They execute trades for all customers. Institutional investors (insurance companies, pension plans, mutual funds, and other large investors) are responsible for the bulk of large-volume trades; but in sheer numbers, the individual investors taking part in the market dominate. They are called "retail" investors because they pay relatively higher commissions than those trading in blocks of 10,000 or more shares at one time.

A trade is executed by placing a call to a broker, or by entering a trade electronically from your home computer. You specify your account identification, the stock, the number of shares, whether you want to buy or sell, and price information. Trades can be made "at market"—meaning at the current available price—or at a specified level. In some orders, the timing is specified. For example, you can instruct a broker to make a trade if and when a certain price level is reached, but to be effective only until the end of the trading day. The variety of trading limits makes it possible to satisfy the trading preferences of almost all investors.

The many methods of selecting and evaluating stocks is not the subject of this book. An options investor should be comfortable in the stock market and should have a fair understanding, at the very least, of how the market works before embarking on an options program. Below is a brief summary of how to read a stock listing from the financial pages, offered here only as a review of what every investor in the market should know well.

The daily listing for every stock includes on one line a great deal of useful information used by analysts to judge the relative health and history of a stock's price and yield. For example, a typical stock exchange listing looks like this:

$$37^1/_4 \ 22^1/_2 \ \text{Ronbar 1} \ 234 \ 33^1/_2 \ 33 \ 33^1/_4 \ -^1/_4$$

All of these items have a meaning. The first two columns summarize the trading range of the past 12 months. During the past 12-month period, the fictitious stock Ronbar traded between its high of $37^1/_4$ and low of $22^1/_2$. Its regular dividend is $1 per share (represented by the "1" after the name). This means a 25-cents-per-share dividend is paid each quarter. The next column, 234, is the volume of the previous day's traded shares. Since this represents the number of trades in equivalent round lots, it reveals that 23,400 shares were traded. The following columns show the high and low prices for the day. In this example, the stock traded in a relatively small range between $33^1/_2$ and 33 (dollars per share). The next column reports $33^1/_4$, which is the day's closing price. Finally, the last column shows $-^1/_4$, meaning the stock lost 25 cents per share, or $^1/_4$ point on the day.

The stock market includes much more than the stock daily listing: Using the possible methods of fundamental and technical analysis can be a full-time job for any investor. The purpose here is simply to review the basics. The abbreviated terminology for the stock market may be universally understood by investors, while a separate series of codes and abbreviations is used in the options market. Even a seasoned stock market investor who is not involved in the options market will be unfamiliar with the specialized coding for options trading.

Understanding Option Abbreviations

Option values are expressed in abbreviated form in listings and in communication between brokers and their clients. The value of a contract is always expressed in fractional value per 100 shares, or for a single option contract. Table 2.1 shows fractions and their equivalent dollar values; 3 means $300 and $2\frac{5}{8}$ means $262.50. Options trade down to fractional values as small as sixteenths of a point, with each sixteenth being equal to $6.25.

The abbreviated expression of options and their terms goes beyond the current premium. Both the expiration month and the striking price are expressed in shorthand form as well. For example, an October option with a striking price of 35 per share is called an OCT 35 option. And a January option with a 50 striking price is a JAN 50. Like the premium value, striking price is expressed without dollar signs.

	TABLE 2.1	Fractional Values	
Fraction	Dollar Value	Fraction	Dollar Value
$\frac{1}{16}$	$ 6.25	$\frac{9}{16}$	$ 56.25
$\frac{1}{8}$	12.50	$\frac{5}{8}$	62.50
$\frac{3}{16}$	18.75	$\frac{11}{16}$	68.75
$\frac{1}{4}$	25.00	$\frac{3}{4}$	75.00
$\frac{5}{16}$	31.25	$\frac{13}{16}$	81.25
$\frac{3}{8}$	37.50	$\frac{7}{8}$	87.50
$\frac{7}{16}$	43.75	$\frac{15}{16}$	93.75
$\frac{1}{2}$	50.00	1	100.00

A complete option description must include the underlying stock, expiration month, striking price, type of call, and current premium: all of the terms and the current value. A sample of this is shown in Figure 2.3. In this illustration, all of the necessary elements are expressed. The terms, when expressed together in this manner, distinguish all options from all other options.

When you call a broker to make an option trade, it is possible to give trading instructions without abbreviations; but that requires the broker to translate your description into abbreviated form before placing the order. Whenever translation is required, the chance of error is increased. So it helps both sides to learn the abbreviations commonly used for option trading, including a series of symbols used to represent expiration month and striking price. Considering the volume of transactions possible for options trading *and* the urgency of timing, abbreviated forms of communication are essential in the options market. Figure 2.4 summarizes the symbols used by virtually all brokerage firm traders when placing buy and sell orders for their customers.

The expiration month is always expressed first, followed immediately by striking price. Note that the striking prices of 5, 105, and 205 have the same symbol. One symbol is used for all three, since the daily price of the underlying stock dictates which of the three prices is applicable to a particular stock.

Example: You want to trade in call options with October expiration and a 35 striking price. The symbol (from Figure 2.4) consists of "J" for the expiration

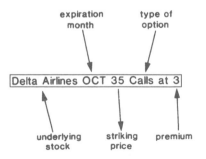

FIGURE 2.3 A complete option description.

expiration month symbols		
MONTH	CALLS	PUTS
January	A	M
February	B	N
March	C	O
April	D	P
May	E	Q
June	F	R
July	G	S
August	H	T
September	I	U
October	J	V
November	K	W
December	L	X

striking price symbols			
STRIKING PRICE			SYMBOL
5	105	205	A
10	110	210	B
15	115	215	C
20	120	220	D
25	125	225	E
30	130	230	F
35	135	235	G
40	140	240	H
45	145	245	I
50	150	250	J
55	155	255	K
60	160	260	L
65	165	265	M
70	170	270	N
75	175	275	O
80	180	280	P
85	185	285	Q
90	190	290	R
95	195	295	S
100	200	300	T
7½	–	–	U
12½	–	–	V
17½	–	–	W
22½	–	–	X

FIGURE 2.4 Option trading symbols.

month and "G" for striking price. Thus, the call option is a JG option. If the option is a put, the correct symbol would be VG.

The complete option quote also includes an abbreviated symbol for the underlying stock. Each listed stock has a unique abbreviation used universally to describe it in trading. Delta Airlines, for example, is abbreviated as DAL. So a Delta Airlines call with a striking price of 35, expiring next October, consists of five letters. As illustrated in Figure 2.5, the stock code is listed first, followed

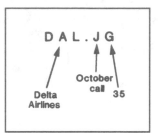

FIGURE 2.5   Example of option quote.

by a period and the two-letter code identifying the month and striking price. Distinction between call and put is included in the month code.

SETTING STANDARDS

Before entering into any option trade, you should establish specific standards for yourself. This is true, of course, for all investing; you need to know when to make decisions and what decisions to make, based on your standards. Having decided what you expect to achieve, decisions are easier. Several questions arise with option investing, such as:

✔ Should the position be closed or allowed to expire?

✔ On what basis should the decision to close be made? Should you establish a minimum acceptable profit level that you will accept, or a minimum loss that you are able to tolerate?

✔ What types of options should you buy, and for what purpose?

✔ How much money should you invest in options and keep at risk?

✔ What portion of your portfolio or available cash should be placed into options?

Setting standards helps you to decide what levels and types of risks are acceptable to you. This is a requirement at every phase of investing. Without setting goals and defining investment standards, you have no means for measuring your success, and to what degree you are succeeding in executing your plan. Without this step, you don't really have a plan at all. Identifying risks is a crucial part of this, and is essential to success in the market, particularly in options investing.

Example: You purchase a call and pay 3 ($300). The option will expire in seven months. In this case, you are accepting the risk that the underlying stock's market value will not go in the money sufficiently to yield a profit higher than the $300 (your original premium cost). No matter what market value existed at the time of your purchase, it must be high enough to yield you the required profit at some point prior to expiration.

The prospect of yielding a profit must be a part of your goal if your only purpose in buying the call is to earn such a profit. For this to occur, price will have to go in the money at some point before expiration; it is dangerous to depend on profiting as a buyer just on time value. That will not happen in normal conditions. Time value rarely increases.

As a buyer of the call in the previous example, you should be willing to risk $300 on the chance that the stock will exceed 3 points of premium value in the money at some point before expiration. So, for example, you might set a standard for yourself in these circumstances that you will sell when the premium is at or above 5 ($500). That action will yield you a profit and also provide a goal. Reaching that goal should generate a sell order. One of the greatest risks in option investing is the greed factor. You might have a poorly defined goal, only to put off action because you believe the potential is there for even more gain. That might be true, but you most likely will end up losing more than you gain if you fail to adhere to established investment standards and personal goals. You should always understand the risks *and* set standards before embarking on the investment.

Example: You have 100 shares of stock in your portfolio, currently valued at $46 per share. You sell a call with a striking price of 45 and receive a premium of 4 ($400). You realize that if the call is exercised, your stock will be called away at $45 per share. The risk is that the stock's market value will increase substantially above that level. However, you are willing to accept that risk in exchange for the certainty of receiving $400 in premium today.

In this example, you have set a standard. It states that you are willing to let the stock go for $45 per share in exchange for $400. You are willing to have your option exercised even if the stock's value climbs far above that level. You can set additional standards as well. For example, you might decide that if the option's value declines by two points, you will buy it and close the position, accepting a $200 profit. This frees you to sell another call if the stock later rises.

You should consider what could happen if you do not set a standard. A pattern might develop in which you can never win. This is a common problem for those who trade options, because some traders discover they cannot resist current trends. Rather than operating from a well planned and firm standard, they react to what appears to be happening from day to day.

Example: You bought a put two weeks ago, believing that the underlying stock's market value would fall. You paid a premium of 2 ($200). Originally, you hoped to double your money, which would require the stock's falling two points or more. Once in the money, the put would increase in value one dollar for each point the stock declined in value. As of last week, the stock's market value had fallen 3 points and your put option was worth 5 ($500). You could have sold it and realized a profit of $300. But you did not sell because you thought the stock might continue its downward movement. Three days ago, the stock rebounded two points, so that your option's value was reduced to 3 ($300). You now see that you could have sold when you had the chance. So you resolved that if that opportunity comes up again, you will sell and take your profit.

Yesterday, the stock's value fell to its lowest point yet, down 4 points. The put was worth 7 ($700). You knew you should sell and take your profit, but again you speculated that the stock might continue to fall, and you did nothing. Today, the stock rebounded several points, and now your put is worth 1 point, half of the price you originally paid.

This type of scenario is not uncommon. Many paper profits have been lost because investors failed to set standards, or failed to observe them once they were set. When the decision point arrives, you need to be able to make your decision with confidence, and take action immediately. The option market is changing constantly, and time does not wait while investors change their minds. You are better off losing future unrealized profit potential than you are losing money today. If you are willing to take greater risks and pass up short-term profits, you also need to be willing to experience more losses than those who set and follow specific rules.

You can set and enforce your own standards with the use of a device called a *stop order*. This order is placed with a broker and will be executed only if the price specified in the order is reached. The stop order does not ensure that the transaction will be made at that price. It happens at that price or above (for a buy) or below (for a sell). Once the threshold price has been reached, the order becomes a *market order*, meaning to buy at the lowest available price or to sell at the highest available price. The market order is the most common form of order. For option buyers, the stop order can serve as a valuable tool for preventing losses arising from hesitation. They can be put into effect as a way of ensuring that you follow your own standards.

stop order
an order from an investor to a broker to buy at or above a specified price, or to sell at or below a specified price level (Once that level has been met or passed, the order becomes a market order.)

market order
an order from an investor to a broker to buy or sell at the best available price

Example: You bought a call last week for 6 ($600) in the hope that the stock's market value would rise. However, you are aware of the risk that the stock will fall, meaning an immediate loss of value in your call. So you place a stop order for 4. If the option's value falls to 4 points or below, a sale will be executed automatically, and as soon as possible. This does not mean you will necessarily receive $400. If the option's value falls rapidly, the premium value could be lower than 4 at the time the sale is executed.

Example: You buy a call for 4 ($400) and place a stop order for 3. If the value falls to 3 or below, a sale will be executed automatically and as soon as possible. There is no guarantee that the sale will occur at 3. The actual sale price could be lower.

You can also specify an exact price. This ensures that a transaction will occur *only* if that price is available. The problem here is that the specified price could be surpassed rapidly and might never be available again. Such an order is called a *stop-limit order*. With such an order, the investor instructs the broker to execute a trade at a specified price, or within a specified price range. For example, you might tell your broker to sell an option after it has fallen to 4 or below, but not below 2.

Stop-limit orders are useful for both buy and sell transactions, and can be used to help you enforce your standards when you can't watch the market and its movements constantly. *A word of caution*: Not every exchange allows the use of stop orders for option trading, and the rules of one exchange might not apply on another. Before devising a strategy including the use of stop orders, check with your broker and make sure that the exchange on which the options are traded allows them.

It is fair to say that the use of these devices makes it easier to enforce a standard. But whether you use stop orders or not, you should establish standards before investing money. Know when to close a position, whether you're winning or losing, based entirely on the formula you develop *in advance*. Many investors try the options market; some succeed and others fail. The majority of those who fail did not establish a standard for themselves. All investing contains a gambling element. But proper research, an understanding of a market's attrib-

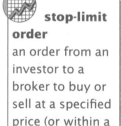

stop-limit order
an order from an investor to a broker to buy or sell at a specified price (or within a specified range)

utes, careful timing, and firm standards all add to your chances of success; the lack of these features virtually ensures failure.

CALCULATING RATE OF RETURN FOR SELLERS

Investors guide themselves and judge their success by their *rate of return*. In a single transaction involving one buy transaction and one sell transaction, rate of return is easy to calculate. Simply divide the net profit by the total purchase amount; the resulting percentage is the rate of return. When you sell options, though, the rate of return is more complicated. Remember, when you sell an option, the sale precedes the closing purchase transaction. Rate of return will vary depending on several possible events, including:

rate of return
the yield from investing, calculated by dividing net cash profit upon sale by the amount spent at purchase

1. Ownership of 100 shares of stock for each option sold.
2. Exercise of the option by a buyer.
3. Closing a position after favorable decline in premium value.
4. Significant change in the stock's market value.

Rate of return should always be studied and compared on an *annualized basis*. Because different investments may be owned for different lengths of time, it is not realistic to simply calculate rate of return and compare them. A 50 percent return in 2 months is much more significant than the same rate of return for an investment held for 10 months. To annualize a rate of return, follow these steps:

annualized basis
a method for comparing rates of return for holdings of varying periods, in which all returns are expressed as though investments had been held over a full year (It involves dividing the holding period by the number of months the positions were open, and multiplying the result by 12.)

1. Calculate the rate of return. Divide the net profit by the amount at purchase, and express the result as a percentage.
2. Divide the percentage rate of return by the number of months the investment position was open.
3. Multiply by 12.

Example: You had a rate of return of 12 percent from an investment. Annualized rate of return will vary depending on the number of months the investment was earned.

1. Three months:

   net profit 12 ÷ 3 = 4

   4 × 12 = 48%   (If you had held this investment and realized the same yield over a full year, the return would have been 48 percent)

2. Eight months:

   net profit 12 ÷ 8 = 1.5

   1.5 × 12 = 18%   (If you had held this investment and realized the same yield over a full year, the return would have been 18 percent)

3. Fifteen months:

   net profit 12 ÷ 15 = .8

   .8 × 12 = 9.6%   (If you had held this investment and realized the same yield only one year, the return would have been 9.6 percent)

As these examples demonstrate, annualized rate of return differs dramatically when the number of months varies. Annualizing works for periods greater than one year, in which case the annualized rate of return should be less than the straight rate (Example 3, above). Just as a short period should be extended and expressed as though it had been realized over a full year, a period greater than one year should be contracted and expressed as though the return applied *only* to one year.

Through annualizing, all rates of return are expressed on a comparable basis. This makes analysis of option trading more realistic. However, annualizing does not always indicate the true overall performance. Remember that for very short periods, an annualized rate of return is of little use for judging overall return.

Example: You recently bought a call for 1 and two weeks later sold it for 3. The profit of 200 percent, expressed on an annualized basis, is 4800 percent. Even though this is an impressive rate of return, it does not indicate the types of returns you earn consistently in every other option investment.

The nature of option investing makes annualized rate of return a tool for use in overall analysis, not in individual transactions. Option investing typically involves several transactions during the year, which might include both long and short positions. A particular strategy could dictate longer holding periods than another strategy. You will discover that application of annualized return over a broad range of transactions and over time is meaningful, but that isolated analysis is not aided by it. Too much can happen to distort the averages. For example, you might have a 4800 percent annualized return this month; but that money may sit idle for three months. In a fair analysis, the idle time has to be counted in overall annualized return. Or you might follow that profit with a 9600 percent annualized loss. Different investment amounts will be involved in each transaction. In short, a variety of factors are involved in the overall combination of strategies option investors use.

Even when reviewing a simple rate of return or anticipating likely outcomes, you sometimes need to make calculations based on more than one possible outcome. When you are considering selling options, you need to judge risks based on two possible outcomes: return if exercised and return if unchanged.

Return if exercised is the return you will realize if the underlying stock is called away by the buyer. *Return if unchanged* is the return you will realize if the underlying stock is not called away through exercise. In both forms of return, the calculation includes income or loss from all sources. The major difference between the two rates has to do with profit or loss on the stock. Return if exercised includes the sale of 100 shares. However, return if unchanged is based on the assumption that the stock price

return if exercised
the estimated rate of return option sellers will earn in the event the buyer exercises the option (The calculation includes profit or loss on the underlying stock, dividends earned, and premium received for selling the option.)

return if unchanged
the estimated rate of return option sellers will earn in the event the buyer does not exercise the option (The calculation includes dividends earned on the underlying stock, and the premium received for selling the option.)

remains out of the money; thus, there is no exercise and no profit or loss from a stock transaction.

In computing return, always remember to include computation of a broker's commission; that can make the difference between profit and loss. Commission rates vary greatly from one broker to another, and if you plan to execute a large volume of transactions, shopping around may be worth thousands of dollars. In the majority of the illustrations presented here, single contract examples are used; in reality, many option traders transact many options at the same time. The greater the number of contracts, the lower the commission. All of these factors should be kept in mind when studying examples.

Example: You own 100 shares of stock originally purchased for $58 per share. Current market value is $63 per share. You sell a call with a striking price of 60 and receive a premium of 7 ($700). Between the time of selling the call and expiration, you are paid two dividends, totaling $68.

Return if Exercised

Striking price	$6000
Original cost	5800
Profit	$ 200
Dividends	68
Call premium	700
Total profit	$ 968

Return if exercised ($968 ÷ $5800) = 16.69%

Return if Unchanged

Call premium	$ 700
Dividends	68
Total profit	$ 768

Return if unchanged ($768 ÷ $5800) = 13.24%

The next step—to accurately compare the two returns—is to annualize. For example, if the time between purchase of the stock and expiration of the option is nine months, annualized return if exercised is:

$$16.69\% \div 9 = 1.85\%$$
$$1.85\% \times 12 = 22.20\%$$

This calculation assumes that exercise occurs at the point of expiration, which is the most likely time. In comparison, return if unchanged is:

$$13.24\% \div 9 = 1.47\%$$
$$1.47\% \times 12 = 17.64\%$$

So, on an annualized basis, we can conclude that return if exercised would be 22.20%, and return if unchanged would be 17.64%. These calculations can be performed in advance of even making the decision to sell a call. From the comparison, you may conclude that exercise would produce a greater return than nonexercise.

A problem in comparing these returns is that one is based on the sale of the underlying stock, while the other involves only option premium and dividend. The comparison is not valid, because you need to assess whether or not you're willing to sell the stock at the striking price. As a general rule, you should not sell a call if you are not willing to release the stock upon exercise. In addition to the flaw in comparison between the two outcomes, the sale of the stock also means there will be a tax consequence, a point to keep in mind when planning outcomes. Make your own comparisons on a net basis, meaning you also calculate the taxes on your profit. Taxes have not been calculated here because tax rates differ vastly for individuals on the federal level, and state and local taxes will be different for everyone as well.

Once an option is exercised, you face another problem—a sum of available cash that you probably will want to reinvest. Depending on the timing and market conditions, exercise could create problems for you that you do not anticipate when simply evaluating option investments. Obviously, the likely outcomes are far from comparative, given that each outcome creates a different set of circumstances for you.

Consider how these computations can be used. In deciding whether or not to enter into a particular option transaction, an understanding of possible outcomes—exercised or unchanged—will help you to judge risks as well as potential profit. With this in mind, the relatively easy calculations are valuable to you whenever you are thinking about an option transaction. In other words, assuming that you are willing to sell the stock, suffer the tax consequences of the profit, and risk the timing of the market and the need to reinvest your proceeds, comparisons of outcome are valuable tools.

In comparing return if exercised and return if unchanged, also note whether you have owned the stock for more than the option period. If you have owned the stock for many years, it is not accurate to include the gain on the stock in the calculated annualization along with the option premium. The longer you have owned the stock, the greater the distortion. Another factor: If the striking price is actually *lower* than the original cost of that stock, then return if exercised involved offsetting an option profit with a stock loss. This also affects annualization, especially if you have owned the stock for many years.

Example: You bought 100 shares of stock last year and paid $37 per share. Last month, you sold a call with a striking price of 35—two dollars below your basis. You were paid a premium of 6; you will also receive a dividend of $40 between now and expiration.

Return if Exercised

Striking price	$3500
Original cost	3700
Loss	$(200)
Dividends	40
Call premium	600
Net profit	$ 440

Return if exercised ($440 ÷ $3700) = 11.89%

As an aware options trader, you need to calculate the risks in advance of entering a trade. You also need to set standards for yourself. In the above example, a return of 11.89% might be considered a reasonable way to profit from the option while also selling stock that has not lived up to expectations. Your own standards may vary, and options can be used to create profits, minimize losses, or expand your opportunities for success in the market. Standards identify the desired level of profit you hope to achieve, while also limiting your exposure to loss. Any options investor who experiences an unexpected loss has failed to evaluate all of the possibilities of a particular strategy. If you set standards and perform your evaluation properly, you will not suffer any unexpected surprises.

Success in the options market means entering an open position with complete awareness of all the possible outcomes. You will also know when to cancel a position with an offsetting closing transaction, based on changes in circumstances; when to exercise and when to allow options to expire; and what will happen to you as a seller in the event of exercise. You need to have complete understanding of the range of outcomes before making any decision. Knowledge of profit potential is not enough. You also need to be aware of all of the risks involved in any strategy and any decision.

Buying Calls

A call grants the buyer the right to buy 100 shares of a specified stock, at a specified striking price, on or before a specified expiration date in the future. The premium the buyer pays acquires that right. As a call buyer, you choose among three alternatives: First, you can sell the call before it expires; second, you can exercise the call and buy 100 shares of the stock; or third, you can allow the call to expire worthless.

You are never obligated to buy 100 shares when you are the buyer. The seller, in contrast, would be required to deliver 100 shares if the buyer exercised the option. The decision you make as the buyer (owner) of a call will depend on:

✔ The actual movement of the underlying stock and the resulting effect on the call's value.

✔ Your reasons for buying the call in the first place.

✔ Your risk posture and willingness to wait out the future movement of the stock and the option, versus taking a sure profit today. (This is where setting and following your standards comes into play.)

UNDERSTANDING THE LIMITED LIFE OF THE CALL

You can become a call buyer purely in the interest of making a profit within a limited period of time. That profit is made by selling the call at a higher price than you paid for it, or by exercising the call to buy 100 shares of stock below current market value. The call can also be used to offset losses in a short position held in the underlying stock. These uses of the call are explained later in this chapter.

Every investor experiences risk, and the risks for buyers are not the same as those for sellers. Before becoming an options buyer, examine the risks and be completely familiar with the potential losses as well as the potential gains. Since the purchased option exists for only a very limited period of time, you will need to achieve your objective before expiration. Otherwise, the investment will quickly become worthless.

Anyone who has purchased stock knows that time is a luxury. In fact, one bit of wisdom about the stock market is that wise investors often must be patient. It takes time for companies to mature, and long-term growth means stockholders often need to settle back and wait for several years before their investment really pays off. The stockholder decides when and if to sell. Most people buy shares of stock for dividend income and long-term appreciation, so the time factor is a benefit. Call buyers, in comparison, cannot afford to wait too long. For the call buyer, time is the enemy.

A simple comparison between purchasing stock and purchasing options defines *speculation*. Typically, speculators accept the risk of total loss for the opportunity to be exposed to potentially substantial profits. Because a relatively small amount of money can be used to tie up 100 shares of stock, it is reasonable to describe call buying as one form of *leverage*. One of the most common examples of leverage is borrowing money to invest. However, buying options is another form. Because options are only rights and include no tangible ownership, and because they exist for only a limited period of time, they are essen-

speculation

the use of money to assume risks for short-term profit, in the knowledge that substantial or total losses are one possible outcome (Buying calls for leverage is one form of speculation. The buyer may earn a very large profit in a matter of days, or could lose the entire amount invested.)

tially side bets in the market. A buyer is betting that the stock's market value will rise, and a seller is betting that market value will fall. Fast—and significant—profits or losses can and do occur for call buyers, and knowing the extent of those potential profits and losses is an important first step.

Knowing what you're getting into, determining that the strategy is appropriate for you, and comprehending the risks involved define the idea of *suitability* for a particular investment or market strategy. Too often, would-be investors understand only the profit potential in a strategy, but are not aware of the risks.

Example: An investor has no experience whatsoever in the market; he has never owned stock before and does not know how the market works. He has $1000 to invest today, and decides he wants to earn a profit as fast as possible. A friend told him that fast and large profits can be earned by buying calls. He needs at least $1500 by September, when a debt will be due. Even though he cannot really afford to risk the $1000, he wants to buy three calls for 3 ($300) each. If the stock goes up at least 3 points, he will double his money; if the stock goes down or does not move at all, he will lose all of his money.

This investor does not meet the suitability standards for investing in options. He does not know what factors cause stocks to rise and fall; he cannot afford to lose the $1000; he is aware of the profit potential, but not aware enough of the loss potential. In this situation, the broker is responsible for recognizing that option buying is not appropriate. The broker should discourage this investor from buying calls and, if the investor persists, the broker should refuse to execute the order.

Call buyers who succeed develop a sense of timing. However, that sense grows from observing how the underlying stock moves. That cycle might not be easy to describe; it occurs in a somewhat predictable pattern, but the astute investor times option decisions based on experience. Not only is the timing important based on movements in the stock, but also the distance between the

leverage the use of investment capital in a way that a relatively small amount of money enables the investor to control a relatively large value (This is achieved through borrowing—for example, using borrowed money to purchase stocks or bonds—or through the purchase of options, which exist for only a short period of time but enable the option buyer to control 100 shares of stock. As a general rule, the use of leverage increases potential for profit as well as for loss.)

suitability
a standard by which a particular investment or market strategy is judged (The investor's knowledge and experience with options represent important suitability standards. Strategies are appropriate only if the investor understands the market and can afford to take the risks involved.)

purchase and expiration may also affect the risk level, and that level could be different for each stock. Because timing is so important for option buyers, the novice tends to suffer more losses than profits.

Example: An investor has several years' experience in the stock market. Even though she has never played the options market before, she has spent a lot of time reading about it, learning the terminology, and learning how to read options listings. She has tracked a few hypothetical option purchases over the past two or three months, and has begun to see the patterns of pricing changes. She also has a portfolio of relatively secure and diversified stocks and shares of mutual funds, and about $1000 in cash that she is willing to risk in the options market. She wants to buy three calls at 3 ($300) each, knowing the extent of potential gain *and* loss.

This situation is vastly different than the first example. This investor understands the market; she can afford to place the $1000 at risk; she knows both the profit and the loss potential. And even though she has no experience, she has spent the time to learn how the options market works, and has tracked a few hypothetical investments. For this investor, a limited experiment in the options market is entirely suitable. She understands that time works against the buyer, and that timing could spell the difference between profit and loss. She will be making an informed decision.

Suitability refers not only to your ability to afford losses, but also to the risks involved in the market. If this investor works with an experienced broker, it would make sense to also listen to that broker's advice about the proposed options investment. However, everyone who wants to become involved with options should also be aware that not every broker understands the market well enough to offer advice. Make sure your broker can really help and be willing to determine the course of your own investment decisions, even with the help of an experienced broker.

JUDGING THE CALL

Most call buyers lose money. Even with the most advanced understanding of the stock and options market, this fact cannot be overlooked. In many cases, the underlying stock's market value rises in value, but not enough to exceed the declining time value in the option. So in some instances, a modestly rising stock value is not enough to produce profits for the option investor.

Example: You recently bought a call for 4 ($400) when it was at the money (meaning the current market value and the striking price were identical)—at $45 per share. By expiration, the stock had risen to $47 per share, but the call was worth only 2 ($200). Why? The entire $400 premium at the time of purchase consisted of time value, and intrinsic value was zero. That evaporated completely by expiration. The remaining value of $200 represents the 2 points in the money and is all intrinsic value. The best action in this case would be to sell the option just before expiration and accept the $200 loss. The alternative would be to lose the entire amount by allowing the call to expire worthless.

Example: You bought a call two months ago at $3/8$ ($37.50) when the stock was 7 points out of the money (current market value was 7 points below striking price). Now the expiration date has arrived. The stock has experienced a 6-point rise, which is dramatic. However, the option is worthless because even with the dramatic rise in market value of the underlying stock the option is still out of the money. The premium at the time of purchase represented time value, and no intrinsic value exists.

Call buyers will lose money if they fail to set goals for themselves. If the premium value falls below their original cost, they have to overcome not only the fallen price, but time as well. That is why it is important to set a bail-out point for yourself, to cut your losses at some point. If the premium value rises above original cost, know in advance when you will sell, and follow that rule. Otherwise, today's profit may disappear tomorrow and the opportunity will be lost. Successful call buyers set and follow goals.

Example: You are the type of investor who believes in setting specific rules and standards. So when you bought a call at 4 ($400), you promised yourself you would sell if the call's premium value fell to 2 ($200), and that you would accept a $200 loss. You also vowed to sell the call if its value rose to 7 ($700), in which case you would have a $300 profit. You reasoned that if you followed your own rules, you would limit your losses and take your profits when available. You know that with options, time is always limited and opportunities might not be repeated. As an option buyer, you often do not get a second chance.

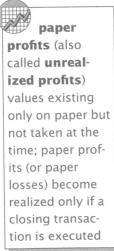

realized profits profits or losses taken at the time a position is closed

paper profits (also called **unrealized profits**) values existing only on paper but not taken at the time; paper profits (or paper losses) become realized only if a closing transaction is executed

Realized profits occur only when a position is closed. For a buyer, that requires an offsetting sale; and for a seller, it requires a closing purchase. As an option buyer, you need to decide at what point you will sell, and that decision has to be made before you enter the position. If you want to succeed, you also need to stick to the standard, and act when the moment arrives. Otherwise, you will only watch the potential for realized profits come and go. You will earn only *paper profits* but end up with realized losses.

Most call buyers study four attributes: current premium value, the portion representing time value, months until expiration, and perception of the underlying stock. For example, you might look through listings in the *Wall Street Journal*, seeking a call available for a premium of 2 or less, that is at the money or close to it, that has at least three months to expiration, and that is available on one of a limited number of companies you consider strong prospects for short-term price increase. However, this method is flawed. The smaller premiums do not always represent the best values.

The best premium bargains for options with the longest time until expiration are those that are the greatest number of points in the money. If the striking price is 40, and the stock is now worth less than $35 per share, you can probably easily find a call with six months until expiration for a very low price. Of course, you will also need that stock's market value to grow substantially in order for the option to have any intrinsic value by expiration. Or, in the alternative, time value needs to grow in the immediate future in order for your position to become profitable.

Trading on time value is a very poor strategy. It is possible that time value will increase in the very short term; but it is more likely that out-of-the-money options will be unresponsive to stock movement below striking price. In other words, if striking price is 40 and the option is trading between 34 and 39, don't expect time value to move much at all. While those price movements are occurring, time is going by. That means that time value will evaporate due to the passage of time and not due to changes in the stock's out-of-the-money value.

Example: You bought a call with a striking price of 40 and paid a premium of 1 ($100). The option will expire in seven months, meaning there is a lot of time in which the stock's market value might change. The stock is now at $34 per share, 6 points out of the money. In order for you to realize a profit on this call, the stock's market value must be greater than $41 per share (before considering broker charges), because you can estimate only the future intrinsic value, and not time value.

In the case above, time is definitely working against you as a buyer. You need the stock to grow by 7 points just to break even, and by more in order for you to realize a profit. If you simply look at the relationship between current premium and time until expiration, you can deceive yourself. Never trade on time value. It will require a substantial and very short-term increase in the stock's value in order for time value to increase enough to create a profit.

It might be possible to profit entirely on time value, meaning buying an option out of the money and hoping for short-term premium growth due to sudden out of the money increases in the stock's value; but you cannot count on that occurring. If the stock were to rise several points immediately after you bought the call, time value would increase as well, and you could close the position with a profit. The greater the distance between current market value of the stock and striking price of the option—in other words, the wider the out-of-the-money range—the greater the chance that you will not be able to realize a profit. Remember that the real leverage value of options is found in the movement of stock and option when the stock is in the money. That's where the point-for-point movements occur. As shown in Figure 3.1, whenever the stock is more than 5 points below the striking price of the call, it is said to be *deep out* of the money. For puts, the number of points is the same but the direction is opposite: "Deep out" refers to the market value of the stock being above the option's striking price. And if the stock is 5 points above the call's striking price (or below the put's striking price), it is said to be *deep in* the money.

deep out
condition when the underlying stock's current market value is 5 points or more below the striking price of the call or above the striking price of the put

deep in
condition when the underlying stock's current market value is 5 points or more above the striking price of the call or below the striking price of the put

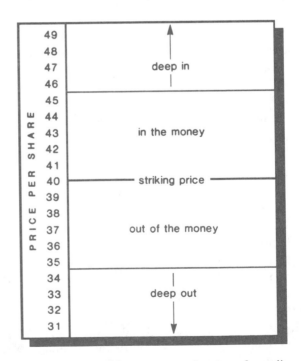

FIGURE 3.1   Deep in/deep out stock prices for calls.

ESTABLISHING GOALS

Most people think of buying options as a purely speculative activity. If the price goes up, you make a profit, and if the price goes down, you lose. While that is essentially true about the speculative nature of buying calls simply to make a profit, calls can also be used for other reasons.

Goal 1: Gaining Leverage

We previously described leverage as using a small amount of money to control a larger investment. This is the perfect description of call buying. For a few hundred dollars, you control 100 shares of stock. By "control" we mean that you may choose to buy those 100 shares at any time before expiration. Leverage is the most common reason for buying calls—that is, calls create the potential for substantial gain through the use of a limited amount of money. This is why so many investors are willing to take the risks associated with buying calls. The potential for profits makes it worthwhile to them. To show just how rapidly profits *can* occur, let's assume you are comparing risks between the purchase of 100 shares of stock, and the purchase of a call that will expire in four months. See Figure 3.2.

The stock is selling at $62 per share. You may either buy 100 shares at a cost of $6200, or purchase a call with a striking price of 60 for a cost of 5 ($500). Of the total premium, 2 points are intrinsic value and 3 points are time value.

If you buy 100 shares of stock, you must pay for the purchase within five business days. If you buy the call, you must make payment on the business day after the transaction. The payment deadline for any transaction is called the *settlement date*.

As a call buyer, your plan is to sell the option before expiration. Like most call buyers, you have no intention of actually exercising the option and buying 100 shares, but are hoping the stock's current market value

> **settlement date**
> the date on which a buyer is required to pay for purchases, or on which a seller is entitled to receive payment (For stocks, settlement date is five business days after the transaction. For options, settlement date is one business day from the date of the transaction.)

will increase enough so that the option's intrinsic value will also grow. That will produce a profit.

For $500, you have control over 100 shares of stock. That's leverage. You do not need to invest $6200 to gain that control. (The stockholder, in comparison, is entitled to dividends and does not have to worry about time.) Without considering the commission costs of buying and selling options, what could happen in the immediate future?

If the stock rises 5 points, the stockholder's $500 profit represents an 8.1 percent return. Because the premium of the option will rise dollar for dollar, the call buyer will realize a 100 percent return in the same situation: 5 points over and above the $500 investment. The profit will occur only if the call's value increases before the 3 points of time value evaporate. Conceivably, if the 5-point gain occurred only at the point of expiration, it would translate to only a 2-point gain:

	STOCK (1)		CALL (2)	
	PROFIT OR LOSS	RATE OF RETURN	PROFIT OR LOSS	RATE OF RETURN
price increase of 5 points	$500	8.1%	$500	100%
price increase of 1 point	$100	1.6%	$100	20%
no price change	0	0	0	0
price decrease of 1 point	-$100	-1.6%	-$100	-20%
price decrease of 5 points	-$500	-8.1%	-$500	-100%

(1) purchased at $62 per share ($6200)
(2) striking price 60, premium 5 ($500)

FIGURE 3.2 Rate of return: buying stocks versus calls.

Original cost	$500
Less: evaporated time value	−300
Original intrinsic value	$200
Plus: increased intrinsic value	+500
Value at expiration	$700
Profit	$200

A point-for-point change in option premium value is substantial. An in the money increase of 1 point yields 1.6 percent to the stockholder in this example, but a full 20 percent to the option buyer. If there is no price change between purchase and expiration, three-fifths of the option premium will evaporate because it is time value. By waiting without price movement, the call buyer risks losses due strictly to evaporation of time value.

As a call buyer, you are under pressure of time for two reasons. First, the option will expire at a specified date in the future. And second, as you approach expiration, the rate of decline in time value accelerates. This is why the chance of loss for the option buyer is high. An increase in the value of the underlying stock is not sufficient. The increase must be enough to offset time value *and* yield a profit above the striking price adequate to exceed the total premium you paid.

You can buy calls that have little or no time value. But to do so, you need to select calls that are close to expiration, meaning you have only a short time for the stock's value to increase.

Example: In the second week of May, the May 50 call is selling for 2, and the underlying stock is worth $51⅝ (1⅝ points in the money). You buy one call. By the third Friday (next week), you are hoping for an increase in the underlying stock's value. If the stock goes up 1 point, the option will be profitable. Because time is short, your chances of realizing a profit are limited. But profits—if they do occur—will be close to dollar for dollar with movement in the stock. So if the stock were to jump 3 points, you could double your money in a day or two. And of course, if the stock were to drop 2 points or more, the option would be worthless.

The greater the time until expiration, the greater the time value premium—and the greater the increase you will require in the underlying stock just to maintain option value. For the buyer, the interaction between time and time value is critical. See Figure 3.3.

Example: You buy an option for 5 when the stock is at or near the striking price of 30. Your advantage is that you have eight months until expiration. For six months the underlying stock remains fairly close to the striking price, and the option's value—all or mostly time value—declines over the same period. Suddenly, the stock moves up to $33 per share. But because much of the time value has disappeared, the option is worth only 3; you have lost $200.

Buying calls for leverage—controlling 100 shares of stock for a relatively small amount of money—offers the potential for substantial gain. But because time value declines as the expiration date comes ever closer, risks are also great.

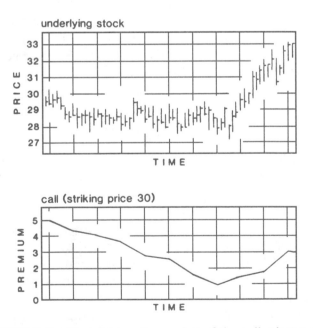

FIGURE 3.3 Diminishing time value of the call relative to the underlying stock.

Even with the best timing and analysis, it is extremely difficult to consistently earn profits through buying calls and hoping for timely price increases.

Goal 2: Limiting Risks

In one respect, the limited amount of money you put into buying calls *reduces* your risk. A stockholder's losses are potentially greater when a stock falls many points.

Example: You bought a call two months ago and paid a premium of 5 ($500). It is scheduled to expire this month and is now virtually worthless, since the stock's market value has fallen 12 points—well below striking price. You expect to lose the entire $500 but, in comparison, stockholders have lost $1200 for every 100 shares owned. You controlled the same amount of stock with a $500 investment, meaning less capital at risk; your loss is limited to only the $500. Offsetting this feature, stockholders can wait for the stock to rebound even if that takes years; you will lose if the stock does not rebound by expiration this month.

The time factor impedes the value of limiting risks. You benefit only so long as the option exists, with expiration a reality you cannot escape. The stockholder has more money at stake, but is not concerned with expiration dates. It would make no sense to buy calls *only* to limit risks. That is a side benefit of leverage. You may assume that if you buy a call, it will be in the expectation of rising stock prices in the immediate future. But in the event you are wrong, your losses are limited to the amount you risk in the form of a premium.

Goal 3: Planning Future Purchases

When you own a call, you fix the price of a future purchase in the event you decide to exercise. This use of calls goes beyond pure speculation.

Example: The market recently experienced a severe drop in value. You have been following one company and

tracking its stock value, which was trading in a range between $50 and $60 per share. You would like to buy 100
shares at today's depressed value, with the stock currently
trading at $39 per share. You believe that when the market
turns around, this stock will prove to be a bargain at that
price. However, you do not have $3900 available to buy
100 shares. You will receive enough cash to make this
purchase in six months. Not knowing what will happen
between now and then, but expecting a rebound, one solution is to buy a call.

To fix the price, you can buy calls while the market
is low, with the intention of exercising that call when you
do have the money. The 40 call is at present selling for 3
($300), and you purchase one contract at that price. Six
months later, the stock has increased to $58 per share.
The option is worth 18 just before expiration date.

In this example, the option buyer has a choice: Either sell the call for 18 and realize an immediate profit of
$1500; or exercise the call and buy 100 shares at $40 per
share. If you seek long-term growth and prefer the permanent value of owning stock, this is one way to use options—that is, to buy calls when you consider prices to be
exceptionally low, and exercise those calls if and when the
stock's market value rises.

The advantage in this strategy is that your investment is limited. So if you're wrong and the stock continues to fall, you lose only the option premium. If you are
right, you pick up 100 shares of stock below market value
by exercising.

Goal 4: Insuring Profits

A final reason to buy calls is to protect a short position in
the underlying stock. Most investors buy stocks hoping
values will rise in the future. At some point, they intend
to sell those shares at a profit. Other investors believe values will fall, and they sell shares by taking a short position. If they are right, values will decline and their short
positions can be closed out at a profit.

Example: An investor sells short 100 shares when market value is $58 per share. A month later, the stock's value has fallen to $52 per share. He makes a closing purchase transaction—buying 100 shares—and realizes a profit of $600.

A short seller's risks are virtually unlimited. If he is wrong and values increase, he can close a position only by buying 100 shares at a higher price than the market value at the time the short sale was made. To protect themselves against this risk, short sellers may buy calls.

Example: An investor sells short 100 shares when the market value is $58 per share. At the same time, she buys one call with a striking price of $65, paying a premium of $7/8$ ($87.50). Her risk is no longer unlimited. If market value rises above $65 per share, the value of the call protects the position. Risk is limited to 7 points (between short sale price of $58 and call's striking price of 65).

In this example, a deep-out-of-the-money call was fairly inexpensive, yet it provided a form of insurance for the short seller. Of course, this protection is good only as long as the call exists. So the short seller needs to decide to exercise the call, buy the stock and close the position, continue without protection, or buy an additional call later. Short sellers reduce and limit risks but also erode their potential profits by buying calls. The premium paid can become an expensive form of insurance. Just as everyone buying any form of insurance needs to assess the cost versus the protection, short sellers need to compare their costs and risks.

Example: A short seller pays a premium of 2 for the call she needs over the next eight months. If the value of the stock declines by 2 points, she would normally sell and take the profit; but because she also paid insurance in the form of buying a call, she will have only broken even at that point:

Profit on the short sale	$200
Loss in the purchase of the call	−200
Net	$ 0

Calls serve an important function when used by short sellers to limit risks. They also take part of the potential profit away from the short selling strategy. In the event the stock falls in value, the short seller will absorb the premium cost. If stock values rise, having the protection of a call can save thousands of dollars.

Example: An investor sold short 100 shares of stock at $58 per share. At the same time, he bought a call with a striking price of 65, and paid a premium of 2 ($200). A few weeks later, the underlying stock rose dramatically on rumors of a merger, to a price of $75 per share. The short sell currently is down $1700 (for shares sold for $58, currently valued at $75). However, the call is worth 10 ($1000) in intrinsic value, plus whatever time value remains as well. To close the position, the investor can exercise the call and pay only the difference between sale price of the stock ($58) and striking price of the option ($65). Without the call, the loss would be $1000 more.

break-even price (also called the **break-even point**) the price of the underlying stock at which the option investor breaks even (For call buyers, this price is the number of points above striking price equal to the call premium cost; for put buyers, this price is the number of points below striking price equal to the put premium cost.)

DEFINING PROFIT ZONES

Whatever strategy you employ in your portfolio, be aware of what is required to create a profit and the ranges of potential loss to which you are exposed. You need to be aware of the *break-even price* as well as the *profit zone* and the *loss zone*. See Figure 3.4.

Example: You buy a call and pay a premium of 3 ($300), with a striking price of 50. What must the stock's price be by the point of expiration, in order for you to break even? What price must the stock achieve in order for you to achieve a profit (assuming only intrinsic value remains by that time)? And at what price will you suffer a loss?

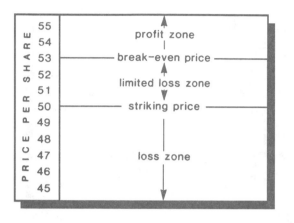

FIGURE 3.4　A call's profit and loss zones.

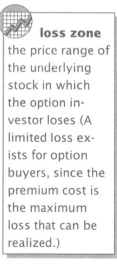

profit zone
the price range of the underlying stock in which the option investor realizes a profit (For the call buyer, the profit zone extends upward from the break-even price. For the put buyer, the profit zone extends downward from the break-even price.)

loss zone
the price range of the underlying stock in which the option investor loses (A limited loss exists for option buyers, since the premium cost is the maximum loss that can be realized.)

In this example, a loss occurs if the option expires out of the money, as is always the case. Because you paid a premium of 3, when the underlying stock's price is 3 points or less above striking price, the loss will be limited; the option will have some intrinsic value, but not enough to produce a profit. So if at expiration the stock is worth $52, the option will be worth 2, which is 1 point below your cost. And if the stock is at $53 per share, you break even (not counting broker fees). When the stock ends up above $53 per share, you are in the profit zone.

Defining break-even price and profit and loss zones helps you to develop a goal with full awareness of the range of potential profit and loss. Be willing to accept limited losses rather than risk losing everything, when expiration is pending. An example of a call purchase with defined profit and loss zones is shown in Figure 3.5. In this example, the investor bought one May 40 call for 2 ($200). In order to profit from this strategy, the call's value must increase to a point greater than the striking price plus the cost of the option (40 plus 2). So $42 per share is the break-even price. Even when buying a call that will expire within a few months, you should know in advance what risks you take and how much price movement is required to yield a profit.

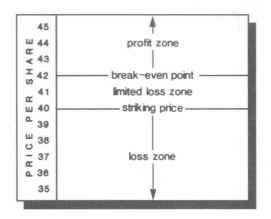

FIGURE 3.5 Example of call purchase with profit and loss zones.

Example: You have been tracking a stock with the idea of buying calls. Right now, you could buy a call with a striking price of 40 for a cost of 2 ($200). The stock's market value is $38 per share, 2 points out of the money. In deciding whether or not to buy this call, you understand that between now and expiration the stock will need to rise by no less than 4 points—2 points just to get to striking price and 2 points to cover your cost. If this occurs by expiration, the option will be worth what you will pay for it today—your break-even price. Remember, when the entire premium consists of time value, the stock must achieve intrinsic value by rising to striking price, and then it must increase in value enough points to more than cover your cost. You might conclude from this that spending $200 is not worth the risk.

Example: Another stock you have been following has an option with a premium of 1 ($100), and is currently at the money. Expiration is two months away and the stock is only 1 point below break-even (because of your premium cost). Considering these circumstances, you might conclude that the potential for profit is worth the risk in this case.

In the first example, a break-even price was actually 4 points away, and the option cost $200. In the second example, only 2 points of price movement are required to create a profit, and the option is available at half the price. In addition, the potential loss is only $100, half the risk in the first example.

You might make as much profit from a $100 investment as you will from an equally valuable $200 investment. The size of initial premium cost cannot be used to judge potential profits; often the premium level is deceptive, and a more thoughtful analysis will reveal the real risk/reward potential.

Before buying any options, you may evaluate the underlying stock's attributes as well. These include price, dividend rate, volatility, and other features that, collectively, define the stock's safety and stability. There is no point in picking what seems a viable option purchase if the stock itself is weak or unpredictable. At the very least, you need to determine from recent history how responsive the stock is likely to be to the general movement of the market as a whole. In a greater sense, options cannot be evaluated apart from their underlying stock; the real value and profit potential in the option is directly a factor of how that stock is likely to perform in the near future.

You may also evaluate the entire stock market before deciding whether your timing is good for investing in options. For example, do you believe the market has recently risen at too fast a rate, and is likely to have a correction soon? You may want to wait before buying calls, or you may want to buy puts in response to that belief. The problem is that all of these judgments are only opinions; no one really knows how market movements will occur in the future, and you might be wrong. The entire process of buying and selling is based on timing and opinion. See Chapter 6 for a more expanded explanation and discussion of stock selection.

Beyond the point of stock and option analysis, you have to learn to manage the time factor for options. Your call will expire within a few months, meaning you have only a very limited time for it to accumulate value. Any time value in the option today will be gone by expiration, and needs to be offset by increased value in the stock itself.

In the next chapter, strategies for buying puts are examined and explained in depth.

Chapter

Buying Puts

You will recall that call buyers acquire the right to *buy* 100 shares of an underlying stock. In comparison, a put grants the buyer an opposite right: to *sell* 100 shares of stock. The premium paid to acquire a put grants that right to the buyer. On the opposite side of this transaction is the put seller, who has agreed to buy 100 shares of the underlying stock at the specified exercise price—if you exercise the put.

As a put buyer, you have a choice to make in the near future. You may sell the put before it expires; you may exercise the put and sell 100 shares of the underlying stock at the exercise price; or you may let the put expire worthless.

You are not obligated to sell 100 shares just by virtue of owning the put. That decision is entirely up to you, and it is a right but not an obligation. The seller, however, would be obligated in the event you decide to exercise the put. The decision you make as a put buyer depends on the same features that motivate call buyers. These are:

✔ The movement in the underlying stock and how that movement affects the put's premium value.

✔ Your motives for purchasing the put, and how today's market conditions meet or fail to meet the purpose.

✔ Your willingness to wait out a series of events between now and expiration and see what happens, versus the desire for a sure profit today.

UNDERSTANDING THE LIMITED LIFE OF THE PUT

Puts can be purchased strictly on speculation. If you believe the underlying stock will be worth less in the near future, you can either sell the stock short, sell calls, or buy puts. As a put buyer, you want the stock to decrease in value, the opposite of the call buyer's desire. In that respect, it is reasonable to consider call buyers optimists and put buyers pessimists.

Short selling of stock is a strategy employed by investors who believe the stock's value will fall. If they are correct, they will be able to close their positions by buying an equal amount of stock at a lower price than the opening sale transaction. Short sellers borrow the stock from the brokerage firm and then sell it. The brokerage firm demands a deposit of a portion of the stock's market value as collateral at the time of the short sale. If the stock's market value rises, the brokerage firm requires that more money be put on account.

The short seller risks the entire amount of the stock's market value. A deposit is required and the short seller has to pay interest on the value of the borrowed stock. So short selling involves even more investment risk than buying stock: Risk is virtually unlimited because the stock's market value might rise to any potential level. The advantage is that short sellers do not have to worry about expiration as option investors do.

Selling short is a very risky strategy because of the unlimited risk. A short seller hopes to gain from price decline. But if that timing is wrong and the stock goes up, the short seller will have to take a loss.

Selling calls achieves the same result and investors who sell calls are subject to the same market changes. However, the call seller can cover a short position by owning 100 shares of the underlying stock. If the sold call is exercised, the 100 shares are available to be called away at the striking price. Selling calls has many similarities to selling short, but risks can be much lower. Call selling is described in greater detail in the next chapter.

The final strategy for those who believe the stock will fall is buying puts. You will have the same risks as call sellers in some respects. Time works against you and time value will evaporate as expiration approaches. If the stock declines but not enough to offset time value, you may only break even or have a limited loss. If the stock rises so that it is out of the money, the put will have no value by expiration. However, your risk is limited only to the amount of the put premium. Unlike short selling of stock or selling of calls, buying puts limits your risks.

Compare the various stock market and option strategies:

You Believe that the Market Will:

	Go Up	Go Down
Stock strategy	Buy shares	Sell shares
Option strategy (long)	Buy calls	Buy puts
Option strategy (short)	Sell puts	Sell calls

Example: You have been following a specific stock over the past few months. You believe it is overpriced today and that market value will fall in the near future. So you instruct your broker to sell short 100 shares. A few weeks pass and the stock has fallen 8 points. You call your broker again and place a closing purchase transaction order to buy 100 shares of stock. Because the price today is lower than when you sold, you realize a profit of $800.

Example: You sold short a stock last month when it was selling at $59 per share. At that time, you believed the stock was overpriced and that it would decline in value. However, a few days ago the company announced a tender offer for the company's stock at $75 per share. The stock immediately jumped to $73. If you enter a closing purchase transaction order now, you will lose $1400 (the difference between your initial sale price and current market value). If the tender offer is accepted or if the stock continues to rise for any other reason, the loss will increase.

Example: You believe a particular stock is going to fall in value, so you sell a call, and receive a premium of 4 ($400). If you are right and the stock falls in value, the value of the call will also decline, and you will either be able to close it by purchasing it for less than the sale price, or wait until expiration when—as long as the stock's market value remains below the striking price—it will expire worthless.

Example: You believe a stock will fall in value, but you do not want to sell a call, fearing that your potential loss could be too significant. You are willing to risk a few hundred dollars in a long position, however. So you buy a put, paying a premium of 3 ($300). If you are right and the stock falls, the value of the put will rise one dollar for each dollar the stock declines (as long as it is in the money). If you are wrong and the stock's value rises, you will lose.

You benefit from a stock's declining market value when you buy puts, and are able to avoid the risks associated with short positions. When you sell short a stock or when you sell a call, you expose yourself to potentially large losses, often for potentially small gains that might not justify the risk. Buying puts allows you to have a potential for gain with only a limited exposure to loss.

The limit of risk is a positive feature in put buying. However, the put—like all options—will exist only for a limited time. If the strategy is to be profitable, price movement in the underlying stock must occur before expiration date—and not just price movement, but *enough* price movement to offset time value and produce a profit. So as a put buyer, you trade limited risk for limited life.

Understanding the potential benefit is only part of the formula necessary to succeed as a put buyer. You also need to understand the risks and know in advance how much price movement will be needed in the underlying stock in order to produce the needed profit. Too many speculators buy puts with high time value, so that many points of decline will be required to produce a profit. If the stock is fairly stable in price movement, chances for profit are greatly reduced.

Put buying is suitable for you only if you understand the risks and are familiar with price history in the underlying stock. You also need to be willing to lose the entire put premium. There should be no doubt: Buying an option is a risky investment, and should be undertaken only if you can afford a loss.

Example: An investor has $600 available to invest, and believes that the market as a whole will fall in the near future. One problem, however: She cannot afford to lose the $600, which is her entire savings account. She buys two puts valued at 3 ($300), spending the entire savings account. The market does fall as she predicted; but the stock on which the puts were written remains fairly stable and the puts gradually lose time value. At expiration date, the puts are worth 1 each, and she sells, receiving $200.

This investor's perception of the market was correct: Prices fell. But the puts were not profitable because the particular stock did not follow the broader trend in the market, so profits were not produced in the limited life span of the options. Additionally, this strategy was inappropriate for the investor; she could not afford to lose the $600. She also failed to analyze the market regarding feasibility of buying puts. Although her belief about market direction was right, that alone was not adequate to justify the decision to invest. She saw the potential for gain and did not also consider sufficiently the potential for loss. She also was unaware of the strength of the underlying stock in a declining market, a factor necessary in selecting the right stock for a particular strategy.

This experience is not untypical. For a number of reasons, investing in options can turn out unprofitably—not because the perception of the investor is wrong, but because there simply is not enough time, because particular circumstances are not right, or because the overall implications of buying options are not understood well enough.

If you understand the risks and can afford to speculate, put buying might have a place in your portfolio. However, it cannot be emphasized too much: You need to understand the evaluation not only of options, but of the stock itself and of the market as a whole.

Example: An experienced investor has a portfolio that is well diversified. He owns several stocks in different industries, shares in two mutual funds, and some real estate. He has been investing for several years and fully understands the risks involved in various markets. He considers his portfolio a long-term investment and has carefully selected stocks with that goal in mind. Short-term price movements do not concern his greatly. Outside of this portfolio, he also has available several hundred dollars for speculation. He believes the market will fall in the near future. So he buys puts, selecting stocks that, in his opinion, are most likely to fall enough to produce a profit.

This investor understands the difference between long-term investment and short-term speculation. He has a base in his portfolio and a thorough understanding of the market. He can afford the losses because he is using money specifically set aside for speculation. Buying puts is an appropriate strategy, given his belief about current conditions and likely price movement in the near future. The money used to buy options is separate from the capital invested long-term. The ability to afford losses, the investor's understanding of the market, and the proper selection of stocks on which to buy puts all add up to a greater likelihood of success.

JUDGING THE PUT

Time works against all option buyers. Not only will your option expire in a few months, but you also have to accept the declining time value that offsets some gain in intrinsic value.

You can select low-priced puts—ones that are out of the money—but that means you need many points more just to produce a profit. Or you can select puts in the money, meaning that if the stock moves upward, you stand to lose on a point-for-point basis.

Example: You bought a put and paid a premium of 5 ($500). At that time, the stock's market value was 4 points below the striking price, or in the money by 4 points. (You will recall that for calls "in the money" means the stock's value is higher than the striking price, and it is the opposite for puts.) However, by expiration, the stock has risen $4^1/_2$ points and the option is worth only $^1/_2$ ($50). The time value has completely disappeared, and you sell on the last day before expiration. Your loss: $450.

Example: You bought a put several months ago, paying a premium of $^1/_2$ ($50). At that time, the stock's market value was 5 points above the striking price (out of the money). By expiration, the stock's market value has declined $5^1/_2$ points, so that it is $^1/_2$ point in the money; its value is then $^1/_2$ ($50). When you bought the put, it had no intrinsic value and only a small amount of time value; at expiration, the time value is gone, and only $^1/_2$ point of intrinsic value remains. You realize no profit, because the net value has not changed; in reality, you will lose money on brokerage fees just for opening and then closing the position.

The problem is not limited to picking the right direction in which the underlying stock will move, although many novice option investors fall into the trap of thinking that is the only issue. Rather, the degree of movement in a limited period of time must be great enough to produce enough price change to offset decreasing time value, to produce intrinsic value above the original cost, and to cover brokerage costs.

Some speculators attempt to bargain hunt in the options market. The belief is that a cheap option is a better buy than an expensive (or higher-priced) option. But this is not always the case; some cheaper options are cheaper *because* they are not good bargains. The question of quality should always be considered when comparing prices of options (and other investments). Some options are low-priced and also low-quality. This means your chances for profit are correspondingly low. All option purchasers need to examine the reasons that particular options are priced at "bargain" levels: The low prices might reflect true value. Just as "bargain" merchandise offered by stores may be junk that no one really wants to buy, options sometimes fall into the same category.

Example: You bought a put last week when it was in the money and paid 6 ($600). You believed the stock was overpriced and was likely to fall. Two days after your purchase, the stock fell 1 point. At that time, you sold and received $700. This represents a return on your investment of 16.7 percent in two days.

Goal-setting for put buyers is as important as it is for call buyers. Do not allow the "greed factor" to distort your views of the market, to take over, or to distract you from your purpose. In the example above, the position is closed after movement of only 1 point; the return is substantial with that modest movement. Hesitation in the hopes of greater profits might work out; it might also mean a large loss. Setting standards gives you targets to aim for; once the targets are hit, the position should be closed.

Example: You bought a put last month and paid a premium of 4 ($400). At that time, you decided to set a few goals for yourself. First, you decided that if the put's value fell by 2 points, you would sell and accept a loss of $200. Second, you promised yourself that if the put's value rose by 3 points or more, you would sell immediately and take your profit. You decided you would be willing to accept a 50 percent loss, but would also close out the position if you could get a 75 percent gain. And failing either of these outcomes, you would sell the put at expiration for whatever its value.

Setting goals is the only way to succeed if you plan to speculate by buying options. Too many speculators fall into a no-win trap because they fail to set standards for themselves.

Example: You bought a put last month and paid 5 ($500). Your plan was to sell if the value went up 2 points or more. A week after your purchase, the stock's market value fell and the put's value went up to 8 ($800)—an increase of 3 points. You didn't sell, though, because you thought the stock's market value might continue to fall, meaning the put's value would rise even further. You didn't want to lose any future profits. The week after that, the stock's value rose 4 points and the put lost 4 points. The opportunity was lost.

Investors who fall into this trap find it impossible to take profits or to cut losses in any circumstances. When the option is more valuable than when they bought it, they fear missing out on additional gains. When it is below their basis, they convince themselves they have to get back to where they started. In this situation, when do you sell?

The lost opportunity might not repeat itself and, with options, usually does not. So potential profits aren't taken and are lost forever. The same logic is applied when a put loses value.

Example: You bought a put last month and paid a premium of 6 ($600), resolving that you would sell if its value rose or fell 2 points or more. A couple of weeks ago, the stock's market value rose and the put's value declined to your bail-out target. You hesitated, though, hoping it would rebound. As of today, the stock has risen a total of 5 points, and your $600 investment is now worth only $100.

Even if this stock did eventually fall, time is working against you. The longer it takes for the turnaround in value, the more time value you lose. The stock could fall a point or two over a three-month period, in which case you would trade time value for intrinsic value, with a net effect of zero. You probably will never get back to an acceptable minimal loss level, and should have taken the smaller loss when the chance presented itself.

The problem of time value is the same problem call buyers experience. It does not matter whether price movement is required to go up or down; time is the enemy, and the movement has to offset time value *plus* produce enough intrinsic value to surpass your purchase price. The relationship between the underlying stock and time premium value is summarized in Figure 4.1.

Example: You buy a put for a premium of 5 ($500) with a striking price of 30. Between purchase date and expiration, the underlying stock rises above the striking price, but then falls to 27, which is 3 points in the money. If you sell the put at expiration, you will lose $200, because time value has evaporated. Even though the stock is 3 points in the money, price movement was not adequate to produce a profit on the $500 investment; for that, the stock would have to be more than 5 points in the money.

The further out of the money the stock price, the cheaper the premium for an option—and the lower the potential for profit. This relationship is not a coincidence; it is predictable. Likewise, the further in the money the

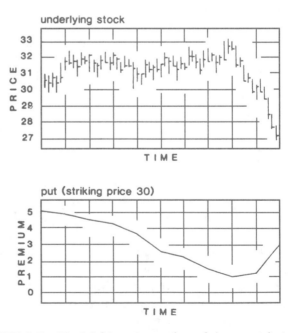

FIGURE 4.1 Diminishing time value of the put relative to the underlying stock.

stock is, the more expensive the option—because you will be paying for both time and intrinsic value.

If you buy an in-the-money put and the underlying stock increases in value, you will lose 1 point of premium value for every point of movement in the underlying stock—as long as it remains in the money—and, by the same argument, for every point the stock decreases in value, the put will gain 1 point of value.

Whether you prefer lower-premium puts out of the money, or higher-premium puts in the money, be aware of the point distance between the stock's current market value and the striking price. For out-of-the-money options, the more points away, the greater your risk.

To minimize this risk, limit your speculation to within 5 points from the striking price. You will see that this seemingly small range is really quite large when you compare premium costs to time until expiration and realize how much price movement is required to produce a short-term profit. As shown in Figure 4.2, you should

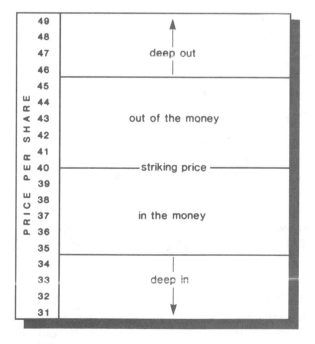

FIGURE 4.2 Deep in/deep out stock prices for puts.

avoid both deep in and deep out puts. The deep in puts are expensive, and the deep out puts are too far from striking price to promise a reasonable chance for profit.

Set goals and stay with them. Consider the premium value, the mix of time and intrinsic value, time until expiration, and the underlying stock's price movement, financial strength, stability, and other features. Do not make the most common speculator's mistakes: shopping for puts based only on premium bargain levels and time until expiration. Look at the entire picture and remember that there is an inescapable relationship between the stock and the put. Volatility and perceptions of that company by the investing public will determine how your put performs between purchase and expiration.

ESTABLISHING GOALS

There are three reasons to buy puts. The first is purely speculative: the hope of realizing a substantial profit in a short period of time. Second, you may buy puts to offset the risk of short selling of stock. Third, puts can serve as a form of insurance against declines in the market value of stock you own.

Goal 1: Gaining Leverage

Most investors who buy puts are hoping to profit from leverage. With a limited amount of money available, the potential for profits is greater through puts than it is through short selling. Risks are also limited. Here's how leverage works in the case of puts:

Example: A stock is currently valued at $60 per share. If you sell 100 shares short and the stock drops 5 points, you can close the position and realize a $500 gain. If you believe the stock will fall but, instead of selling short, you buy 12 puts at $500 each (total $6000), your potential profit is far greater. A drop of 5 points will yield a gain of $6000—a 100 percent return—assuming that no deterioration also occurs due to falling time value.

This example assumes, of course, equal price movement
for both sides: selling short versus buying puts. It also assumes you are willing and able to invest $6000 in either
strategy. While such assumptions will not always apply, the
example makes the point that the use of leverage with options creates the potential for greater profits but also
comes with correspondingly higher risks and the inescapable problem of time value and looming expiration.

If you do not have a large sum of capital available to
make such a choice, you can still use leverage to your advantage.

Example: You buy a put for a premium of 5 ($500) and a
striking price of 60. The stock is currently selling at $60
per share (at the money). Aware of the risks and potential
rewards in this strategy, you made your decision by comparing put buying to the relative risks and rewards of selling short. As shown in Figure 4.3, a drop of 5 points in
the stock's market value would produce a $500 gain with
either strategy (this assumes immediate price movement
for the purpose of comparison, and does not consider
possible decline due to time value).

	STOCK (1)		PUT (2)	
	PROFIT OR LOSS	RATE OF RETURN	PROFIT OR LOSS	RATE OF RETURN
price decrease of 5 points	$500	8.1%	$500	100%
price decrease of 1 point	$100	1.6%	$100	20%
no price change	0	0	0	0
price increase of 1 point	-$100	-1.6%	-$100	- 20%
price increase of 5 points	-$500	-8.1%	-$500	-100%

(1) sold short at $62 per share ($6 200)
(2) striking price 60, premium 5 ($500)

FIGURE 4.3 Rates of return: selling short versus buying
puts.

Because a short sale requires the combination of a deposit equal to part of the stock's value and interest payments on the borrowed stock, the short seller has a time problem just as the option buyer does. While the option buyer is concerned with diminishing time value and expiration, the short seller is paying interest—which has the effect of eroding future profits, which may or may not materialize—and must also live with the threat that the stock might rise rather than fall.

A decline of 5 points—given this example—will produce an 8.1 percent profit to the short seller and a 100 percent return to the put buyer. For that difference in yield, compare the risks. The short seller's risks are unlimited due to the potential that the stock's market value could rise. The put buyer's risk is limited to the $500 investment in the option's premium. A drop of 1 point in the value of the stock will cause a 1.6 percent profit to the short seller, but a 20 percent profit to the put buyer.

Losses can be compared on a similar basis. When a short seller's stock rises in value, the loss can be substantial. But the amount of loss for the put buyer is strictly limited to what was paid to buy the put. Most put buyers never intend to exercise the put. If the put increases in value, the most likely action is to sell that put at a higher price than was paid for it, resulting in a net profit.

Goal 2: Limiting Risks

It is possible to double your money in a very short period of time by speculating in puts. And the leveraging of your money increases even a modest investment's potential. In one respect, leverage increases risks; in another, it decreases risks.

Risks are increased through leverage because you might lose the entire amount invested. The more you invest in buying puts, the more you stand to gain, or to lose.

Example: You recently bought a put and paid a premium of 4 ($400). However, expiration date is coming up soon and the stock's market value has risen above striking price. If the put expires, you will stand to lose the entire

$400. Time has worked against you. You know that the stock's market value might eventually fall below striking price, but not necessarily in time to save the put's value, or to produce enough profit to cover your basis.

Risks decrease with puts when compared to short selling. If a stock rises instead of falling as you expect, your puts will decline in value; but if you sell short, you need to make up the difference when you close the short position. Before closing, you might be required to put up more deposit *and* pay more interest, since the borrowed stock's market value is higher. These considerations could mean your costs might rise well above what you expected. The limited risk of put buying is a considerable advantage.

Example: An investor sold short 200 shares of stock with market value of $45 per share. The stock later rose to $52 and, fearing further price increases, the investor sold. His loss was $1400. If that same investor had bought puts instead of selling short, the potential loss would have been limited to the total premium paid. (Amount of loss depends, of course, on the level of the premium.) The fear of further price increases would not have been a factor, at least not in assessing additional losses. The short seller's potential loss is unlimited. The put buyer, though, can never lose more than the cost of the premium.

This advantage is the privilege of taking a long position over a short position. Although the strategy is employed in pursuit of the same goal, risks are much different. Some investors prefer short selling over buying puts, even with the risks in mind. The short seller's primary advantage is that the position does not expire like a put. The short position can be left open indefinitely, as long as the investor is willing to continue paying interest on the borrowed stock and can afford to keep the deposit on account with the brokerage firm.

The risks of a short position can be reduced by buying calls, as explained in Chapter 3. The risk of rising stock prices is insured against by buying calls since such increases are offset by the rising premium value of the call. However, it becomes expensive to pay interest to the brokerage firm *and* pay a premium on a call that will expire in the near future. So for this level of protection, the short seller has to be willing to risk replacing calls every few months, as older ones expire. Buying calls to protect short positions adds to the cost to a degree that brings the entire strategy into question. The price movement required to produce a profit becomes so high that the relative risks in buying puts (or selling calls) are more affordable.

If you believe a stock's value will fall, you may buy calls and avoid the requirement of placing a deposit with your broker and paying interest on borrowed stock. For the convenience of leverage, you need to accept the possibility of losses when stock goes up instead of down. You should also be willing to live with the disadvantage of time. Your put expires in a few months. Every put buyer has the added disadvantage of having to overcome time value premium. As expiration nears, that value disappears, even when stock values do not change drastically.

Goal 3: Hedging a Long Position

Put buying is not always merely speculative. A very conservative strategy involves buying one put for every 100 shares of the underlying stock owned, as a way of protecting yourself from declines in price. Just as calls can be used for insurance against upward price movement in a short position, puts can be used for insurance against downward price movement in a long position. When a put is used to hedge in this manner, it is called a *married put*, since it is tied directly to the underlying stock.

The risk of declining prices is a constant concern for every investor. If you buy stock and its value falls, you might decide to sell in the belief that the downward movement will continue. Or you might hold, hoping for a rebound. It could take months, even years in some cases, for a stock to recover from a severe decline; some stocks never recover from a serious decline in value. For protection against such declines, some investors buy puts for insurance, which is known as a *hedge* strategy. In the event

married put

the status of a put used to hedge a long position (Each put owned protects 100 shares of the underlying stock held in the portfolio. If the stock declines in value, the put's value will increase and offset the loss.)

hedge

a strategy involving the use of one position to protect another (For example, stock is purchased in the belief it will rise in value, and a put is purchased on the same stock to protect against the risk that market value will decline.)

of decline in stock value, the put can be exercised and the stock sold at the fixed striking price; or the put can be sold at a profit to offset the lowered value of the stock. When you exercise a put, the action is called *put to seller*.

Example: You own 100 shares of stock, which you originally bought for $57 per share. You bought the stock because it is volatile (prone to dramatic price swings). The potential for gain is significant, but so is the risk of loss. To protect yourself against the possibility of a loss in market value, you purchase a put on the underlying stock. You spend $100 and buy a put with a striking price of 50. Two months later, the stock has declined to $36 per share and your option is near expiration. The put has a current premium value of $1400.

> **put to seller**
> action of exercising a put and requiring the seller to purchase 100 shares of stock at the fixed striking price

In this situation, you have two choices:

1. Sell the put and take the $1300 profit. Your original cost for this investment was $58 per share (purchase price of $57 plus $100 for the put). Your net cost is $45 per share ($5800 invested, less $1300 profit on the put). Your basis is now 9 points above current market value. By selling the put, you have the advantage of still owning 100 shares of stock. If that stock's value rises above $45 per share in the future, you will realize a profit. Without the put, your basis would now be 21 points higher than current market value.

2. Exercise the put and sell the stock for $50 per share. In this choice, you sell for 8 points below your original basis. You will lose $100 paid for the put, plus 7 points in the stock.

Regardless of the choice made in this example, you would end up better off having owned the put than you would by simply owning the stock. The put provides you a degree of protection. It either cuts the loss following a severe decline or enables you to actually sell the stock for a price well above current market value. It's still a loss, but a much smaller loss than you would have otherwise.

The two choices—sell the put or exercise the put—both result in losses. The purpose here is to demonstrate that puts can be used to mitigate the damages, not to guarantee that no losses will ever occur. It is also worth noting that not all stocks have options available. This strategy works only for stocks you own on which options are publicly listed.

The put is used in this application to provide *downside protection*, which takes away from your potential profits—because you must pay the put premium to gain the insurance. And if this is a long-term strategy, you will need to replace that put upon expiration. The money invested in a put premium will reduce future profits, so this strategy is useful only when concern for potential losses is severe enough that the cost of buying puts justifies the decision.

In the event the stock's market value rises, your potential losses are frozen at the level of the put's premium, and no more. Whether you exercise the put or sell it at a profit, downside protection establishes an acceptable level of loss and fixes that loss at the striking price, at least for the duration of the put's life.

downside protection
a strategy involving the purchase of one put for every 100 shares of the underlying stock that you own (This insures you against losses to some degree. For every in-the-money point the stock falls, the put will increase in value by 1 point. Before exercise, you may sell the put and take a profit offsetting stock losses, or exercise the put and sell the shares at the striking price.)

Example: You recently bought 100 shares of stock at $60 per share. At the same time, you bought a put with a striking price of 60 and paid a premium of 3 ($300). The total amount invested is $6300. Before making your purchases, you analyzed the potential profit or loss and concluded that your losses would probably not exceed 4.8 percent ($300 paid for the put, divided by $6300, the total amount spent). You also recognize that an increase in the stock's value of 3 points or less will not represent a profit at all. Your total basis is $6300 (combining stock price of $60 per share and the $300 paid for the put). So profits cannot even begin until the stock's market value exceeds $63 per share.

A summary of this analysis is shown in Figure 4.4. Note that regardless of the severity of decline in the stock's market value, the loss can never exceed 4.8 percent of the total amount invested (the cost of the put). That's because for every point of decline in the stock's

PRICE MOVEMENT, UNDERLYING STOCK	PROFIT OR LOSS		NET PROFIT OR LOSS (3)	
	STOCK (1)	PUT (2)	AMOUNT	RATE
down 20 points	−$2,000	$1,700	−$ 300	− 4.8%
down 5 points	−$ 500	$ 200	−$ 300	− 4.8%
down 3 points	−$ 300	0	−$ 300	− 4.8%
no change	0	−$ 300	−$ 300	− 4.8%
up 3 points	$ 300	−$ 300	0	0
up 5 points	$ 500	−$ 300	$ 200	3.2%
up 20 points	$2,000	−$ 300	$1,700	27.0%

(1) stock purchased at $60 per share
(2) put striking price 60, premium 3
(3) return based on total cost of $6300

FIGURE 4.4 Downside protection: selling short versus buying puts.

market value, the put will increase 1 point of intrinsic value. This conclusion applies as long as the option does not expire.

DEFINING PROFIT ZONES

To decide whether buying puts is a reasonable investment strategy for you, always be aware of potential profits *and* potential losses. Pay special attention to the number of points the stock needs to move up or down to produce profits, while also keeping in mind the time remaining until expiration of the option.

Comparing limited losses to potential profits when using puts for downside protection is one analysis that helps determine the value of put buying. And when trying to pick a sound speculative investment, the time until expiration and the distance between current stock value and the striking price—as well as time value—will help you to identify a worthwhile risk.

The profit and loss zones for puts are the reverse of the same zones for a call, because put owners depend on a downward movement in the stock, while call owners anticipate an upward movement. See Figure 4.5.

Example: You buy a put with a striking price of 50 and pay a premium of 3 ($300). Your break-even price is $47 per share. If the underlying stock falls to that level, the option will have intrinsic value of 3 points, the price you paid originally. Your put can be sold when the stock is between $47 and $50 for a limited loss. And if the price of the stock rises above $50 per share, the put will be worthless as of expiration.

Before buying any put, determine the profit and loss zones and break-even price. For the amount of money you will be putting at risk, how much price movement will be required to produce a profit? How much time will be required? Is the risk worth taking?

An example of a put purchase, with defined profit and loss zones, is shown in Figure 4.6. In this example, you buy one May 40 put for 3 ($300). The outcome of this strategy is the exact opposite of buying a call for the same price and same striking price. You will have a profit if the value of the underlying stock falls below the striking price of 40. How-

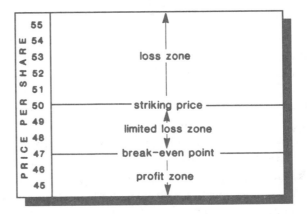

FIGURE 4.5 A put's profit and loss zones.

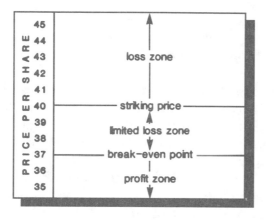

FIGURE 4.6 Example of put purchase with profit and loss zones.

ever, the point decline must be greater than your purchase price, and that level must be reached before expiration. Remember the guideline: Don't depend on time value to produce profits between now and expiration, because it will evaporate. If you do not experience a price decline in the stock equal to or greater than the number of points you paid for the put, you will have a loss. Like call purchasing, time works against you when you buy puts. They will expire within a short period of time. However, your risk is limited to the amount you spend on premiums.

The mistake many investors make is failing to set any standards for themselves. You need to plan to cut losses at a specific, predetermined level, or to sell your put once you reach a specific, predetermined level of profit.

Remember the important points for evaluation when buying puts:

✔ Your motive (leverage, reduction of risk, or downside protection).

✔ The premium and level of time value.

✔ Time until expiration.

✔ Distance between the stock's current market value and striking price.

✔ The number of points needed to yield a profit.

✔ Characteristics of the underlying stock (see Chapter
  6 for guidelines for selecting stocks appropriate for
  your option strategy).

Collectively, these points define an investment strategy
and are tools for evaluation of risks as well as profit potential. Option buyers have the opportunity to earn substantial short-term profits, but they also have to accept the
disadvantage of time.

   On the opposite side of the option transaction from
the buyer is the seller. Unlike buyers, sellers have an advantage in the passage of time, and the evaporating time
value defines opportunities in selling options. Time value
is reduced as expiration approaches, so sellers benefit to
the same degree that buyers suffer losses as time value
goes away. The next chapter explains strategies and risks
of selling calls.

Selling Calls

Most of us think about investing in a precise sequence. First, you buy a security; then, at a later date, you sell. If the sale price is higher than the purchase price, you realize a profit. If it is lower, you have a loss. But when you become a call seller, this sequence is reversed.

If you buy a call and later sell it (see Chapter 3), the transaction conforms with the familiar pattern. In the following chapter the idea of selling first and buying later is introduced. The outcomes of this short position are the same as for the long position: Once both purchase and sale are completed in either sequence, the position is closed. If purchase price is lower than sale price, the result is a profit; if purchase price is higher, the result is a loss.

By starting out with a sale of the option, you are paid at the time you initiate the transaction. You will pay the purchase price later on or, if the option expires worthless, you never have to pay it. If all of this sounds like a pretty good deal, remember that taking a short position also involves some very special risks. These risks are explained in this chapter and examined through examples. You will see that some forms of call selling are extremely risky, while other forms are very conservative.

All sellers enjoy some significant and important advantages over call buyers (and vice versa). The previous two chapters provided numerous examples of how time works against you when you are a buyer. The time factor represents virtually the entire risk element in buying calls. Even if the underlying stock moves in the desired direction, it might not happen soon enough and the extent of that movement might not be enough to make the option purchase profitable. This disadvantage for the buyer is an advantage for the seller.

Because time value evaporates, buyers have to view time as the enemy. For sellers, though, time is an ally. The more time value declines, the more profitable the short position in the option. At the time you initiate a sale (the opening transaction), you want to have the highest possible time value. Remember, while the buyer looks for the lowest cost and the lowest possible time value, sellers want high cost and high time value. You sell calls in the hope that time value will disappear. Remember, because you sell the option *before* you buy it, you want its value to decline. Then you can close the position by buying the option at a lower price in the future.

By selling a call, you grant the buyer the right to buy 100 shares of the underlying stock at the striking price, at any time prior to expiration. That means you assume the risk of being responsible for selling the buyer those shares, potentially at a price far below market value.

Most investment strategies have specific risk characteristics. These are clearly identified and should be understood by anyone undertaking the strategy. The definition of most strategies involves attributes that are unchanging. For example, the risks of buying stocks or bonds are consistent from one moment to another. Experienced investors understand this and accept the consistency of risk. But call selling can be highly conservative or highly risky, depending on how the strategy is undertaken. It is one of the few investment strategies offering an extreme on either end of the risk spectrum—and many variations in between.

SELLING UNCOVERED CALLS

When call selling is looked at in isolation, it is indeed a risky strategy. That is, if you sell calls without also owning 100 shares of the underlying stock, you undertake an unlimited risk. In fact, this is one of the highest forms of risk an investor can take: a short position with unlimited potential for loss.

Remembering that the short position grants a buyer the right to buy 100 shares at the striking price, you need to be willing to deliver those shares if the call is exercised—no matter how high the current price. If you do not currently own 100 shares and you sell a call, you will be required upon exercise to buy 100 shares at current market value and then sell them at the striking price. The gap between those values could be significant.

Example: You enter into an uncovered call position with an opening sale transaction. At that time, the underlying stock is valued at $44 per share. You sell an April 45 call for 5 ($500), but you do not own 100 shares of stock. The day after the order, your broker adds $500 to your account (less brokerage fees). Before the option expires, the stock soars to $71 per share, and your call is exercised by the buyer. You will lose $2100 (current market value of $71, less striking price of $45 per share, and less $500 premium you were paid for selling the call):

Current market value	$7100
Less: striking price	−4500
Less: call premium	− 500
Loss	$2100

When you do not own 100 shares and the call is exercised, you are required to deliver those shares at the striking price. That means you have to buy them at current market value and then sell them at the striking price; thus the loss in the example above. Because upward price movement is unlimited, the per-share price risk is also unlimited.

The risk in selling calls in this manner is extreme.

Because of this, your broker should allow you to sell calls only if you meet specific requirements. These requirements include having enough value in your portfolio and brokerage account to provide protection in the event of an exceptionally high loss; the brokerage firm should believe that it could sell other securities to cover a loss in that event. You also need advance approval from the brokerage firm in order to sell calls; the firm is required to determine that you understand the risks involved and that you are sophisticated and experienced enough to make decisions in any high-risk market.

Thus you will not be allowed to write an unlimited number of calls unless you also own 100 shares of stock. The potential losses to you and to the brokerage firm naturally place a limit on this activity. The requirement that your portfolio include stocks, cash, and other assets is one form of *margin* requirement imposed by your broker. Such requirements apply not only to option transactions, but also to short selling of stock or, most commonly, the purchase of securities using borrowed funds.

When you enter into an opening sale transaction, you are referred to as the *writer*. Call writers hope the value of the underlying stock will remain at or below striking price. If that occurs, the option will expire worthless and the writer's profit will be derived from the evaporation of time value (as well as reduction of any intrinsic value in the option at the time of the write). For the writer, the break-even price is the striking price plus the number of points received for selling the call.

It is conceivable that a written call will be exercised and the writer may still make a profit. For example, if you sell a call for 5 ($500) and the stock is 2 points above striking price as of exercise, the writer will earn $300 upon exercise ($500 premium received, less $200 difference between market value of the stock and striking price):

margin
an account with a brokerage firm containing a minimum level of cash and securities to provide collateral for short positions or for purchases for which payment has not yet been made

writer
the individual who sells (writes) a call (or a put)

Premium received	$500
Less: loss upon exercise	−200
Profit	$300

As the writer, you can cancel out your open position at any time prior to exercise by purchasing the call. The purchase offsets the sale and closes the position. Remember, if you are the writer, you initiated the open position by selling the call; you close the position by later purchasing the same option. If time value declines or the underlying stock's value falls, or if both of these events take place, you will be able to cancel your open position at a profit. There are four events that may cause a seller to close the position:

1. The stock's value falls. As a result, the option's current value falls as well and the investor wants to take a profit.

2. The stock's value remains stable but the option's value falls due to declining time value. The investor wants to take a profit.

3. The option value remains fairly stable due to exchange of time value for intrinsic value. In order to avoid exercise, the investor closes the position, taking neither a profit nor a loss.

4. Stock value rises enough so that exercise is likely or certain. The investor closes the position and accepts a loss, avoiding exercise and the potential for an even greater loss.

Example: You sold a call two months ago and were paid a premium of 3 ($300). The underlying stock's market value has remained below the striking price, even though it has not changed much during the time you have held the open position in the call. Time value has shrunk enough that you now have a choice: You can simply close the position by buying the option at a lower price than you originally paid; or you can wait for expiration and keep the entire premium as profit (risking that the stock might rise between now and then). Purchasing now ensures current profits. Waiting for expiration continues your risk exposure, but could result in greater profits. If you decide to hold, your break-even price is the striking price plus 3 points (the premium you were paid when you sold the call).

naked option
an option sold in an opening sale transaction when the seller (writer) does not own 100 shares of the underlying stock

uncovered option
the same as a naked option—the sale of an option not covered, or protected, by the ownership of 100 shares of the underlying stock

naked position
status for investors when they assume short positions in calls without also owning 100 shares of the underlying stock for each call written

Whenever you sell a call and you do not also own 100 shares of the underlying stock, the option is referred to as a *naked option* or an *uncovered option*. Your risk in a *naked position* is not limited to the option's status only at point of expiration. The buyer has the right to exercise the call at any time. So risk is constant. Most exercises occur on the last trading day prior to expiration, but as a writer you cannot count on that.

Example: You sold a naked call last week with four months to go before expiration, so you were not worried about exercise. However, the underlying stock went into the money yesterday, and your broker telephoned this morning and advised you that the call had been exercised. You are now required to deliver 100 shares of the underlying stock at the striking price. Your option no longer exists.

In this example, you experience a loss on the stock because you must purchase at current market value and deliver at striking price. However, you will have an overall profit or loss based on how much premium you received for selling the call, and how much of a gap there is between market value and striking price. If that gap is lower than the number of points you received for selling the call, you will have a limited profit.

You cannot predict early exercise, since buyers and sellers are not matched up one to one. The selection is random. The Options Clearing Corporation (OCC) acts as buyer to every seller, and as seller to every buyer. When a buyer exercises, the order is assigned at random to a seller. You will not even know it has happened until your broker calls or writes to inform you that the call has been exercised.

In order to give you a profit from selling calls, the underlying stock must act in one of two ways:

1. Its market value must remain at or below striking price of the option, so that time value will evaporate and the option will expire worthless.

2. Its market value must remain at a stable enough

price level so that the option can later be purchased for a lower premium than it was sold for, due to decline in time value.

The profit and loss zones for uncovered calls are summarized in Figure 5.1. Because you receive cash for selling the call, the break-even price is higher than the striking price. (Remember, though, that brokerage transaction fees must also be factored into the calculation.) In this illustration, a call was sold for 5 ($500), hence the break-even price is 5 points higher than striking price.

Your brokerage firm will require you to put on deposit a percentage of the total potential liability for writing calls. For example, if you write one call with a striking price of 40, you have a potential liability. That liability depends on the current market value of the underlying stock at the time of exercise, if that occurs. The price could be $45, $50, or $80 per share, or even higher.

Many of the large stock market losses in October

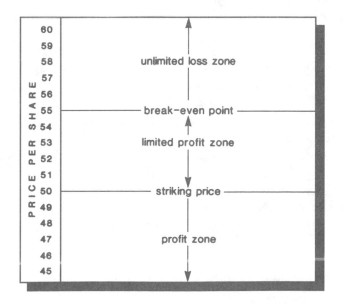

FIGURE 5.1 An uncovered call's profit and loss zones.

1987 occurred because of excessive margin activity, some involving calls or puts, or both. Even brokerage firms did not anticipate the degree of potential loss resulting from a sudden drop of several hundred points in the market. Consequently, many brokerage firms no longer permit public uncovered short selling in options, or they severely restrict this activity by, for example, disallowing such activity in margin accounts. If you want to take high risks, you will be limited by the rules applied by the brokerage firm. When large losses occur and investors cannot cover them, the brokerage firms are forced to absorb those losses. To protect themselves, the firms require pledges of cash or securities, often in higher amounts than in the past.

Example: You have advised your broker that you intend to write uncovered calls. Your portfolio is currently valued at $20,000 in stocks and cash. Your broker will restrict your uncovered call writing activity to a level that, in their estimation, would not exceed maximum losses of $20,000. However, if market conditions change and your portfolio value declines suddenly, you could be forced to either deposit more money or close some uncovered positions.

Example: You would like to write (sell) puts as part of your investment strategy. You own stocks and cash valued at $20,000. Your brokerage firm restricts you to positions that they estimate would not be likely to exceed a $20,000 loss. Because you will be writing puts and not calls, the potential for loss is much more limited—stocks can go down only so far. Offsetting this, however, is a different problem: If the market falls, you will lose value in your uncovered puts, but your stock portfolio will also decline in value.

Writing puts involves limited losses, since the worst outcome is that a stock's value could decline to zero. (In reality, the maximum decline should be considered a decline only to book value of the stock; however, book value is often overlooked by the market.) Puts have a finite worst-case loss, whereas uncovered calls could result in losses much higher than expectations—especially if you write several uncovered calls at the same time.

Assessing Uncovered Call Writing Risks

All investors need to assess their risks. The examples in the preceding section demonstrate that risks can be substantial for uncovered calls. In future chapters and later in this chapter, some alternatives will be presented showing that not all call writing is risky.

For now, consider the risks involved in writing uncovered calls, especially in light of the limitations brokerage firms place upon this activity. As long as your portfolio is limited in value, your call writing activity will be limited as well. This naturally limits the profit potential in call writing, while exposing you to risk in the event the underlying stock rises instead of falling.

The risks of uncovered call writing are:

1. The stock may rise in value, and you will have to buy the call to close the position and avoid further losses or exercise.

2. The stock may rise in value, causing exercise and resulting loss.

3. Although the stock is at or below striking price, it might rise suddenly and be exercised; you are at risk from the moment you sell until expiration.

4. The activity of writing options restricts other activity, because your brokerage firm wants to limit its own risk exposure. As a consequence, you have to pass up other momentary investment opportunities.

5. If your timing or estimation of the market is wrong and you suffer large losses, your brokerage firm may sell other long-term securities in your portfolio to pay for the losses. In this scenario, your short-term losses inadvertently affect your long-term portfolio.

SELLING COVERED CALLS

In the examples of losses writing uncovered calls, the potentially large losses result from being forced to satisfy exercise (or close out positions at a large loss). Typically, uncovered call writers may be required to buy 100 shares at current market value and sell them at a much lower striking price.

Imagine being able to sell calls without that risk. There is a way. By selling calls against stock you own in your portfolio, you *cover* yourself by owning the shares. In the event the option is called, you are prepared to meet the call by simply selling the shares.

You enjoy several advantages with the *covered call*:

1. You are paid a premium for each option you sell, which is cash placed into your account. While this is also true of uncovered option writing, the same risks do not apply. You can afford exercise because you already own the stock and, upon exercise, would not be required to buy it at then-prevailing market value.

2. The true net price of your 100 shares of stock is reduced by the value of the option premium. It is a discount, because you are paid for selling the option. This gives you more flexibility, more downside protection, and more versatility for selling options with high time value.

3. Selling covered calls provides you with the freedom to accept moderate interim price declines, because the premium received reduces your price. Simply owning the stock without discounting through option sales means that even a moderate decline represents a paper loss.

cover
to protect oneself by owning 100 shares of the underlying stock for each call sold (The risk in the short position in the call is covered by the ownership of 100 shares.)

covered call
a call sold to create an open short position, when the seller also owns 100 shares of stock for each call sold

Example: You own 100 shares of stock, which you bought last year for $50 per share. Current market value is $54 per share. You would be willing to sell this stock at a profit. Accordingly, you write a November 55 call and receive a premium of 5 ($500). Once this is done, your real basis in the stock is $45 (original price of $50 per share, discounted 5 points for selling the call, to $45 per share). If the stock's market value remains anywhere between $45 and $55 between now and expiration, your investment will be profitable. In addition, the call will not be exercised under those circumstances, since striking price is 55. If the stock's market value declines, you can buy the option at a profit.

One of three events can take place when you sell a call for every 100 shares of stock you own: an increase in price, a decrease in price, or no significant change. As long as you own 100 shares, you continue to receive any dividends earned regardless of whether you sell an option. The value in writing covered calls should be compared to the value of simply buying and holding stock, as shown in Table 5.1.

Before you undertake any strategy, understand its advantages and disadvantages, including the potential sacrifice of future profits. A call seller can *lock in* the

TABLE 5.1 Comparing Strategies		
	Outcomes	
Event	*Owning Stock and Writing Calls*	*Owning Stock Only*
Stock goes up in value	Call is exercised; profits are limited to striking price and call premium.	Stock can be sold at a profit.
Stock remains at or below the striking price	Time value declines; the call can be closed out at a profit or allowed to expire worthless.	No profit or loss until sold.
Stock declines in value	Stock price is discounted by call premium; the call is closed or allowed to expire worthless.	Loss on the stock.
Dividends	Earned while stock is held.	Earned while stock is held.

lock in
to freeze the price of the underlying stock when the investor owns a corresponding short call (As long as the call position is open, the writer is locked into a striking price, regardless of current market value of the stock. In the event of exercise, the stock is delivered at that locked-in price.)

price of the underlying stock in the event of exercise so that regardless of how far the stock's market price rises, the seller will receive only the striking price value upon exercise.

Assessing Covered Call Selling Risks

The seller of uncovered calls faces potentially large losses. However, when you sell covered calls, your risks are greatly reduced. In many instances, your risk is virtually eliminated—because your profit in the stock more than covers any potential loss in the option.

Many investors are concerned with the risked loss of future profits. In other words, once you sell a call, you risk missing out on the profit in the event the stock rises in value significantly. Owning 100 shares protects the short position in the call; but it is possible to have the stock called away at the striking price, which could be substantially lower than current market value.

By properly structuring a covered call writing strategy, you can learn to accept the risk of losing future profits, in exchange for predictability. The covered call write is a fairly consistent strategy when applied and managed correctly. Some pitfalls to be avoided include:

1. *Setting up the call write so that, if exercised, you create an unintended loss in the stock.* This is possible if you accept a striking price below your actual basis—especially if the option premium is not high enough to offset the difference. For example, if you buy stock at $34 and later sell a call at 30, and receive a premium of only 3 ($300), you could be setting up a loss upon exercise. (Basis of $34 per share, less premium of 3, creates a net basis of $31 per share; but if exercised, the stock is sold for $30 per share, creating a $100 net loss before brokerage fees.)

2. *Becoming tied into positions you cannot afford to close out.* If you become involved in a high volume of call writing, you may want to close out positions later but lack the cash to take advantage of current conditions. Be sure your cash reserves are adequate to provide yourself with flexibility.

3. *Writing calls on the wrong stock.* When you begin evaluating premium values and see exceptionally rich time value, it will be tempting to buy 100 shares just to write calls. However, such stocks tend to be volatile, and that volatility and possible lack of safety are reflected in call premium levels. You might profit on call trades, only to end up with substandard stocks in your portfolio. One moderate correction in the market could wipe out your profits very suddenly.

CALCULATING RATE OF RETURN

If your purpose in owning stock is to hold it for many years, writing calls is not usually an appropriate strategy—although in some instances it can be used to enhance current income with only moderate risks of exercise. The call writer's objective is usually quite different from the objective of the long-term investor and, while the two objectives can coexist, it is more likely that you will use covered options to create current income rather than long-term growth. You have three potential sources of income as a covered call writer:

✔ Call premiums.
✔ Capital gains on stock (limited due to the writing of covered calls).
✔ Dividends.

Example: You bought 100 shares of stock and paid $32 per share. Several months later, the stock's market value rose to $38. You wrote a March 35 call and received 8 ($800). Your reasoning: Since your basis in the stock was $32 per share, if the call were exercised you would have to sell at $35, gaining a profit of $3 per share. In addition, you received money for writing the call, and that represents additional profit. In this case, your option premium sold for $800, of which 3 points were intrinsic value (the difference between striking price of 35 and market value of the stock of $38 per share) and 5 points were time value. If exercised, your total profit would be $1100 ($300 from appreciation in the stock between your original basis and the striking price, plus $800 from the call premium). Two months after you sold the call, the stock's market value rose to $65 per share and the call was exercised. Your profit was frozen at $1100 because you had locked in at the striking price of $35 per share.

This example shows how a potential profit may be lost, a fact that option writers have to accept. Simply owning the stock—without writing any calls—would have produced a profit of $3300 if you sold immediately after the price run-up. Covered call writers limit their upside potential in exchange for certainty regarding a smaller amount of profit. Profits are ensured but limited.

What are the chances of a stock soaring in price? It does happen, but you cannot depend on it. If you sell a call and later limit your profits, have you really lost? Investors will have differing points of view about this. Some will claim that potential future profits not gained *are* losses; however, when one sells a call, there is always a possibility of lost future profits. We may further argue that you lose whenever you fail to buy a stock that later rises in value, or when you sell and take profits immediately before a large price increase.

A more reasoned point of view is one suggested for option investors: Profits exist only if you take them. Covered call writers can consistently earn decent rates of return on their strategy, but they have to learn to live with the occasional missed opportunity. Remember, as an option writer, you seek consistent and decent returns, and you give up the occasional unexpected profit.

By accepting the limitation of writing covered calls, you give up potential gains while you *discount* your price in the stock. This provides a degree of downside protection against interim drops in stock value. You continue to receive dividends. And while you will miss out on the occasional spectacular rise, you settle for consistent and

discount to reduce the true price of the stock by the amount of premium received (A benefit in selling covered calls, the discount provides downside protection and protects long positions.)

better-than-average returns. It is fair to assume that most writers of covered calls will ultimately earn higher profits than those who seek exceptional and sudden increases in stock prices.

A covered call writer should always identify both the profit and loss zones as shown in Figure 5.2, and should also calculate the rate of return under different outcomes. A covered call's profit and loss zones are determined by the combination of two factors: the option's premium value and the underlying stock's market value. If the stock falls below a break-even price (the price paid for the stock, less the premium received for writing the option), then there will be a loss. Of course, when you own stock, you decide when to sell, so such a loss becomes a realized loss only if you sell the stock. You have the luxury of being able to let the option expire worthless, and waiting for the stock's market value to rebound.

You should make one important rule for yourself: Never sell a covered call unless you would be completely satisfied in the event it is exercised. Figure out your *total return* before you sell a call, and enter the transaction only

total return
the combined return including income from selling a call, capital gain from a profit on selling the stock, and dividends earned and received (Total return may be calculated in two ways: return if the option is exercised, and return if the option expires worthless.)

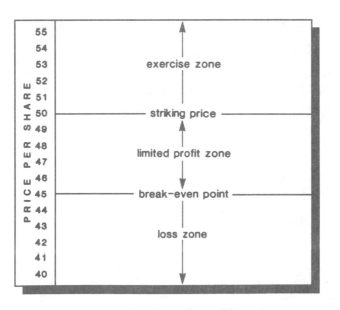

FIGURE 5.2 A covered call's profit and loss zones.

when you are confident that either outcome will be worthwhile.

Total return includes stock appreciation, call premium, and dividend income. If the option expires worthless, one rate of return occurs; if you buy the option and close the position, an entirely different rate of return occurs. Because you do not sell the stock in that second outcome, the rate of return can vary considerably.

Example: You own 100 shares of stock you bought at $41 per share. Current market value is $44 per share, and you are considering selling a July 45 call. The premium value of that call is 5 ($500). Between now and expiration, you will receive a total of $40 in dividends.

If this call were to be exercised, the return would consist of all three elements:

Stock appreciation	$400
Call premium	500
Dividends	40
Total return	$940
Yield	22.9%

If the call is not exercised but allowed to expire worthless, total return will not include appreciation from the underlying stock, since it is still held. (The current value compared to purchase price is a paper profit only and cannot be calculated as a return.) Return in this case would be:

Call premium	$500
Dividends	40
Total return	$540
Yield	13.2%

Although the yield in the second instance is lower, you still own the stock. After expiration, you are free to sell the stock or to write another call—or to take no further action whatsoever.

TIMING THE DECISION

A first-time call writer might be surprised to experience immediate exercise. This can occur at any time you are in the money. It is most likely to occur at or close to expiration date, but you need to be prepared to give up 100 shares of stock for each call sold. That is, after all, the contractual agreement involved in writing the call. This can happen at any time, from the date of the transaction to the last trading day.

As shown in Figure 5.3, during the life of a call, the underlying stock might swing several points above or below the striking price. If you own 100 shares and are considering selling a call, keep these points in mind:

1. When the striking price of the call is higher than the original cost of the stock, exercise is not a negative, since it will automatically create a double profit: from appreciation in the stock and from the call premium.

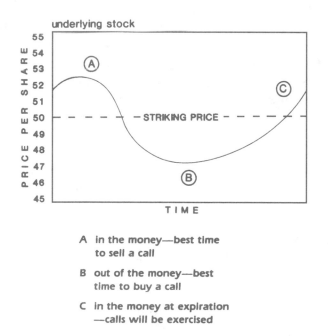

A in the money—best time
 to sell a call

B out of the money—best
 time to buy a call

C in the money at expiration
 —calls will be exercised

FIGURE 5.3 Timing of call transactions relative to price movement of underlying stock.

Example: You bought stock at $38 per share and later sold a call with a striking price of 40. Your option premium was 3 ($300). You are not concerned with exercise, because you know that will produce the double profit: 2 points on the stock plus 3 points on the sale of the option.

2. If you sell a call for a striking price below your original cost of the stock, be sure that the premium you receive is greater than the loss you will experience in the event of exercise.

Example: You bought 100 shares of stock at $43 per share and sold a call with a striking price of 40. If exercised, you will lose $300 on the stock. If the premium you are paid is 3 ($300) or less, you have defeated the purpose in selling calls, because you will lose money. If the premium is 3 or more, you will have a limited profit in the event of exercise.

3. In calculating potential yields, be sure to allow for commission costs on stock *and* option upon both purchase and sale (or exercise).

Example: You bought 100 shares of stock at $53 and later sold a call with a striking price of 50, receiving a premium of 3 ($300). In the event of exercise, the loss in the stock will be offset by a profit in the option premium. But brokerage transaction fees have to be taken into account as well. In reality, if the call is exercised, you will have a loss.

4. For the benefit of producing a consistent profit from writing calls, you give up the potential for larger gains in the event the stock's price rises.

Example: You bought 100 shares of stock at $22 and later sold a call with a striking price of 25, receiving a premium of 4 ($400). However, the stock recently rose to $34 and the call was exercised. Upon exercise, your profit consisted of 3 points for the stock plus 4 points for the call, a total of $700, or 28 percent return (before counting dividends). But if you had not sold the call, your total profit on the stock alone would have been $1200 (if you had sold when the stock rose to $34 per share), a 48 percent return.

You cannot depend on sudden increases in stock value and, as a call writer, you recognize that consistent returns are desirable over the big gain. The way you look at such situations determines whether option selling is appropriate for you. Select calls not in expectation of large price movement in the stock, but with respect to the likely trading range. Selecting an appropriate call depends on the price you paid for the stock, compared to the current price. An option's premium at various price levels varies depending on the striking price and time until expiration.

Example: You buy stock at $51 per share, and it then rises to $53. Rather than sell the stock, you choose to sell a call with a striking price of 50, and receive a premium of 7 ($700).

In this example, the premium is higher than average because it includes 3 points of intrinsic value. This strategy provides several advantages to you:

1. If the stock's current market value falls below your purchase price, you can buy the option to close the position at a profit, or allow the option to expire worthless.
2. By selling the option, you discount your price from $51 to $44 per share, providing yourself with downside protection of 7 points. In the event the stock's price declines, that is a substantial level of coverage.
3. You continue to receive dividends as long as the option is not exercised.

You might also choose to sell a call that is deep in the money.

Example: You bought stock at $51 per share and it is now worth $53 per share. You will receive at least $800 if you were to sell a call with a striking price of 45 (because there are currently 8 points of intrinsic value in the 45 option). That also vastly increases the likelihood of exercise. And for the additional premium, exercise would represent a 6-point loss in the stock:

Purchase price	$5100
Exercise value	−4500
Loss on stock	$−600

If this comparison involved only intrinsic value, it would hardly seem worthwhile to risk exercise for a net profit of only $200 (option premium of 8 points, less loss on the stock of 6 points). However, depending on the time until expiration, the real profit from selling deep-in-the-money calls comes from time value.

Example: You bought stock for $51 and it is currently valued at $53 per share. Now, in the month of January, you can sell a June 45 call and receive a premium of 11 ($1100). In the event of exercise, you will earn a profit on the overall transaction of $500:

Purchase price of stock	$5100
Less: striking price of option	−4500
Loss on stock	$−600
Plus: option premium	1100
Net profit	$ 500

This outcome is not an unreasonable way to create a profit. And remember, this only occurs if the option is exercised. If the stock's market value falls, the option value will also fall point for point, so selling the option provides you with downside protection. You can buy the option and close the position at any time prior to exercise.

Example: Given the same circumstances as above, what occurs if the stock's market value falls 3 points, to $50 per share? The option, sold for $1100, would then be worth $800. You could execute a closing purchase transaction, pay $800, and produce a $300 profit. You still own the stock and are free to sell an option again. If the stock rebounds to $53 per share, you can enter a new option transaction when that occurs.

Always select options and time purchases with all of these points in mind:

✔ Your original cost for the stock.

✔ The amount of the premium.

✔ The mix between time and intrinsic value.

✔ Distance between current market value of the stock and striking price of the option.

✔ Time until expiration.

✔ Total return if the call is exercised, compared to total return if the option expires worthless.

✔ Your objectives in owning the stock, compared to your objectives in selling the call (immediate income, downside protection).

AVOIDING EXERCISE

Assuming that you sell a call on stock originally purchased as a worthwhile investment, you might want to take steps to avoid exercise. First, though, remember the overall rule: Never sell a call unless you are willing to go through exercise, and expect exercise at any time you're in the money. Given that rule, you might be able to defer or avoid exercise while profiting on declining time value.

You avoid exercise in several ways. The following examples are based on the unexpected movement of stock to a position that puts you in jeopardy of exercise. While that outcome would not be altogether negative, we also assume that you would prefer to avoid exercise, if only because the stock's value is now substantially higher than it was when you sold the call.

Example: You sold a May 35 call on stock when the stock's market value was $34 per share. The stock's current market value is $41 per share, and you would like to avoid exercise and be able to take advantage of the higher stock market value.

The first method you can use to avoid exercise involves simply canceling the option by purchasing it. Although this causes you to lose money on the option, it will also be accompanied by an increased value in the underlying stock. If time value has declined, this could be a wise move—especially if the increased value of the stock exceeds the amount of loss in the option.

Example: You bought 100 shares of stock at $21 per share and later sold a June 25 call, receiving a premium of 4 ($400). The stock is at present valued at $30 per share, and the option premium is at 6 ($600). If you buy back the option, you will lose $200 on the transaction (sale at 4, less purchase at 6). However, by avoiding exercise at the striking price of $25, you now own stock with current market value of $30.

In this example, the outcome can be summarized in two ways. First, remember that by closing the call position at a loss, you still own the 100 shares of stock. That frees you to immediately sell yet another call, perhaps one with a striking price of 30—creating more income from the option premium.

You can also analyze this situation by comparing the exercise of the option versus closing the option and selling the 100 shares at current market value. The flaw in this method is that it assumes a sale of the stock, which is not the desired result in avoiding exercise. However, the comparison does enable you to study exercise versus sale on the same basis, namely that the stock is sold:

	Exercise	*Sale*
Basis in 100 shares of stock	−2100	−2100
Call premium received	400	400
Option position closed		−600
100 shares delivered at $25	2500	
100 shares sold at $30		3000
Net profit	$ 800	$ 700

This comparison concludes that it would be better by a difference of $100 to allow exercise of the option. That is true only if you would be willing to give up the 100 shares. However, do not overlook the opportunity to use those appreciated shares to subsequently sell another call. The purpose in avoiding exercise is usually to replace the older position with a newer one.

In this example, the open position in the call also provided downside protection. If the stock had fallen, even to the level of $17 per share, you would have lost no money. Your original basis of $21 per share was protected down to 4 points represented by the option premium. But since the stock's market value rose, closing out the position at a loss may be a smart move, because that leaves open the opportunity to sell other, higher striking price options right away. Considering the current market value of the stock in comparison to striking prices of various options, you certainly have greater flexibility with appreciated stock. Now that market value is $30 per share, by freeing yourself from the short position in the option, you are free to subsequently sell an option with more time until expiration (meaning more time value and a higher premium).

As a second technique, you can avoid exercise by exchanging one call for another, and at the same time make a profit. Since the premium value for the new option is higher when there is more time until expiration, you gain the advantage by trading on time value. This may defer exercise until later while producing more profits, or buy time during which the stock's value might fall—meaning you will make a profit on the new option. The technique of trading on time value is called a *roll forward*.

roll forward
the replacement of one written call with another with the same striking price, but a later expiration date

Example: The May 40 call you wrote against 100 shares of stock is near expiration and is in the money. To avoid or delay exercise, you buy back the May 40 option, canceling that position; then you immediately sell a July 40 call—it has the same striking price but a later expiration date.

You still face the prospect of exercise at any time; however, exercise is always more likely at or near expiration date. In addition, if you think expiration is inevitable, this technique provides you with additional income. Invariably, later expiration dates provide greater time value premium than those about to expire. The roll forward technique can be used whether you have single call contracts or several hundred shares of stock and several calls. The more shares you own in a single underlying stock, the greater your flexibility in rolling forward and adding to your profits. Canceling a single call and rolling forward can produce a marginal gain. However, you increase the gain if you cancel one outstanding call and replace it with two or more with later expirations. That is called *incremental return*. Profits are increased as you increase the number of options sold against your stock.

The roll forward maintains the same striking price and buys time. However, that idea does not always suit present circumstances. Another form of rolling is the *roll down*.

Example: You originally bought 100 shares of stock for $31 per share and later sold a call with a striking price of 35, receiving a premium of 3 ($300). The stock has fallen in value and your call is worth 1 ($100). You cancel (buy) it and realize a profit of $200, and immediately sell another call with a striking price of 30, receiving a premium of 4 ($400).

In this case, the first call was sold at a striking price 4 points higher than your basis. You realize a profit by canceling that position, effectively lowering your basis to $29 per share (purchase price of $31 less the 2-point profit from selling the call). The second call further reduced your basis to $25 per share ($29 less the 4 points received for selling the second call).

Yet another technique is the *roll up*.

Example: You originally paid $31 per share for 100 shares of stock, and later sold a call with a striking price of 35. The stock's current market value has risen to $39 per share. You cancel (buy) the first call, accepting a loss, and offset that loss by selling another call with a striking price of 40.

 incremental return
a technique for avoiding exercise while increasing profits with written calls (When the value of the underlying stock rises, a single call is closed at a loss and replaced with two or more call writes with later expiration dates, producing cash and a profit in the exchange.)

roll down
the replacement of one written call with another that has a lower striking price

roll up
the replacement of one written call with another that has a higher striking price

With this technique, the loss in the original call should not exceed the number of points you pick up in the increased striking price. You will probably need to combine the roll up with the roll forward. In order to make the transaction work, you may need the additional time you get by taking a later expiration date for the option. The rolling technique often involves a combination of later expirations and higher striking prices. Conceivably, this can be carried on indefinitely. See Figure 5.4.

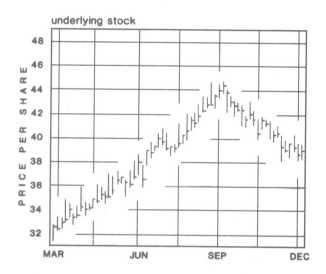

DATE	DESCRIPTION	RECEIVED	PAID
Mar 15	sell 2 Jun 30 calls at 5	$1000	
Jun 11	buy 2 Jun 30 calls at 8		$1600
	sell 5 Sep 35 calls at 6	$3000	
Sep 8	buy 5 Sep 35 calls at 9		$4500
	sell 8 Dec 40 calls at 6	$4800	
Dec 22	Dec 40 calls expire worthless	–	–
	totals	$8800	$6100
	profit	$2700	

FIGURE 5.4 Using the rolling technique to avoid exercise.

Example: You own 800 shares of stock that you originally bought at $30 per share (total basis is $24,000). You expect the value of this stock to rise, but you also believe you can write covered calls and increase your profit while picking up downside protection. So on March 15, you sell two June 30 contracts for a premium of 5 ($500) each, and receive payment of $1000.

On June 11, the stock's market value is at $38 per share and you expect your calls to be exercised shortly. To avoid exercise, you execute a closing purchase transaction, buy the two calls and pay a premium of 8 (total cost, $1600). You replace the canceled calls with five September 35 calls and receive a premium of 6 ($600) each, for a total of $3000.

On September 8, the stock's market value has risen again, and is now valued at $44 per share. You again want to avoid exercise, so you cancel (buy) your five open contracts and pay a premium of 9 ($900) each, for a total cost of $4500. You immediately replace these with eight December 40 calls, receiving a premium of 6 ($600) on each, for a total of $4800.

By December 22, the day of expiration, the stock has declined in value to $39 per share. Your eight outstanding call contracts expire worthless. Your total profit on this series of transactions is $2700 in the calls. In addition, you still own 800 shares of stock now valued at $39 per share, which is $7200 above your basis. Furthermore, you are entitled to all dividends on these shares during this entire period.

For the volume of transactions, you might wonder if the exposure was worth the $2700 profit. It certainly was, considering that the strategy was dictated by the rising price of the stock. While you received a profit, you were also able to avoid exercise in a condition of rising prices. The incremental return combining roll up and roll forward demonstrates how you can avoid exercise while still generating a profit. The example showed a rising stock that happened to fall below striking price in the last series of writes. While you cannot depend on this pattern to occur consistently, it does occur in the market. The investor in the example, we have to assume, would have been happy with exercise at any point along the way. Avoiding exercise when the stock price is rising is a practical strategy. If the investor in this example were to sell the 800 shares at the ending current market value of $39 per share, total profit would be substantial:

Stock

Sell 800 shares at $39 each	$31,200
Original cost	−24,000
Profit on stock	$ 7,200

Options

Sell 2 June contracts	$ 1,000
Buy 2 June contracts	−1,600
Sell 5 September contracts	3,000
Buy 5 September contracts	−4,500
Sell 8 December contracts	4,800
Profit on options	$ 2,700
Total profit	$ 9,900
Yield	41.25%

Whenever you roll forward, higher time value becomes a benefit. Greater premium value will be found because time has value in option premiums, even when striking price is the same. So the longer until expiration, the higher your income from selling calls. In exchange for that higher income, you agree to remain in the risk position that much longer. You are locked in to the striking price until you close the position, go through exercise, or wait out expiration.

The strategies you may employ to defer or avoid exercise combine two dissimilar goals: increasing income while also trying to hold on to the stock that has value above the striking price. This is possible because the time value of longer-term options is higher than the time value of options about to expire.

Example: You own 200 shares of stock originally purchased at $40 per share. You have an open June 40 call you sold for 3. The stock is currently worth $45 per share and you would like to avoid exercise at $40. Table 5.2 shows current values of options available on your stock. A review of this table provides several rolling opportunities.

To begin with, you will need to make a closing purchase transaction, a buy of your June 40 option at 6. This represents a $300 loss on that option. To offset this loss, one of the following strategies can be employed:

1. *Strategy 1: Rolling Up and Forward.* Sell one December 45 call at 5, producing a net income of $200 ($500 for the December call, less $300 loss on the June call).
2. *Strategy 2: Rolling with Incremental Return.* Sell two September 45 calls, receiving $400 and producing net income of $100 ($400 for the two September 45 calls, less the loss of $300 for the June call).
3. *Strategy 3: Rolling Forward Only.* Sell one September 40 call at 8, producing net income of $500 ($800 for the September call, less the $300 loss for the June call).

Note that in these strategies we refer to the *loss* on the June call, and not the actual cash exchange. Because the June call is valued at 6, it requires an outlay of $600 to buy (close) that position. You previously received $300 when it was sold, so your *net* loss is $300; this is the amount used to compare the three available strategies.

If the underlying stock is reasonably stable and its

TABLE 5.2 Current Call Option Values			
Striking Price	Expiration Month		
	June	Sept.	Dec.
35	11	13	15
40	6	8	10
45	1	2	5

market value moves up and down within a range of 5 points or so, it is possible to sell calls in an indefinite series of rolling techniques, canceling one open position and opening another as time value is reduced. Rolling techniques are especially useful when stocks break out of their short-term trading ranges and you want to take advantage of increased market value while still profiting from selling covered calls.

To show how such a strategy might work, refer to Table 5.3. This shows an actual example of a series of trades over a period of 2½ years. The investor owned 400 shares of stock and traded through a discount broker. The sale and purchase prices show the actual amount of cash transacted, including brokerage transaction fees, rounded to the nearest dollar. The total net profit of $2628 occurred after 40 trades (20 buy orders and 20 sell orders). Total brokerage charges were

Calls Traded	Type	Sold Date	Sold Amount	Bought Date	Bought Amount	Profit	Notes
1	Jul 35	3/20	$ 328	4/30	$ 221	$ 107	
1	Oct 35	6/27	235	10/8	78	157	
1	Apr 35	1/15	247	4/14	434	−187	
1	Oct 35	4/14	604	6/24	228	376	1
1	Oct 35	7/31	353	9/12	971	−618	
2	Jan 45	9/12	915	12/16	172	743	2
2	Apr 45	12/16	379	2/24	184	195	
4	Jul 40	3/9	1357	5/26	385	972	3
4	Oct 40	6/5	1553	7/22	1036	517	
4	Jan 40	8/5	1504	9/15	138	366	
		Totals	$7475		$4847	$2628	

TABLE 5.3 Selling Calls with Rolling Techniques

[1] A roll forward: The loss on the April 35 call was acceptable to avoid exercise, since the October 35 was profitable.

[2] A combination roll forward and roll up: The loss on the October 35 call was acceptable to avoid exercise at a low striking price. The number of calls was incrementally increased from one to two.

[3] A roll down combined with an incremental return: The number of calls changed from two to four, and the striking price of 45 was replaced with one for 40.

$722, so actual gross profits were $3350; the figure of $2628 represents the net profit actually realized.

The summary in Table 5.3 shows each type of rolling trade plus an effective use of the incremental return technique. The investor was willing to increase the outstanding number of covered calls on as many as 400 shares of stock, in order to avoid exercise when current market value was greater than striking price. And when the stock's price declined, the investor rolled down but did not write calls below the original striking price of 35.

Any form of covered call writing should be planned well ahead of time. Besides checking the attributes of the option itself, judging the quality of the underlying stock is critical. There is no point in profiting short-term on option writes if the stock itself is of poor quality, without any potential for longer-term price appreciation. If you purchase shares primarily to write covered calls, chances are you will pick issues more volatile than average and more vulnerable to value declines in response to momentary corrections. These issues are likely to offer more attractive option premiums and higher time value because of their underlying volatility and lower safety.

Whether you intend to write uncovered or covered calls, you will be less likely to succeed if you buy overpriced stocks that later fall well below your basis. An example of an uncovered call write, with defined profit and

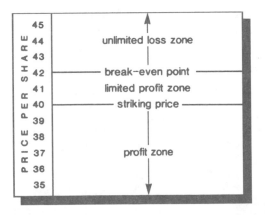

FIGURE 5.5 Example of uncovered call write with profit and loss zones.

loss zones, is shown in Figure 5.5. In this example, one May 40 call was sold for 2. This strategy exposes the investor to unlimited risk. If the stock rises above the striking price and exceeds the number of points equal to premium value, exercise will result in a loss. The stock's market value could rise indefinitely. Upon exercise, the investor has to deliver 100 shares at the striking price of 40 per share, regardless of then-prevailing market value.

An example of a covered call write, with defined profit and loss zones, is shown in Figure 5.6. In this example, the investor owned 100 shares of stock originally purchased for $38 per share. The investor then sold one May 40 call and received 2. This strategy discounts the basis price of the stock to $36 per share. As long as the stock's value is at or below striking price, the call will have no intrinsic value. If that condition lasts until expiration, it will expire worthless. If the stock's market value is above striking price, the call will be exercised and the investor's 100 shares will be called away. In that case, total profit would be $400 (2 points of profit in the stock, plus 2 points received for selling the call). However, selling covered calls also locks in the striking price. In the event of substantial price increase, profits are limited under terms of the option contract.

As a call writer, stock selection is critically important to you. The next chapter explains methods for picking stocks with a call-writing strategy in mind.

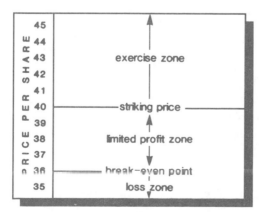

FIGURE 5.6 Example of covered call write with profit and loss zones.

Choosing the Right Stock

Careful, well-researched selection is the key to good investing. This is true for all forms of investment and for all market strategies. Investors whose stock portfolio is not performing as expected might be tempted to augment lackluster profits by becoming involved in options. The short-term income could close a gap, improve yields, and even bail out a small loss by transforming it into a small profit. However, supplementary short-term income is not a valid reason for using options. Your best chance for success as an option investor comes from establishing rules and policies for selection of sound stock investments, fitting a suitable option strategy together with that stock selection, and then following policies designed to maximize profits within a profile of acceptable risks.

Once your investment policy has been established, stay with it. A portfolio of excellent stocks represents a long-term, worthwhile investment. It also offers opportunities for short-term profits in the options market. As a basic rule of thumb, select stocks you would like to hold for many years whether or not you intend to write options.

One common error made by options investors is buying specifically because the current premium for a particular option is attractive. Be aware that the attractive option premium might itself be an indication of problems with the stock. Pricing reflects the opinion of the market at large, and exceptional risk arising from factors like overpriced stock could be represented in unusually high option premiums. For example, a call writer might buy 100 shares of a particular stock just to provide cover for writing a call. If this is done without independent study of the stock involved, it could spell trouble. Because of their attributes, some of the more volatile stocks also are associated with some of the most interesting option premiums and short-term price movement. You should ensure that your personal risk standards are given the highest priority—that they act as a guiding force and not just as a checklist for possible stock selection. While certain option strategies can be highly profitable when the stock's price falls, you also need to look to the longer term. You do yourself no good if you experience option profits but end up with a portfolio of poor-quality stocks.

One of the great advantages to covered call writing is that a minimum profit level is ensured as long as you also remember that stock selection is a critical first step in the strategy.

Example: You bought 100 shares of stock at $38 per share. You bought the stock for reasons independent of any option strategies or considerations. You are thinking about selling a call. One call contract expires in three months and has a striking price of 40 and a premium of 4. During that period, you will also earn a $60 dividend on the stock. Your calculations assure an annualized profit of 48.4 percent (if the call expires worthless) or 69.6 percent (if the call is exercised at the point of expiration). The latter calculation assumes the dividend would be earned even if the stock is exercised, as the calculation assumes exercise at the date of expiration.

If the Call Expires:

Call premium	$ 400
Dividend	60
Total profit	$ 460
Basis in stock	$3800

Yield if the Option Expires

$460 ÷ $3800 = 12.1%

Annualized Return Earned in Three Months

(12.1% ÷ 3) × 12 = 48.4%

If the Call Is Exercised:

Call premium	$ 400
Dividend	60
Capital gain	200
Total profit	$ 660
Basis in stock	$3800

Yield if the Option Is Exercised

$660 ÷ $3800 = 17.4%

Annualized Return Earned in Three Months

(17.4% ÷ 3) × 12 = 69.6%

(Note: Annualized return is calculated by dividing the yield by the number of months the investment was held and multiplying that result by 12.)

DEVELOPING A PRACTICAL APPROACH

Earning a consistently high yield from writing calls is not always possible, even for covered call writers. You might be able to sell a call today that is rich in time value, and to profit from the combination of capital gain, dividends, and call premium profit. But the opportunity also depends on a combination of factors:

1. The price of the underlying stock has to be at the right place in two respects. First, the relationship between current market value and the price you originally paid has to justify exposure to exercise at a profitable level. If exercise would result in a loss, you cannot profitably write a call. And second, the current market value has to be right in relation to the call option you're considering selling, or the time value won't be high enough to justify the transaction.

Example: You bought 100 shares of stock at $43 per share, and would like to write a call with a striking price of 45. If exercised you would profit from the combination of the option premium and a 2-point capital gain on the stock (plus any dividends). As long as the premium is high enough to justify the decision, it will be a worthwhile strategy.

    2. The volume of investor interest in the stock and related options has to be high enough to make the call rich in time value.

Example: The stock you recently bought has had exceptionally high volume lately, because it is rumored as a takeover candidate. For the same reason, call premiums on the underlying stock are very high in time value, the best possible situation for call writing. Note, however, that if the rumors are true, writing calls now has a greater risk than in the past; if the stock rises suddenly because the rumors are true, you could lose potential profits—the trade-off for exceptionally high call premiums now.

    3. The time between now and expiration should fit with your personal goals.

Example: You would like to sell your stock within four months and use the proceeds to pay off a loan. You are confident that the stock's market value will hold up, but in the meantime you would like to augment your income by writing a call. Because you will need the money within four months, that goal limits the practical range of calls to those that will expire within four months or less. You should also note that this deadline restricts your option strategies. Rolling forward will not be a practical available strategy, since you must sell the stock within four months.

These circumstances might not be repeated later. Call writing requires patience and careful timing in certain conditions, and decisiveness in others. You may have to be willing to wait until all of the conditions are right, and then move quickly.

In considering various covered call writing strategies, a common mistake is to assume that today's conditions are permanent. For example, you might earn 48 percent on a single transaction, but you probably will not be able to repeat that outcome every time, because markets are constantly changing. The ideal call write should be undertaken when all four of the following conditions are present:

1. The striking price of the option is higher than your original basis in the stock. Thus, exercise will produce an automatic profit in both the stock *and* the option. If the striking price of the option is lower than your basis in the stock, the option premium must be higher than the difference; it must also contain enough value to cover brokerage fees for both sides of the transaction.

2. The call is in the money. This means it contains some intrinsic value, so that stock movements will be paralleled with dollar-for-dollar price changes in the option premium. While being in the money increases the threat of exercise, it also means higher option premium *and* the likelihood of more time value. The greater the time until expiration, the more valuable this interaction between intrinsic and time value.

3. There is enough time remaining until expiration that the majority of premium in the option consists of time value. So even with little or no movement in the stock, time value will evaporate by expiration, making your call write profitable. Remember, time value will exist whether or not any intrinsic value is also found in the option. It is quite possible to write an in-the-money call option that remains in the money over time, and still produces a profit for the writer—all based on evaporation of time value.

4. Expiration will occur in six months or less, meaning you will not be locked into the position for too long a time. However, the point here is that you don't want to assume that circumstances as they are today will remain into the indefinite future. While six months is an estimation, you should be progressively uncertain about the future as the distance increases. There is no way to know what the future market will look like. Investor moods can change drastically in a few months, but are less likely to change drastically within the near future.

5. The premium is high enough to justify locking in the stock for the period until expiration and to risk exercise due to future price movement in the stock. You might conclude that a small premium, although representing a short-term profit, is simply not worth the risk.

Example: You own 100 shares of stock that originally cost $53 per share. The stock's market value is currently at $57. You write a call with a striking price of 55 that will expire in five months and that offers a current premium of 6. All of the ideal circumstances exist: Striking price is 2 points higher than the stock's original cost; the call is in the money by 2 points, so price movement in the option will be directly responsive to price movement in the stock; two-thirds of current option premium is time value; expiration will take place in less than six months; and the amount of the premium is $600, a rich level. You will earn a substantial return whether the call expires worthless or is exercised. If time value declines, the position can also be closed at a profit.

This example shows a practical and methodical approach to writing covered calls. For the 6 points received from selling the call, you also gain 6 points of downside protection. So the net basis of the stock becomes $47 per share (original cost of $53, less 6 points received for selling the call). Even if the stock were to fall to that level, you would not lose any money.

SELECTING STOCKS FOR CALL WRITING

Some investors choose stocks based only on the potential yield gained from writing covered calls. This is a mistake. Other criteria should be applied because the best-yielding calls often are available only on the most volatile stocks. So if you apply the criterion of yield from call writing as the sole reason for picking one stock over another, you also increase the chances of wide price swings in your portfolio.

Example: You decide to buy stock based on the relationship of current call premium to the price of the stock. You have only $4000 to invest, so you review only those stocks selling for $40 per share or less. Your objective is to buy stock on which the call premium is no less than 10 percent of current value, with calls at the money or out of the money. You prepare a chart summarizing available stocks and options:

Current Value	Call Premium
$36	$3
28	$3^1/_2$
25	1
39	4
27	$1^3/_4$

You decide to buy the stock priced at $28 per share, since the call's value is $3^1/_2$, a yield of 12.5 percent, the best yield available from this range. On the surface, this analysis appears reasonable; however, there are several problems with the approach. Most significant is the fact that no distinction is made among the stocks other than price and yield of their call options. The issue selected was judged not on its own merits, but on that relationship. And by limiting the selection of stocks below $40 per share, the possible market for call writing is severely restricted.

This method also fails to consider time until expiration. You will receive higher premiums when expiration dates are farther away, in exchange for which you lock in for a longer period of time. Another flaw: These calls are not judged in regard to the relationship between striking price and stock market value. The immediate yield appears to be greater when it is in the money, which may deceive the reviewer.

The value of locking in 100 shares to a fixed striking price should be judged in relation to the number of months until expiration. Otherwise, how can you know the real value of that option? For example, a 10 percent or higher yield might be attractive for calls with three to six months remaining until expiration, but less attractive when the call will not expire for eight months. Yield is not a constant; it depends on time.

Comparing yields between current call premium and stock price also ignores the equally important time factor, potential price increase in the stock, and dividend yield. Covered call writing is a conservative strategy, assuming that you first know how to pick high-quality stock issues. The stock should be picked first for its investment value, meaning that option potential is not a major factor in the selection. That is the proper way to select your stock. If you analyze several stock issues and rate them all equally, the option factor can then be brought in to decide which stock to purchase.

Benefiting from Price Appreciation

You will profit from covered call writing when the underlying stock's current market value is above the price you paid for the stock. In that case, you protect your position against a decline in price and also lock in a capital gain in the event of exercise.

Example: You bought 100 shares of stock last year when the price was $27 per share. Today the stock is worth $38.

In this case, you can afford to write in-the-money calls without risking a loss, or you can write out-of-the-money calls if justified by the level of time value. Remembering that your original cost was $27 per share—compared with a value 11 points higher today—you have four possible ways to write calls:

1. Write a call with a striking price of 25. This will yield premiums including a full 13 points ($1300) in intrinsic value, plus whatever time value is available. If the call is exercised, you will lose 2 points in the stock investment (original price of $27 per share, less $25 per share when the option is called), but the entire amount of premium for the option will be profit to you. Meanwhile, if the stock's market value falls before exercise, or if time value evaporates, you can cancel the open position, buying the call for less money than you were paid to sell it. That yields a net profit to you.

Example: You sold a call with a striking price of 25. A few weeks later, the stock has fallen 6 points. You can buy the call and close the position with a profit of at least $600. This offsets the price decline. If any time value has fallen as well, that represents additional profit.

2. Write a call with a striking price of 30. In this case, intrinsic value is 8 points, and you can apply the same strategies as those described above. However, because your position is not as deep in the money, chances for early exercise are reduced and you might also notice a difference in time value premium (this will vary for each case).

Example: You sold a call with a striking price of 30. Two months later, the option has not been exercised, but 3 points of time value have evaporated. You buy the option, closing the position and taking your $300 profit.

3. Write a call with a striking price of 35. With only 3 points in the money, chances for early exercise are fairly low. In the event of even a minimal decline in market value of the stock, you will be able to buy the call and take your profit. Because striking price is fairly close to current market value, time value may be another factor with potential profit in the near future.

Example: You sold a call with a striking price of 35. One month later, the stock has declined only 1 point, but the call has lost an additional 2 points of time value. You buy the option for $300 less than you paid.

4. Write a call with a striking price of 40 or 45. These are out-of-the-money levels, so the entire premium represents time value. The premium amount will be lower for this reason, but this strategy gives you two advantages. First, it will be easier to cancel the position at a profit, because time value will evaporate even if the stock's market value rises but remains at or below striking price. Second, if the stock's market value does rise and the option is exercised, you will receive profit in the 100 shares of stock, because the striking price is higher than current market value.

If you are now holding stock that has appreciated in value since the time you bought it, you face a dilemma every stockholder has to resolve. On the one hand, you can sell now and take your profit. On the other hand, if the trend in this stock continues upward, you do not want to sell too soon.

In this situation, covered calls might be your best way to maximize your position. You provide yourself with downside protection equal to the amount you receive for the premium. You also lock in a capital gain at the striking price, which is higher than your basis (or which is at or near your basis, but accompanied with a write of a call with a lot of intrinsic value).

Example: You bought 100 shares of stock several years ago, paying $28 per share. Today that stock is worth $45 per share. You sell a call with a striking price of 45 and with four months to go until expiration. The premium is 4, all of which is time value. This also discounts your original basis to $24 per share (original cost of $28, less $4 received for selling the option). If the stock were to fall 4 points or less, today's market value of $45 per share is protected by the option premium you received. And if the price of the stock rises and the option is exercised, you would consider the striking price of 45 a decent profit on your investment. Even in the event of exercise, you would consider this a successful rate of return.

In this example, two levels of downside protection are illustrated: First is the protection of the original cost, and second is protection of current market value. When your stock has appreciated well beyond its original cost, it makes sense to protect its current value because most investors would see a decline from that level as a loss—even a paper loss is a loss if you fail to take the profit, or to write options to protect it.

Selection Risks

Picking the best possible option in any situation is difficult. Just as selection of the right stock contains risks, selection of the best possible option depends on several factors:

1. *The current price of the stock, versus your original basis.* This comparison certainly affects the decision about which option to write. If the stock is below what you originally paid for it, writing calls is a problem, because premium has to more than exceed your basis to justify the transaction. When the current price is substantially higher than your original basis, you have vastly more flexibility for creating profits.

2. *Your goals in writing options.* If your stock has appreciated but you have no intention of selling it, writing options may not be appropriate—even if you could use the short-term income. In this situation, you may restrict your option writing to calls out of the money, thus reducing the risk of exercise between now and expiration.

3. *The comparison between intrinsic and time value.* This is always an important test for option selection. The higher the time value, the greater your potential profit; however, higher time value is also accompanied with greater time until expiration. You pay for that time value with longer-term lock in to the option position.

4. *Length of time until expiration.* The longer the time, the more premium you can expect. Compare the number of months to the differences between available options. You might find that for a very slight difference in premium levels, you are expected to give up an additional three months. Many successful option writers profit from transacting short-term expiration contracts, making a profit not only on time value but also on volume. Longer-term options lock in your position too long for a high volume of trades.

5. *Amount of premium, and whether or not the risks justify being locked in.* In some situations, you might find all of the components present signaling the time for selling covered calls, but premium levels are so low that you don't want to expose yourself to the risks. Whenever you have any doubts, waiting until more favorable conditions arise is the more desirable course.

AVERAGING YOUR COST

average up

a strategy involving the purchase of stock when its market value is increasing (The average cost of shares bought in this manner is consistently lower than current market value, enabling covered call writers to sell calls in the money when the basis is below the striking price.)

Your can increase your advantage as a call writer using a strategy known as the *average up*. When the price of the stock has risen since your purchase date, this strategy allows you to sell in-the-money calls on stock you own, on which your average basis is always lower than the average price you paid. (Basis is the overall price paid for all shares currently owned.) So if you buy 100 shares and the price rises, buying another 100 shares reduces the overall cost to below current market value. The effect of averaging up is summarized by example in Table 6.1.

How does averaging up help you as a call writer? When you are writing calls on several hundred shares, you should be concerned about the risk that the stock's price could fall. (While that means you can close out written calls at a profit, it also means your investment in the stock is losing ground.) For example, if you have the capital to buy 600 shares, you can buy all 600 at today's price; or you can buy 100 shares and average the price as it changes by buying an additional 100 shares at various prices. This translates to much higher brokerage fees, but it could also reduce the risk all stock purchasers face. The advantage in buying periodically is in averaging the cost without risking all of your capital in one transaction.

TABLE 6.1 Averaging Up			
Date	Shares Purchased	Price per Share	Average Price
January 10	100	$26	$26
February 10	100	28	27
March 10	100	30	28
April 10	100	30	28$^1/_2$
May 10	100	31	29
June 10	100	32	29$^1/_2$

Example: You buy 600 shares on January 10 at $26 per share. The market value later falls to $20, and you have a loss of $3600. Later, the price rises to $32, changing the loss position to a paper profit of $3600.

Example: You buy 100 shares on the 10th of each month, beginning in January. The price of the stock changes periodically so that by June 10, your average price works out to $29.50 per share.

In the second example, you reduce your risks by buying 100 shares per month. The average price is always less than current market value as long as the trend in stock price is upward. The risk level is built up gradually over time. See Figure 6.1.

By average up and acquiring 600 shares over time, you can also write six covered calls. Because your average basis is 29$^1/_2$ and the current market value as of June 10 is 32, you can sell calls with a striking price of 30 and win in two ways:

✔ When the average price of the stock is lower than the striking price, you will have a profit in the event of exercise.

✔ The call is 2 points in the money, so movement in the stock will be matched dollar for dollar in the call premium level.

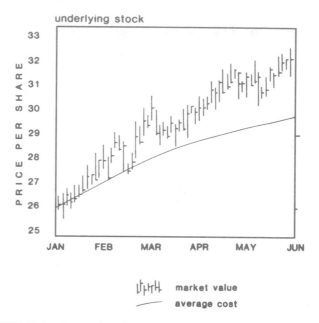

underlying stock

 market value
— average cost

FIGURE 6.1 Example of averaging up.

average down

a strategy involving the purchase of stock when its market value is decreasing (The average cost of shares bought in this manner is consistently higher than current market value, so that a portion of the paper loss on declining stock value is absorbed, enabling covered call writers to sell calls and profit even when the stock's market value has declined.)

You also reduce your risks as a call writer if you *average down* over time. The results of this strategy are summarized in Table 6.2.

One risk in buying stock today is that if its market value falls, you will not be able to afford to sell covered calls later, because striking prices with any worthwhile premium value will have striking prices below your cost basis. If basis is higher than current market value, you will lose money in the event the calls are exercised. And if you sell calls with higher striking prices, premiums will be too minimal to risk the exposure or to justify the strategy. The solution is averaging down.

Example: You buy 600 shares of stock on July 10 when the price is $32 per share. The price rises 8 points and you have a profit of $4800. The stock later falls to $24 per share, and your paper loss is $4800.

Example: You buy 100 shares of stock each month, starting on July 10, when the current market value is $32 per

	TABLE 6.2 Averaging Down		
Date	Shares Purchased	Price per Share	Average Price
July 10	100	$32	$32
August 10	100	31	31^1/$_2$
September 10	100	30	31
October 10	100	30	30^3/$_4$
November 10	100	27	30
December 10	100	24	29

share. By December, after periodic price movements, the current market value has fallen to $24 per share. The average cost, however, is $29 per share.

Your average cost is always higher than current market value if you employ the average down technique, but not as high as it would have been if you had bought 600 shares at the same time. See Figure 6.2.

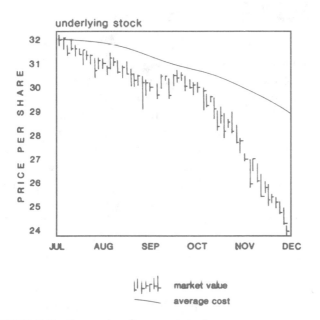

FIGURE 6.2 Example of averaging down.

By owning 600 shares, you can write up to six covered calls. In the first example above, you are at a disadvantage. Your basis is $32 per share, but current market value is 8 points below that. You will have to write calls out of the money and premiums will be drastically reduced as a consequence. To lock in 600 shares at a striking price of 30, for example, would not be worthwhile. If exercised, you will lose 2 points per share on the stock.

In the second example, your average basis is 29. By writing calls with a striking price of 30 in this situation, you will gain 1 point per share in the event of exercise. That is a significant difference when compared to the first example, and this demonstrates how averaging down can be beneficial to call writers.

The average up and average down techniques are important tools, not only for writing calls but for acquiring stock as well. Both techniques are referred to as *dollar cost averaging*. Regardless of price movement, the strategy moderates average price favorably.

ANALYZING STOCKS

Stocks should be selected based on fundamental or technical analysis, or on a combination of both. Too many novice investors buy stocks only on recommendations from others, without understanding the basis for the recommendation, or how that fits with personal investing goals and risk standards. Option investors are especially vulnerable to the temptation to buy stocks for the wrong reason—namely to take advantage of attractively priced options. Some high-premium options may be high-priced specifically because the stock is a high risk.

Fundamental analysis—the study of financial information, management of the company, dividend rate and consistency, volatility and volume, and price history and stability—is the most common method for analyzing stocks. The fundamentals provide you with methods needed for making sound financial estimations of value, safety, and potential for profitable growth and price increase in the future. Collectively, these factors are referred

dollar cost averaging a strategy for buying stocks at a fixed price over time (The result is an averaging of price. If the market value of stock increases, average cost is always below current market value; if market value of stock decreases, average cost is always above current market value.)

to as the "strength" of a company. Financial and economic factors, the company's management, the industry's status and strength, the company's competitive position within that industry, and other tangible indicators are the components of fundamental analysis. The fundamentalist studies the balance sheet and income statement of the company as the primary financial document for judging a stock. Numerous other economic factors often influence judgment about whether or not to invest, such as pending lawsuits or product-related problems, labor strikes, and potential obsolescence of equipment, machinery, and even products—anything that is likely to affect the profitability of a company.

The technician, in comparison, is not as interested in historical information or current financial status as in the indications that can be taken from those numbers to predict the future. The technician uses financial data only to the extent that it can help to affect a trend. Technicians believe that trends provide the key for anticipating the future, that recent events often dictate the direction of a trend. This belief often is applied primarily to actual price movement of the stock. Most market analysts recognize the random nature of price movement in the short term, but the true-believer technician believes that the actual pattern of price movement makes the future predictable. The "chartist" is a technician who studies price movement patterns in an effort to predict the next direction in a stock's price and even watches trading patterns in an attempt to correctly predict the future pricing of a stock. Technicians also track insider trading in the company's stock and watch numerous other technical indicators in following the market.

The relative value of either fundamental or technical analysis can be debated. A fundamental approach assumes that short-term price movement is completely random and that long-term values are best identified by studying a company's financial strength and competitive position. The technical approach relies on patterns of price movement and other indicators not necessarily tied to financial information. By studying support and resistance levels, volume, volatility, trading trends, and other statistics, technicians anticipate market perceptions of value, and their decisions and timing are based on their interpretations.

Many successful investors, recognizing the value in fundamental *and* technical methods, apply combinations of both techniques to make their own judgments and to time purchases and sales of stock. A truly wise investor recognizes that fundamental and technical analysis are merely tools for decision-making, and should never be used to dictate every decision on their own merits without also applying common sense and weighting information according to the circumstances of each case.

Call writers should not overlook the importance of tracking their stock. They tend at times to ignore the stock itself, since the immediate profit or loss will occur in the option premium. So a call writer might be inclined to ignore the trends in stocks in the portfolio when, without the options in play, that same investor would pay more attention to the indicators available for determining what actions to take in the market. Call writers become preoccupied with other matters: movement of stock price, but only in relation to striking prices and premium value; chances of exercise and how to defer or avoid it; opportunities to roll positions based on intermediate stock price changes; and so forth. Such immediate concerns are related to the call value, but do not address the equally important questions every stockholder should ask: Should I keep the stock or sell it? Should I buy more? What changes have occurred in the company, the industry, or the market that might affect the value of this investment?

The time will come when, as a call writer, you will want to close a call position and sell the stock. For example, if you own 100 shares of stock on which you have written several covered calls over the past few years, when should you sell the stock? Perhaps the analysts are now saying they expect a decline in popularity of the industry; or the company itself is no longer in a strong competitive position, and the stock's market value might start to slip as a result. You certainly should be watching for such information in the financial press, since it could be taken as a sell signal. You might need to apply both fundamental and technical tests to keep an eye on the continuing value of the stocks you have selected for your portfolio—regardless of the short-term opportunities in selling calls on those stocks.

Fundamental Tests

The successful call writer not only tracks the everchanging value and status of calls, but also carefully monitors the stocks on which those calls have been written. Several fundamental guidelines should be followed to decide when to buy and when to sell. As a general rule for prudent investing, the stock fundamentals should *always* override any potential gains available in the related option.

The current market value of the stock (often simply called the price) reflects the buying public's and institutional perception of value. This perception is affected by changes in the payment and rate of dividends, and by comparison of current price to earnings.

The *price/earnings ratio* (P/E ratio) is a popular indicator of perceived value, and is most useful when compared in one of two ways: either in relation to other stocks or in relation to previous P/E ratios for the same stock. It is computed by dividing current market value by the most recent *earnings per share* of stock.

Example: A company's recent stock sold for $35 per share. Its latest annual profit and loss statement showed $220 million in net profits and had 35 million shares outstanding. That works out to $6.29 per share. The P/E ratio is:

$$\$35 \div \$6.29 = 5.6$$

Example: A company earned $95 million and has 40 million shares outstanding, so its earnings per share is $2.38. The stock sells at $28 per share. The P/E ratio is calculated as:

$$\$28 \div \$2.38 = 11.8$$

price/earnings ratio a popular indicator used by stock market investors to rate and compare stocks, by which the current market value of the stock is divided by the most recent earnings per share to arrive at the P/E ratio

earnings per share a commonly used method for reporting profits, by which net profits for a year or other period are divided by the number of shares of common stock outstanding as of the ending date of the financial report (The result is expressed as a dollar value.)

The general rule of thumb is that lower P/E ratios indicate lower risk. So in the first example, the P/E ratio of 5.6 will be perceived as a less volatile investment than the second, with a P/E ratio of 11.8. But P/E ratio is not always an accurate measurement, and certainly should not be taken as the only test needed to judge a stock's value, risk, or volatility. As a trend indicator only, it is a useful tool for making comparisons. On a purely mathematical basis, the P/E ratio is problematical. It compares unlike factors derived in entirely unrelated ways. The earnings per share reflect profitability in corporate operations over a period of time, whereas the market value indicates the current perception of value based on supply and demand for the stock at this moment. Obviously, one factor is historical and the other is current.

Still, the use of the P/E ratio does provide good comparative information among various stocks and from one time to another in one stock. The number can give useful indications of relative risk and potential profit. For example, one stock may have had a P/E ratio of 15 last year and only 10 today. That change may indicate that the market value of the stock is a better bargain today than it was last year.

The P/E ratio is an important fundamental test; but you should also consider at the very least three additional tests:

1. As an indicator of current income on the stock, track *dividend yield*. This shows the current yield from dividends expressed as a percentage. It is computed by dividing the dividends paid per share of common stock by the current market value of the stock; the result is expressed as a percentage.

2. Profitability of the company's operations is measured by the *profit margin*. This is the most popular measurement of corporate operations. It is computed by dividing net profits by gross sales; the result is expressed as a percentage.

3. Another useful fundamental indicator is the return to the investor. The *profit on invested capital* shows yield to equity investors. Divide net profits by the amount of outstanding capital; the result is expressed as a percentage.

dividend yield
dividends paid per share of common stock, computed by dividing dividends paid per share by the current market value of the stock

profit margin
the most commonly used measurement of corporate operations, computed by dividing net profits by gross sales

profit on invested capital
a fundamental test showing the yield to equity investors in the company, computed by dividing net profits by the dollar value of outstanding capital

All of these fundamental tests should be reviewed in comparison with past statistics, calculated in the same way. Only then will they have any meaning for you. Analysis of financial information is only worthwhile when you track them over time, and only when they reveal the latest entry in a trend.

The P/E ratio should never be the only indicator you use to decide when to buy or sell. Fundamental analysis should be comprehensive, including complete study of all worthwhile fundamental tests and trends over a period of time.

Technical Tests

Combine fundamental analysis with technical analysis to develop a well-rounded method for judging the market and individual stocks you are thinking of buying, and to help you decide when to trade stocks you already own.

One important technical indicator is the trend in volume of trading on a particular stock. You can also apply volume tests against the entire market, with a different conclusion if volume is high or low, and whether the overall direction in value is on the increase or on the decrease. When volume increases, it indicates increased market interest in that stock. Of course, "interest" does not always mean investors want to buy. High volume accompanied by a decline in the stock's market value means there is a lot of interest, but investors want to sell, not buy. Increased interest in a stock often is accompanied by movement in one direction or the other. At times, you will notice a sudden increase in volume without much price movement in the stock. That means that buyers and sellers agree that the current trading range of the stock is reasonable; but for various reasons, more than average numbers of investors are trading the stock at the moment.

Chartists (technicians who track patterns and trends in a stock's price movement) look for a stock's *support level*, which is the price that has been identified as the lowest likely price under current conditions. The stock's price is not likely to fall below that level. They also try to

support level
the price for a stock identifying the lowest likely trading price under present conditions, below which the price of the stock is not likely to fall

resistance level
the price for a stock identifying the highest likely trading price under present conditions, above which the price of the stock is not likely to rise

breakout
the movement of a stock's price below support level or above resistance level

identify the *resistance level*, which is the highest likely price under current conditions. The stock's price is not likely to rise above that level. Finally, chartists try to identify *breakout* patterns. A breakout occurs when a stock's price moves below support level or above resistance level. Predicting future price movements by watching for patterns and tendencies in the shape and level of pricing helps the chartist to understand how and why stock prices move in the ways they do.

For the options investor, an understanding of support, resistance, and breakout can be valuable. While support and resistance are likely trading limitations, breakouts do occur. But in the short term, and based on past pricing trends, the charting of a stock can help you to identify risks of breakout and thus aid you in finding stocks whose options are reasonably viable for the strategies you want to employ.

Another technical indicator for stocks is the high and low price level. The high and low ranges over the last year provide you with good information about the stock. For one thing, it shows where today's market value is in relation to the trading range. Detailed stock listings generally show the high and low trading prices for the past 52 weeks. So when a stock has had a range between $26 and $45 per share and its current market value is $44, you know that it is very close to its annual high.

Some investors are comfortable buying only when stocks are in the middle of their range, while others look at overall patterns and buy stocks that appear to be trending in a pattern of growth. These types of decisions have to be made by each investor, since one person's opinion about trading range patterns does not always seem right to another. You also need to recognize that some stocks move in patterns of one type, while others—especially in different industries—will tend to act differently.

No single fundamental or technical test should be used exclusively or in isolation. The more information you have available, the better your chances of making a smart decision. You can evaluate your stocks as part of a long-term trend, combining both fundamental and technical tests, by using a stock evaluation worksheet like the one shown in Figure 6.3. After filling in one line for each stock name _____

DATE	DIVIDEND RATE	P/E RATIO	HIGH	LOW	CLOSE

FIGURE 6.3 Stock evaluation worksheet.

week or for each month, you can begin to identify trends in dividend rate and P/E ratio (fundamental tests) as well as the high/low and closing price ranges (technical tests).

The problem with analysis for many investors is that it takes time. There are thousands of available stocks to choose from. As an option investor, you have one advantage: You can limit your analysis to the relatively small number of stocks on which listed options are traded. This is still a healthy number of stocks, but certainly not the thousands that constitute the entire market. You may further reduce the number of likely stocks in your analysis by selecting only those option-listing issues that also are highly rated by one of the analytical services, such as Value Line or Standard and Poor's.

Deciding Which Tests to Apply

Entire books have been written on the hundreds of possible fundamental and technical tests. How do you decide which tests are most meaningful to you? This is a difficult question, because its answer depends largely on your own opinion.

Before deciding how to approach the rather large question of how to pick one form of analysis over another, you should be aware of some facts about the market:

1. Price often has nothing to do with the fundamentals. The stock market is known as an auction marketplace. That means that the price of a particular stock (or option) reflects the current perception of value, and not necessarily the true financial condition or potential of the company. If you evaluate only price-related information, you are not really studying the attributes of the company; you are studying the market's perception of the stock's current value.

2. The real value of assets owned by a company often is not a factor in price. You will observe that in many cases a company's *book value* may have nothing to do with current market value. It is often far less than current market value but in some cases may be higher. Because the market perception of value is what rules price, actual book value per share may be ignored altogether. So an evaluation of a company's tangible worth might not have anything to do with current market value of its shares.

3. The past is not an infallible indicator. You may attempt to predict patterns of price, profits, or competitive

book value
the actual value of a company, more accurately called book value per share; the value of a company's capital (assets less liabilities), divided by the number of outstanding shares of stock

posture within an industry; but in fact the past does not always dictate the direction of the future for any fundamental or technical tests. All of the analysis you perform can serve well as indicators, but there are no guarantees. You can make educated guesses by selecting analysis and conducting it wisely and in comparative form. But you cannot accurately predict the future, even with the best available information about the past.

4. Stock prices may be largely random. Some people believe in the *random walk* theory, which states that all future price movement is random—that there is a 50 percent chance of stocks going up and a 50 percent chance they will go down. The argument is that current price reflects all known information about a company, so future price movement is determined by chance.

> **random walk**
> a theory about market pricing, stating that prices of stocks cannot be predicted because price movement is entirely random

5. Any number of unrelated factors can be studied, and seemingly significant results identified. In the realm of technical analysis, numerous studies have been undertaken in an attempt to correlate market pricing with unrelated social or natural events. Predictions concerning the market have been tied to sports victories, weather patterns, and the distances and thickness of tree rings. None of these unrelated factors are useful in predicting future market movements, and investors are ill-advised to invest money in subscribing to newsletters promoting those theories, let alone acting upon the decisions promoted by their founders.

6. Common sense is your best tool. Investing well requires study, analysis, and comparison. It is not easy. The market is not the place to get rich quick or to make a lot of money without any work. Too often the idea that some scheme or trick will help you amass a fortune without much money, without any risk, and in very little time is appealing and has short-term popular appeal. Making money in the market is hard work, and the risks should never be overlooked. Most of all, use your common sense in making any evaluation. If you proceed with good information, based on research and hard work, and if you make your final decision using common sense, you will beat the averages and succeed in the market.

APPLYING ANALYSIS TO CALLS

To select stocks on which calls will be written, you need to identify an acceptable stock. That usually means you need a degree of short-term price volatility without excessive risk. Volatility is a technical test of a stock's price stability, so it is an excellent tool for call writing. The ideal stock for call writing experiences moderate price volatility in relation to other stocks with similar characteristics. Volatility can and does vary in changing market conditions, and is not a constant. Because price stability is the test for volatility, it is a backward-looking test applied over a period of time. Volatility is expressed as a percentage over a 12-month period, derived by dividing the annual low price into the net change in price during the period.

Example: You want to compute volatility for a stock you are thinking of buying. Its price range over the last 12 months was between $28 and $49 per share. Divide the difference between these high and low prices, by the low. To express the answer as a percentage, multiply the answer by 100:

$$\frac{\$49 - \$28}{\$28} \times 100 = 75.0\%$$

Example: You apply the volatility test to another stock you are also considering buying. Its price range during the past year has been between $67 and $72 per share. Volatility is:

$$\frac{\$72 - \$67}{\$67} \times 100 = 7.5\%$$

The stock in the second example is substantially less volatile than the one in the first example. The percentage summarizes the trading range, making it a useful single-number indicator for call writers. A smaller price range indicates that the second stock is more predictable (less volatile) in price movement. How do you select the best stocks for call writing? With little or no volatility, call premiums will be low and not worth the risk. For extremely volatile stocks, premiums will be much higher but the risks will be greater as well. You need to identify a middle range of moderately volatile stocks that offer healthy call premiums without also being overly risky as indicated by price volatility.

Fundamental and technical tests can be applied not only to identifying good values in underlying stocks, but also to the timing of selling covered calls. In addition to volatility, also study a stock's *beta*, which is a test of relative volatility. While price volatility looks only at one stock's price trend, beta compares a stock's price movement to the entire index of stocks. A beta of 1 tells you that a particular stock tends to move in the same degree as the market as a whole. A beta of 0 implies that the stock's price changes independently of the market, and does not react to overall price changes. A beta of 2 is calculated for stocks that react or overreact strongly to market trends, often by moving to a greater degree in the direction of the overall market.

beta
a measurement of relative volatility of a stock, made by comparing the degree of price movement in comparison to a larger index of stock prices

Example: Over the past year, the composite index—the overall value of the stock market—rose by approximately 7 percent. Your stock also rose 7 percent, so its beta is 1. If your stock rose 14 percent, its beta would be 2.

As a general rule, more volatile stocks will also tend to have higher time value in their options. That is, time value will also decline at a sharper rate for high-beta stocks than for average stocks. The higher time value premium is also a reliable indicator of greater risks. If you buy high-beta, high time value stocks and sell calls, you may receive higher premiums, but you also end up with a more volatile portfolio.

Because time value is usually high for a high-beta stock, premium value—like the stock's market value—is also less predictable. Exceptionally high time value that also tends to fall rapidly in a short period may seem like an advantage to call writers. But that advantage may be offset by volatility in the stock's price.

Example: You own 100 shares of stock you bought at $62 per share. You recently sold a May 65 call and received a premium of 5. Last week, the stock fell 6 points and your call's value went down to 1. You buy, realizing a profit on the call of $400. However, you lost $600 in the underlying stock.

delta
the degree of change in option premium, in relation to changes in the underlying stock (If the call option's degree of change exceeds the change in the underlying stock, it is called an "up delta"; when the change is less than the underlying stock, it is called a "down delta." The reverse terminology is applied to puts.)

Besides volatility and beta of the stock, covered call writers can follow the trend in a call's *delta*. When the option premium and the underlying stock price change by the identical number of points, delta is 1.00. As delta increases or decreases for the option, you can judge the responsiveness (volatility) of the option to the stock at the current pricing in relation to underlying stock price and striking price, fluctuations of time value, and changes in the delta as expiration approaches. This type of analysis provides you with insight as to how a particular stock and its options interact.

The inclination of the typical option is to approach a delta of 1.00 as it goes deep in the money. So for every point of stock movement, you would expect a change in option premium very close to 1 point. Time value tends not to be a factor in option premium changes in deep-in-the-money situations. The time value then changes more in regard to the approach of expiration and not to movement in the underlying stock.

When the option is at the money, you can judge the option activity by observing delta. For example, if the option's delta is at 0.80 when at the money, you would expect a change of $8/10$ point in the option for every point change in the stock. This would vary as expiration approaches and time value disappears; in addition, the direction of stock movement may also affect response in the option premium.

Example: You are tracking an in-the-money call. Its striking price is 35 and the underlying stock's current market value is $47 per share. You notice that each point of movement in the stock's current market value is paralleled by a corresponding change in option premium value. The only variance is evaporation of time value.

Example: Another option is currently at the money. You observe that as the underlying stock's market value changes, it tends to affect the option premium value by about 80 percent. This option's delta is 0.80.

Example: A third option is out of the money. Its striking price is 65 but the stock's current market value is $52 per share. Minor changes in the stock's market value have little or no effect in the option's premium level, which consists entirely of time value. As striking price and the stock's current market value widen, you notice that there tends to be less effect on premium movement. This option is experiencing a declining delta as it moves farther out of the money.

Being aware of the delta enables you to take advantage of conditions and also improves your timing, whether you're a buyer or a seller.

Open interest is another useful technical indicator you can use. Simply the number of open option contracts, it gives you the current status of market interest in a particular option. For example, for one stock the July 40 calls had an open interest last month of 22,000 contracts; today, only 500 contracts remained open. The number changes for several reasons. As status moves farther away from at the money, the number of contracts tends to decline due to exercise, closing sale transactions, or rolling forward. Sellers tend to sell as time value evaporates; buyers tend to close out positions and take profits or accept losses. And as expiration approaches, fewer new contracts are opened. In addition, changes in open interest indicate changing perceptions of the stock for sellers or buyers. Unfortunately, the number of contracts itself does not tell you the reasons for a change in the trend, nor whether the change is being driven by other buyers or other sellers.

open interest
the number of open contracts of a particular option at any given time, which can be used to measure market interest in that option

Applying the Delta

The delta of a call option should be 1.00 whenever it is deep in the money. As a general rule, you can expect the call to parallel the stock's price movement point for point. In some cases, the option's delta will change unexpectedly. For example, if an in-the-money call increases by 3 points, but the stock has increased only 2 points (a delta of 1.50), this change in time value is a sign that investors perceive the option to be worth more than the previous price (relative to the stock's movement). See Figure 6.4.

Time value will not move in a predictable pattern and generally does *not* increase with time. This general observation varies from one option to another, and from one time to another. The market's overall perception of future value (both of the call and of the underlying stock) changes, and that change will often affect time value as well.

You can track the delta of a call to identify and time a covered call write.

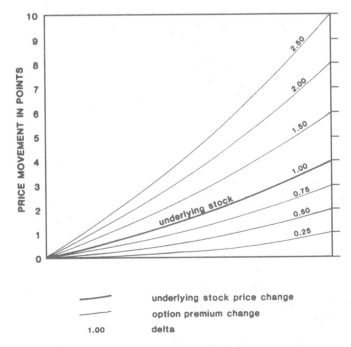

FIGURE 6.4 Changes in an option's delta.

Example: You bought 100 shares of stock at $48 per share. During yesterday's market the stock rose from $51 to $53, based largely on rumors of higher profits than the analysts previously estimated for the company. The option with a striking price of 60 rose from 4 to 8, an increase of 4 points. The delta was 2.00: The stock rose only 2 points, and the option increased in value by twice as much (200 percent).

If a call's premium exceeds the movement in the stock, it could serve as a signal to open a covered call position with an opening sale transaction. You can use the delta to track market perception and then take advantage of distortions in time value. Those distortions may be very momentary, subject to correction within a very short time.

The same strategy can be applied when you have an open covered call and you are thinking of closing the position. For example, your call is in the money and the stock falls 3 points. At the same time, the option's premium falls 3 points, a delta of 1.50 in a downward trend. If this is a temporary distortion of delta, meaning time value is artificially reduced temporarily, you can profit by closing the position immediately. As this is a possible shift in market perception of the stock, the option, or both, it could also serve as a warning that the stock's risk level might be changing.

FOLLOWING YOUR OWN PERSPECTIVE

All analysis of stocks and calls is a matter of estimates. You cannot time decisions perfectly, but must depend on a combination of fundamental and technical tests to give yourself an edge in the market. As a call writer, do not ignore the importance of studying stocks for more than today's call values. Buy stocks for the same reasons you would as a long-term investor who will not be writing calls. Value should always rule your decision. The stock, by itself, should be an attractive investment without considering the opportunities in call writing.

Also recognize that covered call writing is one way

to provide partial downside protection, and to improve overall return on your stock investment. In exchange, you give up potential gains if the stock were to suddenly increase in value. The fixed striking price ensures you a limited, consistent profit but may prevent you from realizing the larger gains that occur from time to time. If writing calls is contrary to your long-term objectives or even your short-term beliefs, you should not enter this market. For example, if you buy stock because you believe it is grossly under its fair price and will jump in the near future, you should not sell calls and fix your striking price.

Example: You bought 300 shares of stock last year as a long-term investment. You have no intention of selling that stock and, as you hoped, its market value has been inching up consistently. Your broker is encouraging you to write calls against those shares, pointing to the potential for additional profits as well as downside protection. Your broker points out that if exercised, you will still profit. Remembering that your reason for buying the shares in the first place was long-term growth, you reject the advice. Call writing is contrary to your established reason for buying and will not fulfill your investment goal.

You usually can avoid exercise in an open call writing position by rolling up and rolling forward. But you may also run into a situation where price increases are substantial enough that exercise in unavoidable. Or the call could be exercised early. As a call writer, you need to realistically understand these risks; the loss of potential future profits might not be worth the premium income. Exercise is always a possibility when you have sold a call. You need to be satisfied with the yield from the combination of call premium, limited capital gains, and dividends, and exchange certainty for potential. You also have to be completely willing to give up 100 shares of stock for each call you write in the event of exercise.

Do not overlook the importance of tracking stocks and evaluating them on their own merit. By preparing a performance chart like the one shown in Figure 6.5, you can track price movement by week. A completed chart

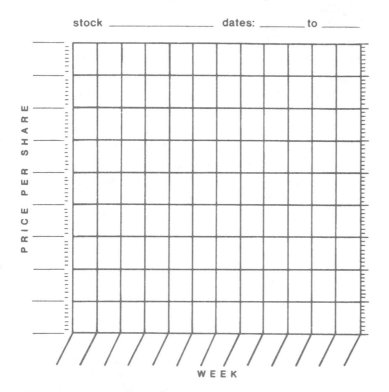

stock _____ dates: _____ to _____

PRICE PER SHARE

WEEK

FIGURE 6.5 Stock performance chart.

helps you identify and time decisions to sell or, if you continue to hold the stock, when to write covered calls.

To succeed as a call writer, you should track both the stock and the option. Making a large percentage profit in calls is of no real value if you end up with losses in your stock portfolio, or with depressed stocks that might not increase in value in the near future.

Example: You bought 100 shares in each of four companies last year. Within the following months, you wrote covered calls in all four cases. Today, three out of the four have market values below your original cost, even though the overall market is higher. You add up the total of profits on calls you wrote and dividends you have earned, only to discover that those profits are lower than the paper losses in market value of the stocks. If you were to sell all 400 shares today, you would lose money.

Certainly, in this case those losses would be higher if no calls had been written. That is a viable argument. However, you need to look at the original basis for buying those particular stocks. Were options one reason? Are these companies too volatile to justify having purchased them just to write calls? Would you have bought these stocks if no options were available? Relatively stable, safe stocks tend to have very little time value in their options, making them appear less attractive for option writing. More volatile issues tend to have higher time value.

Perhaps the greatest risk in call writing is the tendency to buy stocks because calls appear to be attractively priced for the seller. Your best chance for overall success in call writing is to think of it as a secondary strategy.

First, pick stocks wisely and hold them for a while, giving them an opportunity to increase in value. That gives you much greater flexibility in the selection of a call and ensuring yourself profit from all sources: call premium, dividends, and capital gains on the stock. Thorough analysis and comparison should be the basis for your stock selection. Listen to good advice, read research reports, study fundamental and technical indicators, and define what you consider an acceptable level of risk.

Second, time your decision to sell calls on stocks you already own to be preferably when current market value is higher than both your basis and the striking price of the call.

Patience is a good attribute for the call writer to cultivate. Opportunity presents itself eventually, but too many novice call writers are impatient. They want to act now, and as a result, mistakes can be made.

Putting Your Rules Down on Paper

Setting goals helps you to succeed in the market. This is true for options and also for the selection of stocks. You will improve your chances of success by defining your personal rules and then putting them down on paper. Write down your standards in several areas:

1. Long-term goals for your entire portfolio.

2. Methods you believe will help you reach those goals.

3. Percentages of your portfolio to be placed in each type of investment.

4. Definitions of "risk" in each of its several forms.

5. Purchase and sale levels for each investment you make.

6. Guidelines for review and possible alteration of your goals.

Those investors who write down their rules tend to succeed more than others, while those who don't write down their personal rules tend to ignore them or not follow their own guidelines in the first place. Everyone knows someone who does not use goals, and can observe that their lives are without direction. The same principle applies in the market. Rules and standards help us set a course, define the necessary steps to follow, and succeed.

The next chapter explains how the strategy of selling puts can be used for several different goals, including protection of long positions.

Chapter

Selling Puts

In Chapter 5, the special risks involved with selling calls were examined in depth. Every call seller needs to recognize the fact that the underlying stock could rise indefinitely. For uncovered call writers, that represents an unlimited risk. And for covered call writers, that could mean lost opportunities for future profits.

Selling puts is an entirely different matter. A put seller hopes that the value of the underlying stock will rise. If that occurs, the value of the put will diminish and the seller will realize a profit. But what about the risk that the stock's market value could fall? Because the lowest possible value is zero, the maximum theoretical risk is easily identified: It is the difference between the striking price and zero. But in reality, the risk is limited to the difference between striking price and book value per share. Even a drastic decline in the underlying stock's market value has limited consequences. The put seller's real liability is limited in the event of a decline in market value, because a lower book value of the stock represents the real lowest likely point of decline.

Book value per share is the real support level. Many popular stocks trade well above book value, however, so a market risk for put selling is still a factor to keep in mind. The book value per share should be thought of as a dependable realistic floor for the risk in selling puts. You might assume that, except in a rare case, the stock's market value should never fall below book value per share. So a stock currently selling at $50 per share that has a book value of $20 per share may be looked at as having maximum risk of 30 points (market value per share less book value per share).

A put is an option to *sell* 100 shares of the underlying stock. So when you sell, or write, a put, you grant the buyer the right to sell 100 shares of that stock to you, at the predetermined striking price, by expiration date. In other words, in exchange for receiving a premium, you are willing to buy 100 shares at the striking price, even if the stock falls below that level. The risk, of course, is that the stock's market value will fall below striking price and you will then be required to buy 100 shares—when market value is much lower.

As a put seller, you can reduce your exposure by selecting puts in a specific striking price range. For example, if you sell puts with striking prices of 50 or more, your maximum loss range will be 50 points, or $5000 per 100 shares. But if you sell puts with striking prices of 25 or below, your maximum loss per put will be only 25 points.

EVALUATING STOCK VALUES

If you consider the striking price to be a fair and reasonable price for 100 shares of stock, selling puts has two advantages:

1. You receive immediate cash income from selling the put.
2. The premium discounts the price of the stock, reducing the risk.

If you are willing to purchase stock at the striking price—meaning you consider that price to be reasonable—then selling puts at that striking price is a good strategy. You would be willing to pay that price for the stock and, in the event of exercise, you will be required to do so. The risk is that the price may fall below that level.

If the put is exercised, you will end up with 100 shares for which market value is below your cost.

Buying shares above market value may be acceptable if you plan to hold the stock as a long-term investment. You will need to accept a temporary paper loss, however, in the belief that over the long term your investment will be profitable. Identifying this risk may or may not make put writing acceptable. For the immediate income, you risk filling your portfolio with stocks you bought above current market value. So you will have to wait out the market, and that could take time. Hopefully, the risk is justified by selling puts only on stocks you would like to own.

Example: You sold a put with a striking price of 55 and were paid a premium of 6 ($600). You considered $55 per share a reasonable price for this stock. Before expiration, the stock's market value fell to $48 per share and the put was exercised. You were assigned 100 shares and paid $5500 for them, 7 points higher than the stock's current market value.

Several particulars are worth mentioning in this case:

1. The outcome is acceptable as long as you still believe that $55 per share is a good price for the stock. You would then also believe that current market value represents a temporary depression in the market for that stock, and that it will rebound in the future. If your assumption is correct, the paper loss is only temporary and should not represent a problem for you.

2. The premium of $600 paid when you sold the put discounted your real basis in the stock to $49 per share (stock basis of $55, less option premium of $6 per share). So your true basis in the stock after exercise is only 1 point above current market value.

3. If the stock's market value had risen, you would have made a profit from selling the put. It would not have been exercised and would have eventually expired worthless. In that outcome, the $600 premium would have been a clear profit. Thus, selling puts in a rising market can produce profits for investors not as interested in buying 100 shares, with limited risk exposure.

Put sellers who seek only the income from premiums should select stocks that they consider have the best chance of rising in value. Fundamental and technical tests on stocks and on the market in general can be applied to the selection of underlying stocks and their put options in order that if you do end up buying shares upon the exercise of a written put, you will have selected puts on stocks you are willing to own. The income received from premiums is only one-half of the total test. You also need to sensibly evaluate the stocks themselves, or the risks are too great to justify the strategy.

EVALUATING RISKS

In Chapter 6 we demonstrated how stock selection contains certain risks for call sellers. Specifically, the more attractive premiums will be found on the more volatile stocks. This means that covered call sellers may be prone to picking the higher-risk stocks primarily to get high time value opportunities.

The same risks apply to put sellers. You will find that higher time value premiums for puts exist on stocks with higher than average volatility. The direction of movement is different for selling puts than it is for selling calls, but the risks on the underlying stock are the same. Selecting stocks for put writing is subject to the same cautions as selecting stocks for selling calls—covered or uncovered. In the case of puts, your risk is that a stock's market value will fall. The more drastic the fall, the greater the loss. However, a put seller's perception of risk has to be different. The key to selecting puts to sell should not be the size of the premium, but that seller's willingness to buy the stock.

With this in mind, the evaluation of risk is different than it is for call selling. The put seller should apply the same fundamental and technical tests to a stock that the call seller applies. The difference, however, is that while covered call writers own the stock when they write the call, the put writer is only willing to buy the stock should exercise occur. So because not every put will be exercised, put sellers enjoy greater leverage than call sellers. Your only limit is the degree of short position risk you are willing to assume at one time—and, of course, the level of risk your broker will allow you to carry as well. A short position is always risky, because if the market trend suddenly turns downward, all short puts in your portfolio will increase in value (not a good outcome for a seller), and if too many are exercised, it could be impossible for you to meet your obligations. If that were to occur, the broker would have to pick up the shares—at a loss.

SETTING GOALS

There are four possible goals you may have in mind for selling puts: to produce short-term income, to make use of idle cash deposits in a brokerage account, to buy stocks, or to create a tax put.

Goal 1: Producing Income

The most popular reason for selling puts is also the most apparent: to earn short-term profits from premiums. The sale is made and, in the ideal outcome, the put declines in value so it can be purchased (closed) at a lower price, resulting in a profit. Time is on your side when you're a seller, so when you sell puts with large time values your potential for profit is increased. A corresponding higher risk is usually associated with higher time values.

Example: Last January, you sold a June 45 put and were paid a premium of 4. At that time, the underlying stock's market value was $46 per share. Because market value was higher than the striking price, the entire premium represented time value. (Remember that for puts, the in-the-money condition is opposite than for calls.) If the stock's market value remains at or above $45 per share, the put will eventually expire worthless. If by exercise date the stock is valued at between $41 and $45, you will earn a limited profit or you will break even. The $41 per share price is the difference between striking price and the amount you received in premium.

A short position can be canceled at any time. As a seller, you can close the position simply by purchasing the same contract at current premium value. However, remember that an open option can also be exercised by the buyer at any time. So whenever you sell a put, you are exposed to exercise and you must be willing to accept the stock if exercise occurs. If the market value falls below striking price, exercise can occur at any time. For the premium you are paid upon sale of the put, you accept the risk that market value of the stock will fall below striking price, and that you will be required to buy 100 shares above current market value.

A smart put seller is always aware of the potential profit or loss zones, and will decide ahead of time at what point to close a position and when to keep it open. If a profit becomes impossible, the best possible outcome could become one of limiting losses. An example of profit and loss zones for put selling is shown in Figure 7.1. In this case, striking price was 50 and the put premium was 6. This creates a 6-point limited profit zone between $44 and $50 per share; below that, you will experience a loss.

Example: You sold a put with a striking price of 60 and received a premium of 5. Your profit zone in this case is any price at or above striking price. If the stock's market value falls below $60 per share, but remains at or above $55, you will have a limited profit (because you received 5 points for selling the put). If the stock's market value falls below $55 per share, it will be in the loss zone.

Conceivably, you could select stocks that will remain at or above striking price and earn profits repeatedly over time by selling puts, without the threat of exercise. However, it takes only one dip in price to be exposed to exercise, and this risk cannot be overlooked. Remember the

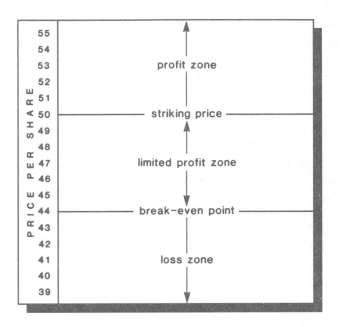

FIGURE 7.1 Put selling profit and loss zones.

basic guideline for selling puts: You should be willing to purchase 100 shares of stock at the striking price, which you consider a fair price for the stock. If current market value is lower than striking price, you should believe market value will eventually rebound, justifying the purchase.

One of the greatest risks in selling puts is exercise, which could create a problem for you as an investor. You could end up with a significantly overpriced portfolio. It will take time for market values to catch up to your basis; meanwhile, your capital is invested in stocks purchased above market value.

Example: You sold several puts over the last few months. This month, the market fell dramatically in what analysts are calling a correction. Five of your puts were exercised at the same time, and you have been assigned a total of 500 shares. Your entire available capital is now tied up in these shares, all of which were purchased in the money. Consequently, your entire portfolio's basis is higher than current market value, and prices seem to be moving slowly or not at all. Your portfolio is overpriced even considering the premiums you received. The drop in market values was sudden and unexpected, so your losses were significant. You have no choice but to sit out the market and hope it rebounds in the future.

The net cost level for stock acquired through exercise of puts is the striking price, minus premiums received for selling the puts. Allowing for transaction fees paid to the brokerage firm (both for selling the put and for buying the stock) further reduces your net basis. In the event of a large drop in market values, the possibility of ending up with substantially overpriced stocks should not be overlooked. Even when you believe the striking price is reasonable, that is today's judgment. You might believe differently after the market decline; time will be required to recover from a large price drop.

Your broker will probably require a cash deposit or commitment of securities in order to satisfy margin requirements when you sell puts. Whenever short positions are opened, brokerage firms want to be protected in the event of adverse outcomes. If you have a number of short position puts open, the brokerage firm has to be assured that in the event of exercise you will be financially able to honor the requirements of the puts and buy the shares assigned to you. From the brokerage firm's point of view, if you are not able to keep that commitment, the firm will be required to absorb the loss.

You need to limit the number of puts you sell at any one time, if only from the point of view of the broker's risks and margin requirements. In addition, no investor can afford unlimited exposure to risk. You cannot exceed your capacity for buying stock at the combined striking prices of all puts you have open in short positions at any one time.

Example: You have $12,000 available to invest in the market today. Taking the traditional route, you could buy shares to the extent that you can afford, with current market value of $12,000 or less. However, if you want to write puts instead, you will be expected to place in reserve some amount of cash determined by the potential striking price value of the puts you want to write. In this case, you cannot exceed 120 points in striking price value (which translates to $12,000).

This limitation can consist of three options, each with striking prices of 40 or less; or one option with a striking price of 120; or any combination that does not exceed the total. This raises another point: spreading the risk among several different puts reduces your risk. In comparison, selling a single put means all of your potential risk lies in one company.

A broker might allow you to exceed your maximum available cash level in written puts. However, if the puts are exercised and you exceed your purchase ability, you will be required to finance the balance in a margin account—essentially, borrowing the money from the brokerage firm and paying interest. This further increases your loss in puts.

Whenever you sell puts, you accept the risk of exercise and cannot cover your position as you can with calls. A call write can be covered by buying 100 shares of stock. An uncovered call, in comparison, exposes you to unlimited potential losses. It is a different matter with puts, however. Written puts cannot be directly covered (except through the purchase of other options, which is discussed in Chapter 8). The term "covered call" refers to the combination of selling calls and owning stock, and a similar strategy is not possible with puts. (The strategy called a "covered put," consisting of selling a put and also selling short 100 shares of the underlying stock, protects only the number of points equal to the amount the seller receives for the put. If the put's value rises above that level, then the short position is not completely covered. So in practice you cannot "cover" a short put as you can a short call. And considering the many ways you can use options, the "covered put" strategy is not a practical idea.)

Put sellers need to view their strategy differently from call sellers. With covered call writing, exercise is not necessarily a negative; at times, it is a welcome outcome and even a desired outcome. Profits can be built into the strategy. But when a put is exercised, stock is always assigned to the seller at a value higher than current market value, without exception. That is only advantageous when the assignment occurs in the limited profit range. That means that the net basis (striking price less premium received) makes your basis lower than current market value. Considering brokerage fees for both option and stock, this profit will be marginal at best.

As a put seller, you can avoid exercise using the same techniques used by call sellers. Rolling forward buys you time and might help to avoid exercise, at least until the stock's price rises. You should avoid increasing the number of puts in a short position on any one issue, however, unless you can afford to buy a greater number of shares above current market value and you are willing to take that risk. It is a mistake to increase your exposure to loss just to avoid exercise.

Example: You sold a put two months ago and received a premium of 4. The stock recently declined below striking price and you would like to avoid exercise. The original put is now valued at 6. In order to forestall or avoid exercise, you close the original position by buying the put. This produces a loss of $200. At the same time, you sell two additional puts currently valued at 4 each, producing a premium total of $800.

The problem in this technique for avoiding exercise is that your risks are doubled. Now, instead of being at risk for one put and assignment of 100 shares, you have two puts and might eventually be required to buy 200 shares—above market value. An alternative is to roll forward the one put and reduce potential losses. You could replace the original put with another of the same striking price but later expiration date. That reduces the pending risk of expiration (although exercise can still occur at any time), but also produces more premium income due to higher time value. Alternatively, you can simply close the position by buying the put and accepted a $200 loss. This decision rests with how you now look at the stock and how much risk you are willing to have. In some cases, the $200 loss might be the best outcome for the transaction. Do you still consider the stock reasonably priced at the striking price (regardless of current market value)? If so, then exercise would not be entirely negative, assuming current market value did not fall too drastically below its current level.

Compare potential losses to the number of points of difference between current market value and striking price. For example, if striking price is 45 and the stock has declined to $38 per share, that is a 7-point difference. Let's say that closing the put will produce a $400 loss. In this case, your question should be: Is the $400 loss better or worse than having to buy 100 shares of stock at 7 points above current market value? As owner of the stock, you can afford to wait for the price to increase. However, once you are free of the open short position in the put, you can always sell another, offsetting your $400 loss. This decision depends on your risk tolerance and what you believe about the stock's potential for future price movement.

Goal 2: Using Idle Cash

When investors sell options, their brokerage firms require deposits of cash or securities for at least a portion of the risk. With puts, the maximum risk is easily identified. It is the striking price of the put.

In some instances, investors keep their money on the sidelines because they believe that stocks they would eventually like to buy are at present overpriced. The dilemma is that, if they are wrong and those stock prices increase, they miss an opportunity *and* their money is idle. If they are forced to wait for the next opportunity, how long will that take?

These are problems that cannot always be foreseen, and the answers are never known. One way to deal with the unknown factor is by selling puts on targeted stock. You may wish to keep your investment capital on the sidelines, fearing that the underlying stock's price is currently too high. By selling puts, you will make a profit if prices go higher still, and you risk buying stock at the striking price if the stock's market value does go lower. In either event, you keep the premium received for selling the put.

Example: You are interested in buying stock as a long-term investment. However, you also believe that the overall market has increased in value too quickly, and that a correction is likely to occur in the near future. You also believe that the price of the stock you want is reasonably low at this moment. Your solution: Sell one put for every 100 shares you want to buy, instead of buying the stock. Place your capital on account with the brokerage firm as security against your short position in the puts. If the current market value of the stock rises in the future, your short puts will lose value and can be bought at a lower price than you sold them for, or allowed to expire worthless. In this way, you benefit from a rise in market value without risking all of your capital.

If the market value of the stock declines, you will be assigned the shares. But as long as the striking price represents what you believed to be a reasonable market value at the time you opened the position, a decline in price should not concern you; as a long-term investor, you are confident that the price will rise in the future, and your paper loss will be offset partially by your profit on the puts.

Goal 3: Buying Stock

The third reason for selling puts is to intentionally seek exercise. Selling a put discounts the purchase price and your basis in the stock by the amount of the premium, and you will not be concerned with price drops between the time of selling the put and expiration date.

Example: You have been tracking a stock for several months, and have decided you are willing to purchase 100 shares at $40 per share. The current price is $45 per share. You may wait for the stock to drop without result. However, you decide to sell a November 45 put and are paid a premium of 6. The effect of this transaction will depend on whether the stock's market value rises or falls. If it rises, the put will become worthless and the entire $600 sale price will become profit; you are then free to repeat a short transaction with the same arguments as before. If the stock's market value declines, the option will be exercised. When you subtract the option premium you received from the striking price of $45 per share, your net cost is only $39—one dollar per share *below* your target price (not allowing for brokerage fees).

In this example, the put was sold at the money and the premium—all time value—was high enough to reach your target purchase price on a net basis. Even if the stock's current market value fell below $40 per share, your long-term plans would not be changed. Remember, in this example, you originally thought that $40 per share was a fair price. Intermediate dips are not of concern to long-term investors. However, if the stock's market value rose and the put expired worthless, the $600 premium would all be profit, giving you the flexibility to adjust your purchase goal. If you were to purchase the stock at $46 per share, the net basis to you remains at $40 ($46 per share less $6 per share already received in profit from selling the put). In theory, you could repeat the success in this strategy indefinitely, as long as the stock's value continued inching upward, and as long as puts were available with adequate premium value to cover the rise in stock market value. You miss buying opportunities as long as the stock's market value is rising, but you also cover all or part of that lost opportunity.

Example: You are interested in acquiring a stock at $40 per share. However, current market value is $45. You sell a put with a striking price of 45 and receive a premium of 6. You hoped the value would fall and that the option would be exercised, giving you ownership at a net cost of $39 per share. However, instead of falling, the stock's market value rises 14 points.

In this example, the put would expire worthless and the $600 premium would be all profit. But if you had bought the shares in the first place instead of selling a put, you would have earned $1400 in profit. Once the put expires, though, you can sell another, offsetting part of the lost opportunity of this rise in market value. If the stock seesaws up and down, you can realize an overall profit and still not miss any opportunities.

To succeed as a put seller, you need to be willing to risk losing future profits in two ways due to unexpected price movement in the stock:

1. If the price of the underlying stock rises beyond the amount you receive in premium, you miss the opportunity to make a profit on the stock. You settle for premium income only. However, when this occurs, you still have your original capital plus the premium; and you can always sell a subsequent put, continuing the strategy.

2. If the price of the underlying stock falls drastically, you will be required to buy 100 shares for each put sold, at a price above current market value. It may take considerable time for the stock's market value to rebound; meanwhile, your investment capital will be tied up in a stock you bought above current market value.

While the risks of put selling are much more limited than those associated with uncovered call selling, you could miss opportunities to make profits in the event of stock movement in either direction.

Goal 4: Creating a Tax Put

A fourth reason to sell puts is to create an advantage for tax purposes, which is known as a *tax put*. However, before employing this strategy, you should first check with your tax adviser to determine that you will be timing the transactions properly and legally—and to ensure that you know the risks and potential liabilities involved.

An investor who has a paper loss on stock (when current market value is lower than the original purchase price) has the right to sell that stock and create a loss at any time, even to create a loss to reduce income taxes. Such losses can be deducted up to annual limits. At the

tax put
a strategy combining the sale of stock at a loss—taken for tax purposes—and the sale of a put at the same time (The premium received on the put offsets the stock loss; if the put is exercised, the stock is purchased at the striking price.)

same time, those same investors may sell puts on the stock, so that the premium received offsets the loss.

One of three results is possible:

1. The stock's market value rises, and the option expires worthless. In this outcome, the loss on the stock is offset by the option premium received; however, the stock loss is deducted in the current year, whereas the profit on the short put is taxed the following year.

2. The stock's market value rises and the investor closes the position, creating a profit because the purchase price is lower than the sale price.

3. The stock's market value falls below the striking price, and the investor is assigned the stock. In this case, the basis in the stock is discounted by the amount received for selling the put.

You may assume that if the stock's current market value is lower than its original cost, the put will have a striking price that is also lower than that cost. So upon exercise, not only does the investor keep the option premium, but the basis in the stock is also discounted.

The advantage in the tax put is twofold: First, you take a current-year loss in the year the stock is sold, deferring the gain on the put sale until the following year. This deferral is advantageous because it reduces this year's taxes by writing off the stock loss, while putting off the tax on your option profit for a full year. Second, you profit from selling the option, as shown in Figure 7.2, in the following two ways:

1. The premium income offsets the stock loss.
2. In the event of exercise, your true basis in the stock is discounted from the level of striking price.

Example: You originally bought stock at $38 per share, and it is now valued at $34. You sell the stock, realizing a $400 loss. At the same time, you sell a put with a striking price of 35, receiving a premium of 6. If exercised, the result of this strategy is, first, that your $400 loss in the stock is offset by the $600 profit in put premium. Net adjusted

DATE	ACTION	RECEIVED	PAID
Aug. 15	buy 100 shares at $50		$5000
Dec. 15	sell 100 shares at $47	$4700	
Dec. 15	sell 1 Feb 50 put at 6	600	
	total	$5300	$5000
	net cash	$ 300	

PRICE MOVEMENT	RESULT
stock rises above striking price	$300 profit
	put is bought at a profit
stock falls below striking price	put is exercised at $50, net cost $47 (with $300 profit from tax put)

FIGURE 7.2 Example of tax put.

basis is $36 (original purchase of $38 per share, less $200 net profit from the tax put). Second, when the put is exercised, you will buy 100 shares of the stock at the striking price of 35, which is only 1 point below your adjusted basis.

Put sellers enjoy an important advantage over call sellers: Their risk is not unlimited by potential indefinite market value increases in the underlying stock. That stock can fall only to the point that it becomes worthless.

An example of a put write, with defined profit and loss zones, is shown in Figure 7.3.

Example: You sold one May 40 put for 3. The outcome of taking this short position will be profitable as long as the stock remains at or above striking price. If, at expiration, the value is lower than $40 per share, you will be required to buy 100 shares at the striking price. As a put seller, you assume a limited risk. Compared to writing un-

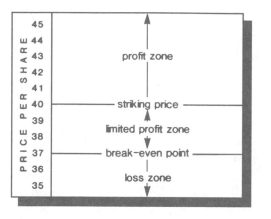

FIGURE 7.3 Example of put write with profit and loss zones.

covered calls, in which the current market value of the underlying stock could rise indefinitely, the downside risk is limited. Since you received $300 when you sold this put, your break-even price is 3 points below the striking price.

The most significant risk faced by put sellers is that the stock might become worthless. While this may seem an extreme claim, it is true. If the stock were to fall to zero, you would have an exercised put at the striking price for stock worth nothing. But as long as you select stocks in well-managed companies, the risk of a zero value is remote. The realistic risk level is the book value per share, which is often close to the current market value. *A word of caution:* In the reality of short-term expirations, it *is* possible (rarely) to experience exercise *below* book value, because current market value is a reflection of the market's perception of value and not of the financial realities (the company's tangible worth). To avoid ultimate risks, select stocks with fundamental strength, but remain aware that the limited risk associated with market factors is ever present.

As with all option strategies, the best stocks to select for put writing are those that tend to move within a rather limited trading range, thereby offering enough volatility to create short-term profits from declining time value, but not enough movement to represent risk of large value losses that could take months or even years for recovery.

Put sellers should be willing to accept the 100 shares represented by the put contract, because if you sell puts, in all likelihood you will eventually experience exercise. And when exercise occurs, you will be buying 100 shares above current market value. As long as you believe the striking price is a reasonable price, the short-term current market value movements are not important in the long run. If you have thoroughly studied the company's strength and prospects for future growth, selling puts can be a smart way to increase current income, discount the price of stocks you end up buying, and benefit from price increases without having to buy stock now.

In the next chapter, you will see how buying and selling strategies can be combined to increase income and reduce—or increase—risks.

Combined Techniques

Option investors or speculators can employ only four basic strategies: buying calls, selling calls, buying puts, and selling puts. In previous chapters, you have seen how these basic ideas can be modified and applied in various ways, and how a number of variations on these themes can be employed for different reasons. For example, risks are modified when you compare covered and uncovered calls.

The reasons for buying or selling options define the types of risks you are willing and able to take. In that respect, the utilization of an options strategy defines a completely separate investment. In other words, the way you use options defines the risk level, the expected outcome, and the way you use available capital. Consider, for example, the difference between one investor interested only in profits from selling calls or puts and another who wants exercise as a way to either buy or sell shares. Their perceptions of risk, desired outcome, and method of selection are entirely different.

This chapter expands on the variations of these four basic strategies, and shows you how they can be further structured and combined in many ways. Long and short positions can be engaged in at the same time, so that risks offset one another. Some combined strategies are designed to create potential profits in the event the underlying stock moves in either direction; others are designed to

spread
the simultaneous purchase and sale of options on the same underlying stock, with different striking prices or expiration dates, or both (The purpose of the spread is to increase potential profits while also reducing risks in the event that the value of the underlying stock does not move as anticipated, or to take advantage of the timing of the stock's price movement.)

vertical spread
a spread involving different striking prices but identical expiration dates

money spread
alternate name for the vertical spread

produce profits if the stock remains within a specific price range. Other strategies that will be explained and illustrated in this chapter are designed to minimize risks while still providing potential profits for option investors.

You will learn about three different combined strategies. The first is the *spread*. This is the simultaneous opening of both a long position and a short position in options on the same underlying stock. The positions, in order to be correctly called a spread, should involve options that have different expiration dates, different striking prices, or both. When the striking prices are different but the expiration dates are identical in a spread, it is called a *vertical spread*. The vertical spread is also called a *money spread*.

Example: You buy a call with a striking price of 45 and, at the same time, sell a call with a striking price of 40. Both options expire in February. Because the expiration dates are identical, this is a vertical spread.

Example: You buy a put with a striking price of 30 and, at the same time, you sell a put with a striking price of 35. Both options will expire in December. This is also a vertical spread.

You may also create a spread by buying and selling options that have different expiration dates, or that have a *combination* of different striking prices and expiration dates. Spreads come in a wide variety of formations, and these will be described later in the chapter.

The second combined strategy is the *straddle*. This involves the simultaneous purchase and sale of the same number of calls and puts with identical striking prices and expiration dates. While the spread requires a difference in one or more of the terms, the straddle requires that they be identical, with the exception that one side represents calls and the other side represents puts.

The third type of combined strategy is the hedge. This involves the opening of one position specifically to protect against loss in another open position. The hedge is used to reduce risks. In some respects, spreads and straddles have hedging features because two dissimilar positions are opened at the same time; so movement that reduces the value in one side of the transaction tends to increase value in the other side. In the options market, buying one put per 100 shares owned is a form of hedge, because the put protects you in the event that the stock's value declines. The put, in this application, is a form of insurance.

Many investors new to the options market will want to keep their strategies fairly simple at first. If you decide to venture beyond basic strategies, you will be most likely to start out with a vertical spread. Other, more advanced strategies are complex and beyond the scope and intention of this book. They are included here only to explain the entire range of possibilities in option trading; however, they often produce minimal profits per contract. Many of these marginal outcomes are not appropriate for the average individual investor, because potential profits are going to be limited by the nature of the transaction. They are used in transactions involving large amounts of money and thousands of option contracts, and are not commonly applied in the average portfolio. The risks, commission costs, and analysis required for these advanced strategies exclude all but the most experienced investors.

Remember, too, that what might look safe and simple on paper does not always work out the way you might expect. Changes in option premium levels are not as logical or predictable as one might hope, and short-term variations may occur for any number of reasons. This is what makes option investing so interesting; it also makes the use of advanced strategies particularly daunting. If you do combine any strategies and use spreads, straddles, or hedges, you should first ensure that you understand the scope of risks and costs that will be involved, and that you have the experience and knowledge—as well as the proper risk tolerance—to proceed.

combination

any purchase or sale of options on one underlying stock, with terms that are not identical

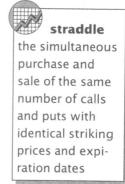

straddle

the simultaneous purchase and sale of the same number of calls and puts with identical striking prices and expiration dates

UNDERSTANDING VERTICAL SPREADS

Option investors use spreads to take advantage of the predictable course of changes in premium value. These changes are predictable because everyone knows that time value evaporates as expiration approaches. And when options are in the money, you can usually assume that changes in premium value will be far more responsive than when they are out of the money. This relationship between intrinsic value (which exists only in the money) and time value makes the spread an interesting and challenging tool for the option investor.

You have an advantage when offsetting long and short positions in the spread. The side of the transaction that is in the money will tend to change in value at a different rate than the side that is out of the money. This is the key to the successful spread strategy. If you observe how premium values change on each side, you will be able to anticipate the advantage you can gain with a spread strategy, whether the market is moving up or down.

Bull Spreads

bull spread
a strategy involving the purchase and sale of calls or puts that will produce maximum profits when the value of the underlying stock rises

A *bull spread* provides the greatest profit potential if and when the underlying stock's market value rises. In this approach, you buy an option with a lower striking price and, at the same time, you sell one with a higher striking price. You can use either calls or puts in a bull spread.

Example: You open a bull spread using calls. You sell one December 55 call and buy one December 50 call, as shown in Figure 8.1. At the time of this transaction, the underlying stock's market value is $49 per share. After you open your spread, the stock's market value rises to $54 per share. When that occurs, the December 50 call increases in value point for point once it is in the money. The short 55 call does not change in value as it remains out of the money and, in fact, is inclined to lose time value. Because of the advantage the spread creates at the point the stock is at $54 per share, both sides of the spread are profitable. The long call (at 50) rises in value, creating a profit; and the short call (at 55) remains out of the money and loses time value, again creating a profit.

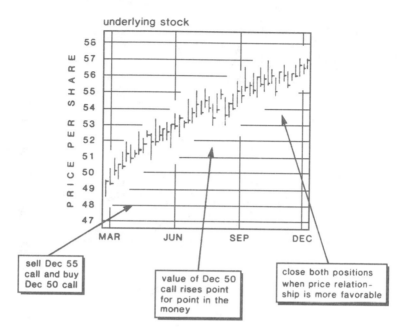

FIGURE 8.1 Example of bull spread.

This example describes the ideal situation, in which both sides of the spread became profitable. Of course, that will not always happen. Even when only one side is profitable, however, the strategy is justified as long as you achieve an overall profit.

A bull vertical spread will be profitable when the price of the underlying stock moves in the direction anticipated. For example, a bull spread may involve buying a lower-priced call option in the hope the stock will increase in value between now and expiration. That call will be in the money and thus will grow in value at a faster rate than the higher striking price call sold at the same time.

A detailed bull vertical spread, with defined profit and loss zones, is shown in Figure 8.2.

Example: You sell one September 45 call for 2 and buy one September 40 call for 5. The net cost of this is $300. When the stock rises in the zone between $40 and $45 per share, the value of the September 40 call will rise dollar for dollar

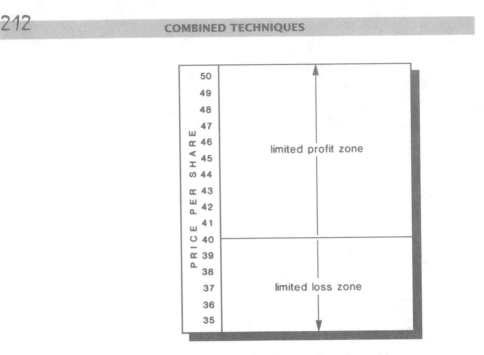

FIGURE 8.2 Bull vertical spread profit and loss zones.

with the stock, while the short September 45 option will still have no intrinsic value; in fact, as time goes by, the time value premium will diminish in this option. As long as the stock's market value remains above $40 and below $45 per share, both sides can be closed at a profit (as long as the difference in the value of the two options exceeds the net cost of $300). Above the $45 per share level, the 5-point spread in striking prices is offset by the short and long positions. Thus, maximum profits *and* maximum losses are both limited by this strategy.

A bull spread can also be entered into using puts, in which case the put in the money should be expected to lose value more rapidly than the lower, long put. It is the same strategy as that for calls, but using puts instead. In either case, you depend on diminishing time value premium to create a profit, while limiting potential profit and loss overall.

Example: You enter into a bull spread using puts. You sell one November 45 put and buy one November 40 put. The stock's market value at the time you open these positions is $42 per share. Since the higher striking price, the November 45 put, is in the money, premium value is higher than the lower put, which is out of the money. If the stock's price rises, the short position will lose its premium value at a faster rate than the long put, because it will move dollar for dollar with the stock. That would enable you to close the position at a profit.

Bear Spreads

Compared to bull spreads, the *bear spread* will produce profits if and when the stock's value falls. In this version of the spread, the higher-value option is always bought, and the lower-value option is always sold. The bear spread can employ either calls or puts.

bear spread
a strategy involving the purchase and sale of calls or puts that will produce maximum profits when the value of the underlying stock falls

Example: You open a bear spread using calls. You sell one March 35 call and buy one March 40 call. The stock's market value was $37 per share at the time you opened these positions. The premium value of the lower call, which is in the money, will decline point for point if the stock's market value declines. If the stock's market value does fall, you will be able to close that position at a profit.

Example: You open a bear spread using puts. As shown in the example at Figure 8.3, you sell one December 50 put and buy one December 55 put. The underlying stock's current market value is at $55 per share. As the price of the stock moves down, the value of your long put will increase point for point with movement in the stock's declining value. By the time the stock's value declines to $51 per share, this position can be closed at a profit.

A detailed bear vertical spread, with defined profit and loss zones, is shown in Figure 8.4.

Example: You sell one September 40 call for 5 and buy one September 45 call for 2, receiving net proceeds of $300. As the stock's market value falls below the level of

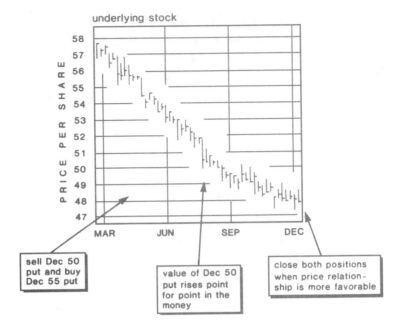

underlying stock

sell Dec 50
put and buy
Dec 55 put

value of Dec 50
put rises point
for point in the
money

close both positions
when price relation-
ship is more favorable

FIGURE 8.3   Example of bear spread.

$45 per share, the short call (at 40) will lose value point
for point; the lower long call will not react to the same degree. As the $40 per share level is approached, the spread
can be closed at a profit.

Consider how the above example would work with puts
instead of calls. In that case, the higher long put, which
would be in the money, would have increased point for
point with a decline in the stock's market value.

In the example employing calls, profits are frozen
once both calls are in the money. When the underlying
stock's market value falls below $40 per share, changes in
value for long and short positions will offset one another
point for point.

In all of these examples, the significant risk is that
the stock might move against the desired direction of the
spread. You should be prepared to close the spread in that
outcome before the short position gains in value (meaning you will lose as a seller). However, if the underlying
stock's market value changes too quickly, you risk exercise

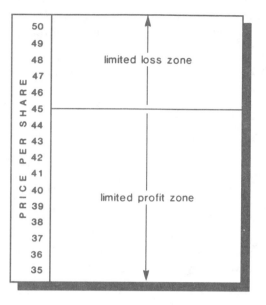

FIGURE 8.4 Bear vertical spread profit and loss zones.

or might have to close at a loss or reduced profit. In that event, your maximum risk will be limited to the difference in the two striking prices, multiplied by the number of option spreads involved. In our examples, we have used 5-point differences in striking prices, which is normally the practical distance for the spread, so that maximum risk is 5 points, or $500. See Table 8.1.

Example: You open a spread by buying one option and selling another. The difference between striking prices of each position is 5 points. Your maximum risk if the stock movement goes in the wrong direction is $500 plus brokerage costs.

Example: You open a spread by buying four options and selling four others. The difference between striking prices is 5 points. Your maximum risk before brokerage fees is $2000. (The difference between striking prices is multiplied by the number of option spreads involved; in this case, 5 points multiplied by four spreads equals $2000.)

TABLE 8.1 Spread Risk Table		
Number of Option Spreads	Striking Price Interval	
	5 Points	10 Points
1	$ 500	$ 1,000
2	1,000	2,000
3	1,500	3,000
4	2,000	4,000
5	2,500	5,000
6	3,000	6,000
7	3,500	7,000
8	4,000	8,000
9	4,500	9,000
10	5,000	10,000

Box Spreads

You can open a bull spread *and* a bear spread at the same time by using options on the same underlying stock. In that case, your risk is still limited, whether the stock rises or falls in value. This strategy is called a *box spread*. A limited profit will be earned if and when the stock's market value moves in either direction.

box spread
the combination of a bull spread and a bear spread, opened at the same time on the same underlying stock

Example: As illustrated in Figure 8.5, you create a box spread by buying and selling the following contracts:

1. *Bull spread:* Sell one September 40 put and buy one September 35 put.
2. *Bear spread:* Buy one September 45 call and sell one September 40 call.

If the price of the underlying stock moves significantly in either direction, portions of the box spread can be closed at a profit. Of course, this action could also leave you with

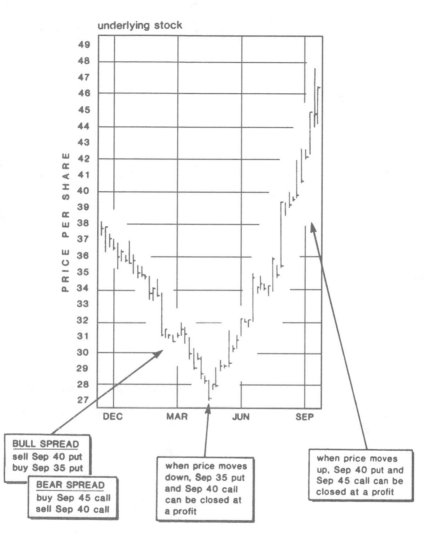

underlying stock

BULL SPREAD
sell Sep 40 put
buy Sep 35 put

BEAR SPREAD
buy Sep 45 call
sell Sep 40 call

when price moves
down, Sep 35 put
and Sep 40 call
can be closed at
a profit

when price moves
up, Sep 40 put and
Sep 45 call can be
closed at a profit

FIGURE 8.5 Example of box spread.

an uncovered option, depending on direction of price
change and resulting closing actions you might take.
However, if the stock moves first in one direction and
then in the other, you could profit from both price movements.

The detailed profit and loss zones of a box spread are
summarized in Figure 8.6. The net proceeds from this box
spread result from the following outcomes:

credit spread
any spread in which receipts from short positions are higher than premiums paid for long positions, net of transaction fees

debit spread
any spread in which receipts from short positions are lower than premiums paid for long positions, net of transaction fees

calendar spread
a spread involving the simultaneous purchase or sale of options on the same underlying stock, with different expirations

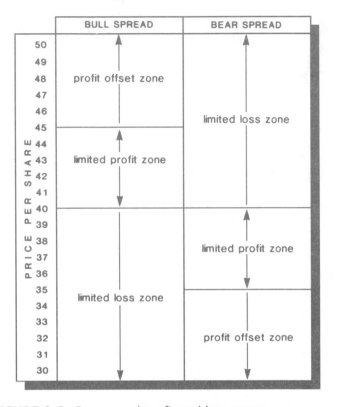

FIGURE 8.6 Box spread profit and loss zones.

1. *Bull spread:* Sell one September 45 put for 6 (+$600) and buy one September 40 put for 2 (–$200).
2. *Bear spread:* Sell one December 35 put for 1 (+$100) and buy one December 40 put for 4 (–$400).

If the stock rises to between $40 and $45 per share, the bull spread can be closed at a profit. Above that level, the difference in bull spread values will move in the same degree in the money. If the stock falls to between $35 and $40 per share, the bear spread can be closed at a profit. The long position—December 40—in the money will increase in value point for point with movement in the stock's price. Below the level of $35 per share, the difference of 5 points in striking prices will be fixed, limiting profit and loss on both sides.

Debit and Credit Spreads

The simultaneous transacting of long and short positions involves offsetting receipt and payment of premiums. And while it is always desirable to receive more money than you pay out, that is not always possible. Some strategies involve a net payment. A spread position should be entered into not to create positive cash flow in every case, but to build potential profit and, at the same time, to limit potential losses.

A spread in which more cash is received than paid out is called a *credit spread*, while the opposite is called a *debit spread*.

time spread
alternate term for the calendar spread

UNDERSTANDING HORIZONTAL AND DIAGONAL SPREADS

In the previous section, vertical spreads were explained and illustrated. (A vertical spread involves options with identical expiration dates but different striking prices.) Another type of spread involves simultaneous option transactions that have different expiration months. This variation is called a *calendar spread* or a *time spread*. The calendar spread can be further broken down into two types:

horizontal spread
a calendar spread in which offsetting long and short positions have identical striking prices but different expiration dates

1. *Horizontal spread:* Options that have identical striking prices but different expiration dates.
2. *Diagonal spread:* Options that have different striking prices *and* expiration dates.

Example: You enter into transactions to create a horizontal calendar spread. You sell one March 40 call and receive 2; and you buy one June 40 call and pay 5. Your net cost is $300. Two different expiration months are involved. The earlier, short call expires in March while the long call does not expire until June. This means your loss is limited in two ways: amount and time. This point is illustrated in Figure 8.7. If, by the March expiration date, the first call expires worthless, you have a profit in that position and the second phase goes into effect. With the short position

diagonal spread
a calendar spread in which offsetting long and short positions have both different striking prices and different expiration dates

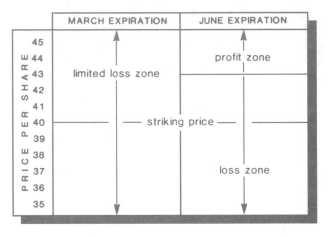

FIGURE 8.7 Profit and loss zones for an example of horizontal calendar spread.

eliminated, only the long position remains. If the stock then rises 3 points or more above striking price, the long position can be sold at a profit.

Example: You create a diagonal calendar spread. You sell one March 40 call and receive 2; you also buy one June 45 call and pay 3. Your net cost is $100. This transaction involves different striking prices *and* expiration months. If the earlier-expiring short position is exercised, the long call can be used to offset the assignment. In other words, as the owner of the long position, you can exercise the option in response to your short position being exercised against you. Until the earlier call's expiration occurs, your risk is limited to the net cost of the two calls, which is $100. After expiration of the earlier short call, your break-even price is the higher striking price plus the cost for the overall transaction. In this example, striking price is 45 and net cost is $100, so $46 per share is the break-even price. This is illustrated in Figure 8.8. Once the underlying stock's market value rises above this level, the June 45 call can be closed at a profit.

Giving different spread strategies the names vertical, horizontal, and diagonal helps to distinguish them and to visualize what it means in terms of expiration dates and

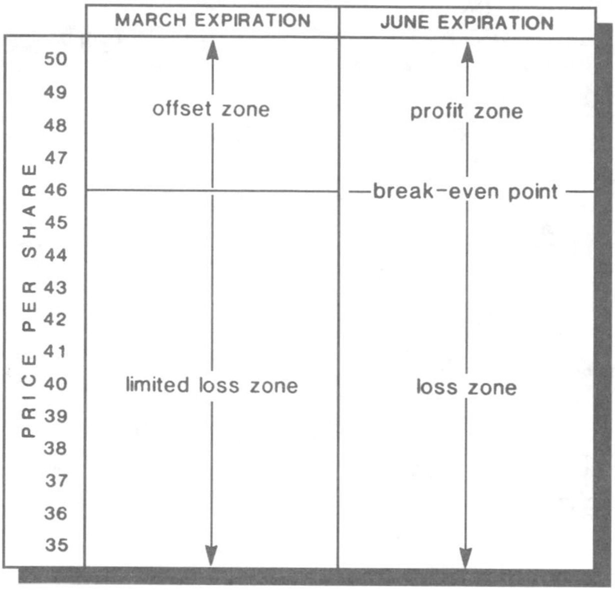

FIGURE 8.8 Profit and loss zones for an example of diagonal calendar spread.

striking prices. These distinctions are summarized in Figure 8.9.

A horizontal spread is a good strategy to employ when the premium value between two related options is temporarily distorted, or when a later option's features protect the risks of an earlier-expiring short position.

Example: You enter into a horizontal spread using calls. You sell a March 40 call and receive a premium of 4. You also buy a June 40 call, paying a premium of 6. Your net cost is $200. If the market value of the underlying stock rises, the long position protects you against the risks in the short position. No longer is that risk unlimited. Thus, maximum risk is limited to the 2-point cost of entering this position. If the stock remains at or below the striking price between now and expiration of the short position call, it will expire worthless. However, you still own the June 40 call. If the market value of the underlying stock then rises above the striking price before expiration by 2 points or more, you will be able to close at a profit.

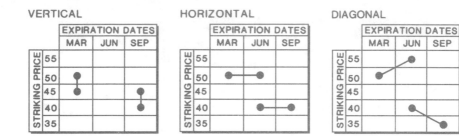

FIGURE 8.9 Comparison of spread strategies.

A horizontal spread can be useful for reducing existing risks when one option position is already open. For example, if you have previously gone short on an option and the stock moves in the opposite direction than you expected, you can limit your risks by buying an option to create a horizontal spread.

Example: You sold a covered June 45 call last month. The stock's market value is now above the striking price. You do not want to close the position and take a loss, but you also would like to avoid exercise. You protect your position by buying a September 45 call, creating a horizontal spread. If the stock continues to rise, your short call will be exercised. However, since you now own a later-expiring call, you could respond to the exercise by exercising that call; you could also sell that call at a profit and allow your 100 shares to be called away. The horizontal spread limits your potential losses and creates a separate profit opportunity.

A diagonal spread combines vertical and horizontal features. Long and short positions are opened with different striking prices and expiration dates.

Example: You create a diagonal spread. You sell a March 50 call and receive 4; you also buy a June 55 call and pay 1. You receive a net of $300, minus brokerage fees. If the stock's market value falls, you will profit from the decline in value in the short position. But if the stock rises, the long option's value will rise as well. Your maximum risk in these options is 5 points. However, because you received a net of $300, your real exposure is only 2 points (5 points between striking prices, less 3 points you were paid). If the earlier, short call expires worthless, you will still own the long call, which also has a longer term so you might profit from later price appreciation.

ALTERING SPREAD PATTERNS

The vertical, horizontal, and diagonal patterns of the typical spread can be employed to reduce risks, especially if you keep an eye on relative price patterns and can recognize temporary distortions. Going beyond the reduction of risk, special techniques can be employed through some advanced strategies.

Varying the Number of Options

The *ratio calendar spread* involves employing a different number of options on each side of the spread and using different expiration dates as well. The strategy is interesting because it creates two separate profit and loss zone ranges, thus broadening the opportunities for interim profits.

ratio calendar spread a strategy involving a different number of options on the long side of a transaction from the number on the short side, when the expiration dates for each side are also different (This strategy creates two separate profit and loss zone ranges, one of which disappears upon the earlier expiration.)

Example: You enter into a ratio calendar spread by selling four May 50 calls at 5 and buying two August 50 calls at 6. You receive a net of $800 ($2000 less $1200) before brokerage fees. Between now and the May expiration, you hope that the underlying stock's market value will remain below striking price; that will produce a profit on the short side. Your break-even price is $54 per share.

If the stock is at $54 at point of expiration, you will break even due to the ratio of four short calls and two long calls. Upon exercise, the two uncovered calls will cost $800—the same amount as the credit you received when the position was opened. If the price of the stock is higher than $54 per share, the loss occurs at a 4 to 2 ratio. If the May expiration date passes without exercise, the four short positions will be profitable, and you will still own two August 50 calls.

The profit and loss zones in this example are summarized in Figure 8.10. Note that no consideration is given to the following factors:

✔ Brokerage costs.

✔ Time value of the longer-term premiums.

✔ Outcome in the event of an unexpected early exercise.

A complete ratio calendar spread strategy, with defined profit and loss zones, is summarized in Figure 8.11.

Example: You sell five June 40 calls for 5, receiving $2500; and you buy three September 40 calls for 7, spending $2100. Your net proceeds amount is $400. This ratio calendar spread involves long and short positions and two expiration months. The short position risk is limited to the

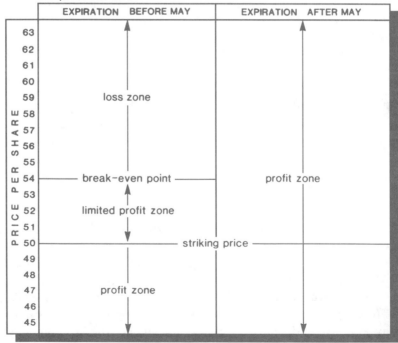

FIGURE 8.10   Example of ratio calendar spread.

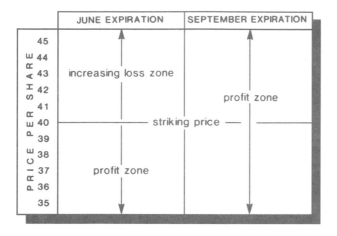

FIGURE 8.11 Ratio calendar spread profit and loss zones.

first expiration period, with losses partially covered by the longer-expiration long calls. As long as the stock's market value does not rise above the striking price of the June 40 calls, the short calls will expire worthless. However, you have two uncovered calls in this example up to that point.

Once the June expiration date passes, the $400 net is all profit, regardless of stock price movement after that time. However, if the stock's market value then rises above the long calls' striking price, you will earn 3 points for every point in the money (three calls).

Table 8.2 provides a summary of values for this strategy at various stock prices as of expiration. If the stock remains at or below the level of $40 per share, the proceeds of the ratio calendar spread will be profitable. However, the profit is limited and will never exceed that level. The loss, however, increases in the event of price increase in the underlying stock, by 2 points for every point of change in the stock's market value. This limited profit with growing loss reflects the degree of the ratio. There are more short position options than long position options.

Expanding the Ratio

The ratio calendar spread can be expanded into an even more complex strategy, called a *ratio calendar combination*

ratio calendar combination spread a strategy involving both a ratio between purchases and sales and a box spread (Long and short positions are opened on options with the same underlying stock, in varying numbers of contracts and with expiration dates extending over two or more periods. This strategy is designed to produce profits in the event of price increases or decreases in the market value of the underlying stock.)

TABLE 8.2 Profits/Losses for Ratio Calendar Spread Example			
Price	June 40	Sep. 40	Total
$50	−$5000	+$3000	−$2000
49	− 4500	+ 2700	− 1800
48	− 4000	+ 2400	− 1600
47	− 3500	+ 2100	− 1400
46	− 3000	+ 1800	− 1200
45	− 2500	+ 1500	− 1000
44	− 2000	+ 1200	− 800
43	− 1500	+ 900	− 600
42	− 1000	+ 600	− 400
41	− 500	+ 300	− 200
40	+ 2500	− 2100	+ 400
39	+ 2500	− 2100	+ 400
38	+ 2500	− 2100	+ 400
lower	+ 2500	− 2100	+ 400

spread. This adds a dimension to the ratio calendar spread by adding a box spread to it.

Example: As illustrated in Figure 8.12, you open the following option positions:

✔ Buy one June 30 call at 3 (pay $300).
✔ Sell two March 30 calls at $1^{3}/_{4}$ (receive $350).
✔ Buy one September 25 put at $^{3}/_{4}$ (pay $75).
✔ Sell two June 25 puts at $^{5}/_{8}$ (receive $125).

The net result of these transactions is a receipt of $100, before figuring brokerage fees. This complex combination involves 2 to 1 ratios between short and long positions on both sides (two short options for each long position). In the event of unfavorable price movements in either direction, you risk exercise on some part of the strategy. The

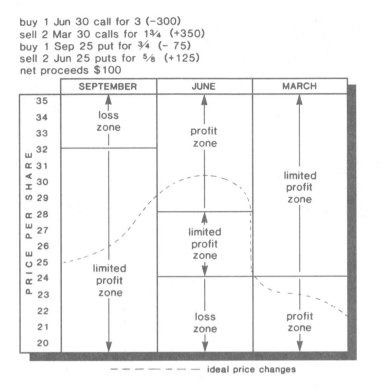

buy 1 Jun 30 call for 3 (−300)
sell 2 Mar 30 calls for 1¾ (+350)
buy 1 Sep 25 put for ¾ (− 75)
sell 2 Jun 25 puts for ⅝ (+125)
net proceeds $100

FIGURE 8.12 Example of ratio calendar combination.

ideal price change will enable you to close segments of the total combination before expiration dates at a profit.

Because of commission costs, entering into combinations with only one or two options is a costly strategy. Considering the risk exposure, potential profits do not justify the action in most cases. However, for the purpose of illustration, we limit our example to one-option and two-option spreads. In reality, such combinations may involve much higher numbers of contracts.

Risks of exercise are somewhat reduced by owning shares of the underlying stock, which provides full or partial coverage on short call positions. For example, when writing two calls and buying one, the risk of a price increase is eliminated if all call positions are covered by either owning shares or offsetting long calls.

Example: A complete ratio calendar combination spread, with defined profit and loss zones, is shown in Figure 8.13. In this example, you conduct the following transactions:

✔ Buy one July 40 call for 6 (−$600).
✔ Sell two April 40 calls for 3 (+$600).
✔ Buy one October 35 put for 1 (−$100).
✔ Sell two July 35 puts for 2 ($400).

Net proceeds in this example are $300.

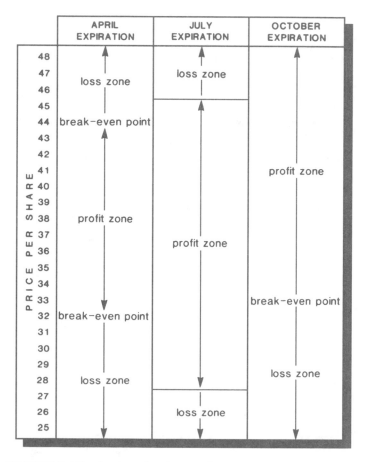

FIGURE 8.13 Ratio calendar combination spread profit and loss zones.

This ratio calendar combination spread consists of two separate ratio calendar spreads, boxed together. Profits could occur if the stock's market value moves in either direction, while losses are limited. Three separate expiration dates are involved. One danger in this strategy is that, as earlier options expire, the later option positions become exposed to uncovered loss, so risks could increase. This situation can be reversed—so that chances for later profits are greater—by building a combination using later long positions instead of short positions. Table 8.3 provides a breakdown of profit or loss that is produced at various prices as of expiration for the ratio calendar combination spread in Figure 8.13.

A Strategy with a Middle Range

Another technique calls for opening offsetting options in middle striking price ranges, with opposite positions above and below. This is known as the *butterfly spread*. It may involve long or short positions in either calls or puts. There are four possible versions of the butterfly spread:

> **butterfly spread**
> a strategy involving open options in one striking price range, offset by transactions at higher and lower ranges at the same time

1. Sell two middle-range calls and buy two calls, one with a striking price above that level and one with a striking price below that level.
2. Sell two middle-range puts and buy two puts, one with a striking price above that level and one with a striking price below that level.
3. Buy two middle-range calls and sell two calls, one with a striking price above that level and one with a striking price below that level.
4. Buy two middle-range puts and sell two puts, one with a striking price above that level and one with a striking price below that level.

Example: You sell two September 50 calls at 5, receiving a total premium of $1000. You also buy one September 55 call at 1 and one September 45 call at 7, paying a total of $800. Net proceeds are $200. This is a credit spread, since you received more than you paid. You will profit if the underlying

	April 40	July 40	July 35	Oct. 35	
Price	Call	Call	Put	Put	Total
$47	+$100	−$800	$ 0	+$400	−$300
46	0	− 600	0	+ 400	− 200
45	− 100	− 400	0	+ 400	− 100
44	− 200	− 200	0	+ 400	0
43	− 300	0	0	+ 400	+ 100
42	− 400	+ 200	0	+ 400	+ 200
41	− 500	+ 400	0	+ 400	+ 300
40	− 600	+ 600	0	+ 400	+ 400
39	− 600	+ 600	0	+ 400	+ 400
38	− 600	+ 600	0	+ 400	+ 400
37	− 600	+ 600	0	+ 400	+ 400
36	− 600	+ 600	0	+ 400	+ 400
35	− 600	+ 600	0	+ 400	+ 400
34	− 600	+ 600	0	+ 200	+ 200
33	− 600	+ 600	+ 100	0	+ 100
32	− 600	+ 600	+ 200	− 200	0
31	− 600	+ 600	+ 300	− 400	− 100
30	− 600	+ 600	+ 400	− 600	− 200
29	− 600	+ 600	+ 500	− 800	− 300
28	− 600	+ 600	+ 500	−1000	− 500
27	− 600	+ 600	+ 500	−1200	− 700
26	− 600	+ 600	+ 500	−1400	− 900

TABLE 8.3 Profits/Losses for Ratio Calendar Combination Spread Example

stock declines in value. And no matter how high the stock's market price rises, the combined long positions' values will always exceed the values in the two short positions.

Butterfly spreads often are created when one position is later expanded by the addition of other calls or puts. It is very difficult to find opportunities to create riskless combinations, especially a position that yields a credit as well.

Example: You sold two calls last month with striking prices of 40. The underlying stock's market value has declined to a point that the 35 calls are cheap, so you buy one to partially offset the risk in holding short calls. At the same time, you also buy a 45 call, which is far out of the money. This creates a butterfly spread.

The transaction fees charged by brokerage firms make butterfly spreads difficult to produce in a profitable manner. A credit is even less likely. The potential gain should be evaluated versus the limited potential profit, commission cost, and risk exposure.

Butterfly spreads can be created with either calls or puts, and structured with a bull or bear attitude. A bull butterfly spread will be the most profitable if the underlying stock's market value increases, and the opposite is true for a bear butterfly spread.

A detailed butterfly spread, with defined profit and loss zones, is summarized in Figure 8.14. In this spread, the following transactions are involved:

✔ Sell two June 40 calls for 6 (+$1200).

✔ Buy one June 30 call for 12 (−$1200).

✔ Buy one June 50 call for 3 (−$300).

The net cost is $300. This butterfly spread will either yield a limited profit or result in a limited loss. It consists of offsetting a position at one striking price with a higher and a lower position. In many instances of butterfly spreads, potential profit ranges are limited and too small to yield a profit after commissions; thus it is difficult to justify the strategy with a limited number of option contracts. In this example, the limited profit and loss ranges involve three different exercise prices.

Table 8.4 summarizes profit or loss at various prices of the underlying stock (assuming point of exercise and no remaining time value). If the stock's market value rises to $50 or more, the short position losses are offset by an equal number of long positions. And if the stock's market value declines, the maximum loss is $300, which is the cost of opening the butterfly spread.

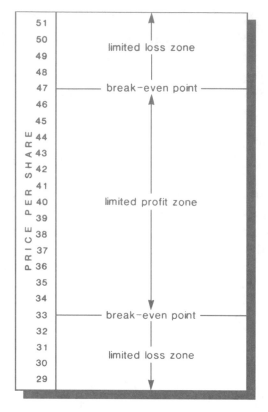

FIGURE 8.14 Butterfly spread profit and loss zones.

UNDERSTANDING HEDGES

Whenever options are bought or sold as part of a strategy to protect another open position, the combined positions are properly described as a hedge.

The Two Types of Hedges

A *long hedge* protects you against price increases, while a *short hedge* protects against price decreases.

Example of a long hedge: You have gone short on 100 shares of stock. You are at risk of loss if the stock's market value rises, so you buy one call. In the event of an increase in the stock's price, the call with increase as well, protecting against loss.

	TABLE 8.4 Profits/Losses for Butterfly Spread Example			
Price	June 50	June 40	June 30	Total
$51	+$900	−$1000	+$100	$ 0
50	+ 800	− 800	0	0
49	+ 700	− 600	− 300	− 200
48	+ 600	− 400	− 300	− 100
47	+ 500	− 200	− 300	0
46	+ 400	0	− 300	+ 100
45	+ 300	+ 200	− 300	+ 200
44	+ 200	+ 400	− 300	+ 300
43	+ 100	+ 600	− 300	+ 400
42	0	+ 800	− 300	+ 500
41	− 100	+1000	− 300	+ 600
40	− 200	+1200	− 300	+ 700
39	− 300	+1200	− 300	+ 600
38	− 400	+1200	− 300	+ 500
37	− 500	+1200	− 300	+ 400
36	− 600	+1200	− 300	+ 300
35	− 700	+1200	− 300	+ 200
34	− 800	+1200	− 300	+ 100
33	− 900	+1200	− 300	0
32	−1000	+1200	− 300	− 100
31	−1100	+1200	− 300	− 200
30	−1200	+1200	− 300	− 300
29	−1200	+1200	− 300	− 300
lower	−1200	+1200	− 300	− 300

Example of a short hedge: You own 100 shares of stock and, due to recent negative news, you are concerned about the possibility that market values will fall. To hedge against that, you have two possible courses of action: you can buy one put or sell one call. Both positions hedge your 100 shares. The put will provide unlimited protection, while the call hedges only in the same number of points received for the sale.

Long hedges protect investors by covering their short positions in the event of price increases; the original and hedged positions offset one another, so that unexpected price movement is matched on the other side. Short hedges are the opposite; they protect investors against price decreases that adversely affect long positions.

An expanded example of a long hedge, with defined profit and loss zones, is summarized in Figure 8.15. In this example, you sell short 100 shares at $43 per share, and you buy one May 40 call for 2. This long hedge strategy assumes that the underlying stock's market value has declined since the position was opened, to the point that the combined time and intrinsic value of the call are equal to only a premium of 2. Under this assumption, you accept a reduced overall profit to eliminate the risk of future losses, but without closing the position. The risk is eliminated only until the expiration of the call, while the short position in the stock may be continued beyond that date.

If the underlying stock's market value increases, the profit potential is limited to the pricing gap between the stock and the call. It will never increase beyond that point spread before expiration date. Increasing value in the shorted stock will be exactly offset by increasing premium

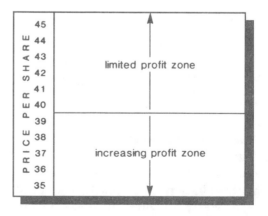

FIGURE 8.15   Long hedge profit and loss zones.

value in the option. If the stock's value falls, the short stock position will be profitable, minus the 2 points paid for the hedge provided by the call.

Table 8.5 summarizes the hedged position's overall value at various price levels for the underlying stock.

Hedging beyond Coverage

Hedges can be modified to increase potential profits or to minimize the risk of loss.

A *reverse hedge* involves providing more protection than that needed just to cover the position. For example, if you are short on 100 shares of stock, you need only one call to hedge the position. With a reverse hedge, you would buy more than one call, providing both protection of the position and the potential for gains that would outpace adverse stock movement (2 points for every 1 point of price change with two calls; with three options, the advantage would be 3 to 1).

An expanded example of a reverse hedge, with defined profit and loss zones, is summarized in Figure 8.16. In this example, you sell short 100 shares of stock, which

reverse hedge
an extension of a long or short hedge in which more options are opened than the number needed to cover the stock position; this increases profit potential in the event of unfavorable movement in the market value of the underlying stock

TABLE 8.5 Profits/Losses from the Long Hedge Example			
Price	Stock	Call	Total
$45	−$200	+$300	+$100
44	− 100	+ 200	+ 100
43	0	+ 100	+ 100
42	+ 100	0	+ 100
41	+ 200	− 100	+ 100
40	+ 300	− 200	+ 100
39	+ 400	− 200	+ 200
38	+ 500	− 200	+ 300
37	+ 600	− 200	+ 400
36	+ 700	− 200	+ 500
35	+ 800	− 200	+ 600

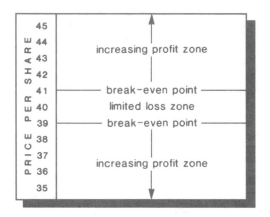

FIGURE 8.16   Reverse hedge profit and loss zones.

now is at $43 per share, and you buy two May 40 calls at 2, which cost $400. This reverse hedge strategy solves the problem you face when you utilize a long hedge. That is, the reverse hedge will produce profits if the stock's value increases or decreases—by enough points to offset the cost of buying calls. In this example, 100 shares were sold short at $43 per share, and two May 40 calls were bought. (As in the previous example, we assume that the stock's price has declined since the short sale, so that enough profit exists in the position to justify the cost of the hedge.)

In this example, the reverse hedge creates its advantage in two ways: First, it protects the short position in the event of a price increase; second, including the second call adds profit potential to the position. Now, if the stock's market value falls, further profits will accrue in the stock. And if the stock's market value rises, a two-to-one profit will be realized in the calls.

Table 8.6 summarizes the position's value as of expiration at various prices of the underlying stock.

Hedging Option Positions

Hedging can protect a long position or a short position in an underlying stock, or it can reduce or eliminate risks in other option positions. Hedging is achieved with various forms of spreads and combinations described previously in this chapter. By varying the number of options on one

TABLE 8.6 Profits/Losses from Reverse Hedge Example			
Price	Stock	Call	Total
$45	–$200	+$600	+$400
44	– 100	+ 400	+ 300
43	0	+ 200	+ 200
42	+ 100	0	+ 100
41	+ 200	– 200	0
40	+ 300	– 400	– 100
39	+ 400	– 400	0
38	+ 500	– 400	+ 100
37	+ 600	– 400	+ 200
36	+ 700	– 400	+ 300
35	+ 800	– 400	+ 400

side or the other, you can create a *variable hedge*—a hedge involving both long and short positions. However, one side will contain a greater number of options than the other.

Example: You buy three May 40 calls and sell one May 55 call. This variable hedge creates the potential for profits while entirely eliminating the risks of selling uncovered calls. If the underlying stock's market value increases beyond the $60 per share level, your long positions, containing three contracts, will increase three dollars for every dollar of loss in the short position. If the stock's market value decreases, the short position can be closed at a profit.

Long and short variable hedge strategies with defined profit and loss zones are illustrated in Figure 8.17. In the long variable hedge example, you buy three June 65 calls for 1, spending $300; and you sell one June 60 call for 5; net proceeds are $200. This long variable hedge strategy will achieve maximum profit if the underlying stock's market value rises. Above the striking price of 65,

variable hedge
a hedge involving a long position and a short position in related options, when one side contains a greater number of options than the other (The desired result is reduction of risks or potentially greater profits.)

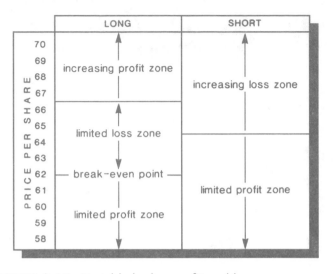

FIGURE 8.17 Variable hedge profit and loss zones.

the long calls will increase by three dollars for every point increase in the underlying stock. If the stock's market value declines, all of the calls will lose value, and the net proceeds of $200 will be profitable. Table 8.7 summarizes this position's value as of expiration, at various stock price levels. The problem in this strategy is that the short position expires later than the long positions; that is normally the only way to create a credit in a variable hedge. So you need to see price movement to create an acceptable profit before expiration of the long positions, or be prepared to close out the short position when the long positions expire.

In the short variable hedge example in Figure 8.17, you sell five June 60 calls for 5, receiving $2500; you also buy three June 65 calls for 1, paying $300; net proceeds are $2200. This short variable hedge strategy is a more aggressive type than the previous example, with a higher level of proceeds at the front end and a correspondingly higher risk overall. When the offsetting call positions are eliminated, two of these calls are uncovered. A decline in the underlying stock's market value will result in a profit; if the price remains below striking price until expiration, the entire $2200 net proceeds will be profit. However, a rise in price will create a growing level of loss. Beyond striking price, the loss is 2 points for every point of movement in

TABLE 8.7	Profits/Losses from the Long Variable Hedge Example		
Price	Stock	Call	Total
$70	+$1200	−$500	+$700
69	+ 900	− 400	+ 500
68	+ 600	− 300	+ 300
67	+ 300	− 200	+ 100
66	0	− 100	− 100
65	− 300	0	− 300
64	− 300	+ 100	− 200
63	− 300	+ 200	− 100
62	− 300	+ 300	0
61	− 300	+ 400	+ 100
60	− 300	+ 500	+ 200
59	− 300	+ 500	+ 200
58	− 300	+ 500	+ 200

the stock's price. Outcomes of the short hedge at various price levels as of expiration are summarized in Table 8.8.

Partial Coverage Strategies

Another form of hedging involves cutting partial losses through partial coverage. The strategy is called a *ratio write*. When an investor sells one call for every 100 shares owned, the strategy provides a one-to-one coverage. A ratio write exists when the relationship between long and short positions is not identical. The ratio can be greater on either the long side or the short side. See Table 8.9.

ratio write
a strategy for partially covering one position with another for partial rather than full coverage (A portion of risk is eliminated, so that ratio writes can be used to reduce overall risk levels.)

Example: You own 75 shares of stock and you sell a call. Because some (even a minority) of your shares are not covered, you have two separate positions: 75 shares of stock, and one uncovered call. However, if the call is exercised, your 75 shares can be sold to satisfy three-quarters of the assignment. For practical purposes, your short position is 75 percent covered. The ratio write is 1 to $^3/_4$.

TABLE 8.8 Profits/Losses from the Short Variable Hedge Example

Price	Stock	Call	Total
$70	−$2500	+$500	−$2000
69	− 2000	+ 400	− 1600
68	− 1500	+ 300	− 1200
67	− 1000	+ 200	− 800
66	− 500	0	− 500
65	0	− 300	− 300
64	+ 500	− 300	+ 200
63	+ 1000	− 300	+ 700
62	+ 1500	− 300	+ 1200
61	+ 2000	− 300	+ 1700
60	+ 2500	− 300	+ 2200
59	+ 2500	− 300	+ 2200
58	+ 2500	− 300	+ 2200

TABLE 8.9 Ratio Writes

Calls Sold	Shares Owned	Percent Coverage	Ratio
1	75	75%	1 to 3/4
2	150	75	2 to 1 1/2
3	200	67	3 to 2
4	300	75	4 to 3
5	300	60	5 to 3
5	400	80	5 to 4

Example: You own 300 shares of stock and you recently sold four calls. The positions are viewed as having three covered calls and one uncovered call, all on the same underlying stock. Or the position can be viewed as a 4 to 3 ratio write.

An expanded example of the ratio write, with defined profit and loss zones, is summarized in Figure 8.18.

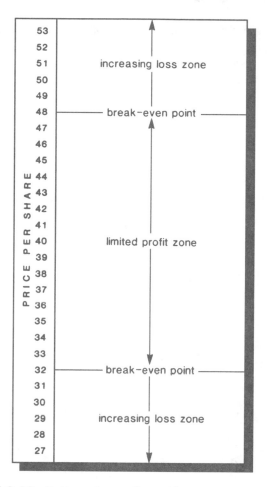

FIGURE 8.18 Ratio write profit and loss zones.

In this example, you buy 50 shares of stock at $38 per share, and you sell one September 40 call for 3. This ratio write strategy creates a partially covered call. Half of the risk in the short position has been offset by the 50 shares in the long position; the other half of the risk is uncovered. If the value of the underlying stock increases, the degree of risk is cut in half by owning 50 shares, as they can be used upon exercise. However, if the stock's market value falls far enough, a loss in the stock will offset the premium received from selling the call. A summary of this strategy is provided for various price levels at expiration (Table 8.10).

| | July 40 | July 40 | |
Price	Call	Put	Total
$50	+$600	−$700	−$100
49	+ 550	− 600	− 50
48	+ 500	− 500	0
47	+ 450	− 400	+ 50
46	+ 400	− 300	+ 100
45	+ 350	− 200	+ 150
44	+ 300	− 100	+ 200
43	+ 250	0	+ 250
42	+ 200	+ 100	+ 300
41	+ 150	+ 200	+ 350
40	+ 100	+ 300	+ 400
39	+ 50	+ 300	+ 350
38	0	+ 300	+ 300
37	− 50	+ 300	+ 250
36	− 100	+ 300	+ 200
35	− 150	+ 300	+ 150
34	− 200	+ 300	+ 100
33	− 250	+ 300	+ 50
32	− 300	+ 300	0
31	− 350	+ 300	− 50
30	− 400	+ 300	− 100

TABLE 8.10 Profits/Losses from the Ratio Write Example

long straddle
the purchase of an identical number of calls and puts with identical striking prices and expiration dates, designed to produce profits in the event of price movement of the underlying stock in either direction adequate to surpass the cost of opening the position

UNDERSTANDING STRADDLES

While spreads involve buying and selling options with differing terms, straddles are the simultaneous purchase and sale of options with the same striking price and expiration date.

Middle Loss Zones

A *long straddle* involves the purchase of calls and puts to create a straddle. Because you pay to create the long position, it creates a loss zone above and below the striking price, and profit zones above and below that range.

Example: You enter into a long straddle. You buy one February 40 call and pay a premium of 2. You also buy one February 40 put and pay 1. Your total cost is $300. If the underlying stock's market value remains within 3 points of the striking price, either above or below, the straddle will not be profitable. The 3 points of intrinsic value for either option offset your cost. If the stock's market value is higher than the striking price by more than 3 points, or if it is lower than the striking price by more than 3 points, the long straddle will be profitable. This example does not provide for brokerage fees.

An example of a long straddle, with defined profit and loss zones, is illustrated in Figure 8.19. In this example, you buy one July 40 call for 3, and one July 40 put for 1; net cost is $400. This long straddle strategy involves assuming a long position in both calls and puts of the same stock, with the same striking price and expiration date. It will become profitable if the underlying stock's price movement exceeds the number of points involved in

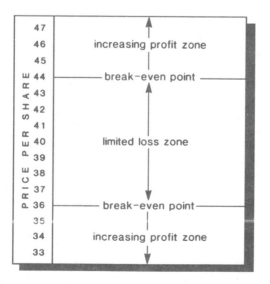

FIGURE 8.19 Long straddle profit and loss zones.

opening the position—in this example, 4 points. That price movement can occur in either direction. Table 8.11 provides a summary of outcomes at various stock prices as of expiration.

Since both sides are long, you can sell off one position at a profit and hold onto the other, hoping for movement in the other direction. For example, if the underlying stock's market value moves up 2 points, the call can be closed at a profit; if the stock's market value later falls below the striking price by 3 points, the put can also be sold at a profit. The important price to watch, however, is the net price of the overall strategy. In order to profit, you need to have overall price movement exceeding the cost. Because time is running, there might not be enough time for the desired price movement in *both* directions; long strategies are designed to be profitable in either direction, but you cannot depend on profiting on both sides.

TABLE 8.11	Profits/Losses from the Long Straddle Example		
Price	July 40 Call	July 40 Put	Total
$47	+$400	–$100	+$300
46	+ 300	– 100	+ 200
45	+ 200	– 100	+ 100
44	+ 100	– 100	0
43	0	– 100	– 100
42	– 100	– 100	– 200
41	– 200	– 100	– 300
40	– 300	– 100	– 400
39	– 300	0	– 300
38	– 300	+ 100	– 200
37	– 300	+ 200	– 100
36	– 300	+ 300	0
35	– 300	+ 400	+ 100
34	– 300	+ 500	+ 200
33	– 300	+ 600	+ 300

Middle Profit Zones

In the previous example, two related long positions were opened, creating a loss zone on either side of the striking price. The same idea applies on the short side; you can create a limited profit zone by opening a *short straddle*. This involves selling an identical number of calls and puts on the same underlying stock, with the same striking price and expiration date. This creates a middle range of profit on either side of the striking price. Beyond that range, the position will create a loss. Short straddles provide potential profits in stocks that do not move too many points, while maximizing time value advantage. Because time value evaporates over time, the short straddle will become profitable as long as the stock's underlying market value does not move too many points in either direction.

short straddle
the sale of an identical number of calls and puts with identical striking prices and expiration dates, designed to produce profits in the event of price movement of the underlying stock only within a limited range

Example: You create a short straddle. You sell one March 50 call for 2; you also sell one March 50 put for 1; net proceeds are $300. As long as the underlying stock's market value remains within 3 points of striking price—on either side—any intrinsic value in one option will be offset by the other option. But if the current market value of the stock exceeds the 3-point range in either direction, the short straddle will result in a loss.

This theory does not take into account the cost of transacting options. So the limited range would be even smaller in practical application, since brokerage fees reduce the profit range. And upon exercise, those fees would be even higher. Exercise is more likely in this case than a simple short position, since one option or the other will probably be in the money at expiration. This strategy will work best if and when the stock's market value remains within the range long enough for you to close both positions with lower time value. A thin margin of profit might be desirable, but you need to ask whether that margin is worth the risks involved in having both short positions open.

An example of the short straddle, with defined profit and loss zones, is summarized in Figure 8.20. In this example, you sell one July 40 call for 3, and you sell one July 40

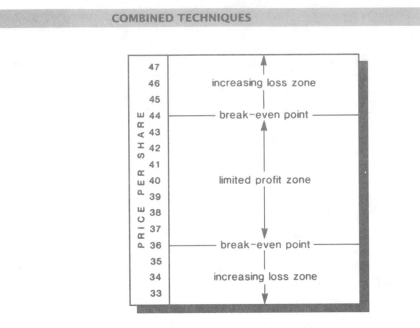

FIGURE 8.20 Short straddle profit and loss zones.

put for 1; net proceeds are $400, which creates a 4-point profit zone on either side of striking price. The short strategy as illustrated by this example is exactly the opposite of the long straddle. The position consists of two short positions—one call and one put on the same underlying stock, with identical striking price and expiration date. The middle range is a profit zone instead of a loss zone. As long as the underlying stock's market value remains within that profit zone, the strategy will be profitable overall. In this example, the zone extends 4 points above and below striking price.

Unless the underlying stock's market value is exactly at striking price at the time of expiration, the risk of exercise is very real for one option or the other. Table 8.12 shows in summary the outcome for the short straddle at various stock price levels as of expiration.

Actual profits and losses have to be adjusted to allow for brokerage fees. Those fees will be charged for opening and for closing each position, and if either position is exercised, additional fees will be charged. So a thin margin of profit could be eliminated altogether by such fees, which have not been calculated in the sample outcome. See Figure 8.21 for a comparison between long and short straddles and profit and loss zones.

	TABLE 8.12 Profits/Losses from the Short Straddle Example		
Price	July 40 Call	July 40 Put	Total
$47	−$400	+$100	−$300
46	− 300	+ 100	− 200
45	− 200	+ 100	− 100
44	− 100	+ 100	0
43	0	+ 100	+ 100
42	+ 100	+ 100	+ 200
41	+ 200	+ 100	+ 300
40	+ 300	+ 100	+ 400
39	+ 300	0	+ 300
38	+ 300	− 100	+ 200
37	+ 300	− 200	+ 100
36	+ 300	− 300	0
35	+ 300	− 400	− 100
34	+ 300	− 500	− 200
33	+ 300	− 600	− 300

THEORY AND PRACTICE OF COMBINED TECHNIQUES

Advanced option strategies expose you to danger, especially when they involve short positions. If you decide to attempt any of these theories, remember the following critical points:

1. Brokerage charges are part of the equation.

Brokerage charges will reduce profit margins significantly, especially when you have only single-option contracts. The more contracts involved, the lower the brokerage charges per contract—and the greater your market risks. A marginal potential profit could even be entirely wiped out by fees, so be aware of the real, net effect of a strategy before opening any positions. There are

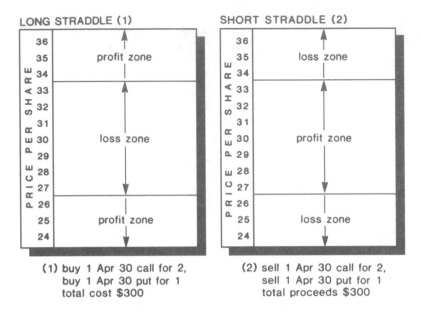

LONG STRADDLE (1)

36	profit zone
35	
34	
33	
32	loss zone
31	
30	
29	
28	
27	
26	profit zone
25	
24	

(1) buy 1 Apr 30 call for 2,
buy 1 Apr 30 put for 1
total cost $300

SHORT STRADDLE (2)

36	loss zone
35	
34	
33	
32	profit zone
31	
30	
29	
28	
27	
26	loss zone
25	
24	

(2) sell 1 Apr 30 call for 2,
sell 1 Apr 30 put for 1
total proceeds $300

PRICE PER SHARE

FIGURE 8.21 Comparison of long and short straddle strategies.

no sure ways to have a profit in every case, and it is a mistake to ignore the effect of brokerage charges.

2. Early exercise can change everything.

Buyers have the right of exercise in calls and puts at any time, not just at expiration. It is easy to forget this, and to assume that exercise always occurs at expiration. Never ignore the exercise risk. What seems a simple, easy strategy can be thrown into disarray by early exercise, and early exercise does occur. Be sure that when you evaluate a strategy and its possible outcomes that you also consider the effects of possible early exercise. As long as your strategy involves short positions in calls or puts, exercise is a constant possibility. Also consider what will happen to the balance of your positions if and when early exercise occurs.

3. Potential profit and risk are always directly related.

Many option investors tend to pay attention only to potential profits, while overlooking potential risks. Remember that the greater the possibility of profit, the greater the potential for loss. The relationship is inescapable.

4. Your degree of risk will be limited by your brokerage firm.

You can devise a complex series of trades that, in your view, limit risk while providing the potential for significant gain. However, remember that as long as that strategy includes short positions, your brokerage firm will restrict the degree of risk you will be allowed to assume. You will be required to meet minimum margin requirements, and failing that, your broker has the right to close out positions in the event the market moves against you—even if you believe that price movement is only temporary. So you need to be able to commit cash and securities to cover short positions according to the rules of your brokerage firm.

5. You need to thoroughly understand a strategy before opening positions.

Never employ any strategy until you completely understand how it will work in all potential outcomes. You need to evaluate risk levels for all outcomes, and not only for the limited range of possibilities you think are most likely. You also need to identify in advance what actions you will need to take in the event of each and every outcome. In that way, you will know what to do when price movement occurs, whether in a positive or a negative direction. It makes sense to devise reaction strategy in advance when you have time to think it through. Many mistakes are made under pressure by those investors who have not thought through their strategies ahead of time. Think of this process as best case/worst case planning.

6. It doesn't always work out the way it was planned on paper.

When working it out on paper you can convince yourself that a particular strategy simply cannot fail—or at least that failure is only a remote possibility. Then, when you enter the transaction, prices don't move as you expect, or option values don't respond as they are supposed to. Risk is only understood when it is experienced directly. Only experience can demonstrate the difference between theory and reality in options trading. Sudden changes in the market value of an underlying stock, or large corrections or run-ups in the market as a whole, will affect profitability and throw paper models into disarray.

Options add a new dimension to investing. You can protect existing positions, insure profits, and take advantage of momentary opportunities. These outcomes are all positive and informed, aware investors can profit using options wisely. However, also remember that each potential profit has another side, the offsetting risk. Only with evaluation and analysis will you be able to identify those few strategies that will work for you, that make you comfortable, and that you believe will be profitable.

The next chapter explains why each investor needs to devise a personalized, individual strategy. No one approach is universally right or appropriate for all investors.

Chapter

Choosing Your Own Strategy

You will ultimately decide to employ options in your portfolio upon concluding that they are appropriate in your particular circumstances. And if your personal risk tolerance and goals profile dictate that you should *not* employ options at any level, then you should not pursue the idea. Keep in mind, though, that there are a broad range of reasons to use options.

Your success as an investor depends on how well you are able and willing to set policies based on your goals; how accurately you identify the strategies appropriate for your goals (assuming also that you accurately select your goals in the first place); and most of all, how disciplined you are in staying with the course you have set for yourself: not only following the strategies appropriate to your overall goals, but also following the strategic rules you set in advance, and ignoring the temptation to deviate from that course.

With options, perhaps more than with other forms of investing, the establishment of strict and well thought out policies is critical. There are so many different ways to use options, from highly speculative and risky to very conservative and low-risk, that you need to examine with great care what you really need and what you can afford; and you also need to be able to follow your rules once you set them. Most important among these policies is the definition of acceptable risk. Your personal risk standards reveal what forms of option investing, if any, will fit your portfolio and your financial plan. Perhaps they fit today but will not fit tomorrow. Perhaps the reverse is true. Your financial plan is dynamic; it should change as your own circumstances change. Your risk standards will change as well, as your financial strength is altered and as you have experiences in the market.

Options might provide you with a very convenient form of diversification, protection, or income—or all of these benefits in various forms and combinations. But first, you need to decide what type of investor you are today, and what type of investor you want to be in the future. Option investing contains many traps. It has a complex language, it is highly mathematical, and it moves and changes quickly. Thus, it is easy for some people to become lost in terminology, to enjoy the theoretical probabilities more than profits, and to face unintended risks because they don't monitor the market regularly or react decisively enough when conditions demand action. So it is not enough to define yourself. You also need to keep focused on what is important.

If you are a speculator, you will favor short-term income potential and you will have little interest in potential profits over the longer term. So higher risks will get your attention. Selling uncovered options or buying near-expiration cheap positions will be especially appealing. As a speculator, you will also gravitate towards spreads and straddles for profit potential with minimum exposure to larger losses. If you speculate in your stock portfolio as well, you might also want to use options to offset potential losses in volatile stocks or to cover short positions. The danger is that you might be attracted to exotic strategies because they are exotic and not necessarily because they are appropriate.

If you are conservative and you seek income over long-term growth, you can achieve a consistently high rate of return through covered call writing. To protect the value in long-term portfolio positions, extremely conservative investors can use options as insurance to ride out temporary market corrections. This provides downside protection along with short-term income potential, often for little additional cost. By buying puts, for example, you do not risk exercise as you do by writing calls, but you achieve the same protection. While long puts are used for insurance, short calls are more appropriate for providing income and a higher than average rate of return but come with the risk of exercise in the event that the underlying stock's market value rises.

KNOWING THE RANGE OF RISK

Options serve the entire spectrum of risk profiles and can be used to speculate or to insure the value of an underlying stock. In order to identify how options can best serve your personal investing requirements, three steps are involved:

1. Become thoroughly aware of the various types of option investing. Before actually taking positions in options, prepare hypothetical variations and track the market to see how you would have done. Track options through the financial press or with an interactive system from your home computer providing direct quote service. Become so familiar with option quotations that you do not need to think about what they mean. See how values change from day to day.

2. Identify your personal investment and risk policies and set standards for yourself that conform to those zones. Based on the goals you devise as part of a personal financial plan, limit your market activities to those strategies and actions that fit. Also be aware that your goals and policies should change over time as your financial conditions change. Be prepared to throw out yesterday's plan *and* yesterday's perception of risk, and to look at all of the questions with a fresh point of view.

3. Identify and understand the specific risks involved with options in each and every variation possible, including contingent risks beyond unexpected movement in the market value of the underlying stock. Avoid the all-too-common trap of assuming a simplistic point of view. Develop a deeper sense of the options market by tracking it and, ultimately, by experiencing it directly. In most forms of investment, perceptions of risk are fixed. In option investing, it all depends on the position you assume. For example, as a buyer, time is the enemy; as a seller, time is your best ally. This is because the essential point to remember about options is how time value changes over time.

The obvious risk in each and every option position is that the underlying stock will move in a direction other than the one you expect or, with some strategies, that short-term movement will be too little or too much to attain the ideal profit zone outcome. This danger is accepted by speculators seeking immediate income, and by the conservative investor who uses options to lock in a rate of return or to insure the value of a related position.

Beyond these obvious risks, several other forms of risk should be kept in mind whenever you become involved with options.

Margin Risks

Most investors think of margin investing as buying stock on credit. That is, indeed, the most familiar form. In the options market, margin requirements are different and margin is used in a different manner. Your brokerage firm will require that any short position you assume be covered through collateral (unless the short position is already covered in your portfolio).

Whenever you open uncovered short positions in options, the brokerage firm will require that you place cash or securities on account to protect a portion of the potential loss. For example, when you sell uncovered calls your brokerage firm requires that you maintain a specified level of security in your account (this may vary between firms, subject only to minimum legal requirements). The balance above the margin requirement is at risk, both for you and for the brokerage firm. So if the stock involved experiences an increase in value, the margin requirement will go up as well.

The risk here is that in the event of an unexpected increase in the market value of the underlying stock, you will be required to deposit additional money or securities to meet the margin requirement. This limits every investor's potential involvement in the market to the amount of capital he or she has available. Margin requirements generally must be met within the immediate future. Before entering into any short position—uncovered calls or puts, spreads, straddles—you should determine the margin requirements that will be imposed, and ensure that you can afford to enter the position.

Personal Goal Risks

Successful investors establish personal goals, review them regularly, and select strategies that meet their risk profile. They then set rules for themselves and follow those rules consistently. Investing is a formula, not something that is made up along the way. If you do not adopt this point of view, then your chances for gaining consistent profits in option trading will be reduced significantly.

Example: You establish a number of personal goals and then set standards for yourself. One of your investing policies states that you will use no more than 15 percent of your portfolio's value to speculate in options. You begin a program of buying calls and puts after careful analysis and selection. Over time, you earn a respectable profit. Then, unexpectedly, the market enters into a severe correction and you find yourself heavily invested in calls. They all lose value rapidly. Upon review, you discover that you had about 30 percent of your portfolio invested before the correction, and it looks like you are going to lose it all. Somewhere along the way, you lost sight of your policy. You lost more than you could afford because you did not monitor your portfolio.

Your standards should include identifying the point where you will close any open position. Avoid breaking your own rules by delaying action in the hope of greater profits in the future. That is a constant temptation, but if you give in, it virtually assures that you will lose. Establish two price points: *minimum gain* and *maximum loss*. When either point is reached, close the position.

Unavailability of a Market Risk

A discussion of any option strategy assumes that you will be able to open and close positions when you want. Timing is the essential element of all option trading. But as an option investor, you need to accept the continuous risk that a market could be unavailable for several reasons.

Example: On October 19, 1987, the stock market experienced the worst decline in its history until that point. Volume exceeded 600 million shares and brokerage firms fell behind several days in completing orders. Investors who wanted to enter trades were unable to reach their brokers by telephone, and even already-placed orders often were delayed several days. During the following week, prices of stocks and options moved through an extremely broad range of prices. Option investors, notably speculators, suffered tremendous losses due not only to the violent decline in value, but also to the unavailability of a market. They were not able to cut their losses because the market was unavailable to place a closing transaction.

Since that time, procedures have been changed so the market shuts down automatically when trading levels reach certain points, so this situation cannot be repeated. In addition, the use of computers for direct order placement has improved the overall efficiency of the market. Still, the nature of the options market means that a specific price is not necessarily going to be available. For example, you might want to make a trade at the price that is offered at this moment. However, actual execution might occur a half point away from the desired level. Because the market changes quickly, you cannot always get immediate prices in each case. In deciding on a specific trade, you need to allow a margin of adjustment with this in mind.

Disruption in Trading Risks

Another risk you face as an option investor is that trading will be halted in the underlying stock. For example, there may be rumors that a company is a takeover candidate, and the stock of the company is apt to rise substantially if the rumors are true. When that occurs, trading in the stock is halted, often for more than a day. And all related options trading is halted as well. This situation presents a particularly severe risk for options investors.

Example: You sold an uncovered call last month and received a premium of 11. Your strategy was to close the position if the stock rose 8 points or more, or to hold until expiration. But yesterday a tender offer was made on the company at a price per share 20 points higher than current market value. You called your broker immediately to cancel your position. But you were told that the exchange halted trading in the stock, so you were barred from trading any options. You were not able to escape the short position. Now you realize that when trading is reactivated, your option will probably be worth 20 points more than it was yesterday. It will probably be exercised.

In the same circumstances, a call buyer will not be able to close a position and take profits until trading is resumed. Meanwhile, the tender offer might fall apart and the option's value will no longer be 20 points higher.

Brokerage Risks

If your brokerage firm becomes insolvent or if a regulatory agency takes over its operations, you might find yourself unable to close positions at will. Or your positions might even be closed without your authorization to eliminate the risk of losses to the firm itself. These are not everyday occurrences, but such events do happen.

In the event of a widespread brokerage insolvency, the Options Clearing Corporation would not necessarily be able to honor the exercise of all option contracts. The system of margin requirements and limitations on individual option positions in effect does limit this risk. But every option investor should recognize that the risk does exist.

Another form of brokerage risk involves the conduct of your personal broker. You should never grant unlimited trading discretion to *any* broker, no matter how much trust you have. Option trading, with its varied and special risks in a fast-moving market, is not appropriate for every investor, and even competent brokers cannot possibly know the mind of his or her clients in every instance. Instances have occurred of abuse by brokers who were granted trading authority for customer accounts, and abuses will no doubt occur in the future. You also face the very real risk that an individual broker will assume trading authority that you have not granted. Unfortunately, when too much trust is placed in a broker, the problem will not be discovered until after losses have occurred. It is always a mistake to allow a broker, by virtue of experience or knowledge, to dictate positions in options or any other security without your consent in advance, or outside of your control.

Commission Risks

A calculated profit zone has to be reduced to allow for the cost of trading. And every loss zone has to be expanded for the same reason. Remember, brokerage charges apply on both sides of the trade. If you trade in single-option contracts, you reduce risk and exposure, but you also increase your costs.

We have used examples in this book involving single contracts for the most part, but only to illustrate the application of particular strategies as clearly as possible. Trading expense has been excluded for the same reason. However, as you enter into trades you will discover that the cost has to be included because thin margins of profit can quickly turn into losses when the *net* transaction clears.

You risk losing sight of the cost of trading, so that marginally profitable trades don't work out as you thought. This is especially true when stock is assigned, meaning you will be charged a fee for the option *and* for the stock. For the overall risk assumed when you open a position, you might realize very little or nothing for your efforts. Always calculate the risk and potential for profit with trading costs in mind. And always add enough price value to cover all trading costs involved in opening and closing positions.

Lost Opportunity Risks

One of the most troubling aspects of option investing involves lost opportunities. These arise in several ways, the most obvious being in selling covered calls. You risk losing profits from price increases if the stock's market value suddenly rises after you have opened a position. Covered call writers have to accept a consistent, ensured, but limited profit while being willing to lose opportunities that might arise in the future.

Example: You originally bought 100 shares of stock at $34, and it is now valued at $42. You sell one call with a striking price of 40, reasoning that even if exercised, you will profit on both the call and the stock. However, the stock later rises in value to $65 per share and the call is exercised; you are required to sell your shares at $40 per share, while current market value is $65.

In this example, you entered the position with good reasoning and in recognition of the built-in profit. However, for the premium you were paid, you accepted the opportunity risk that would (and did) arise if the stock's market value increased.

Opportunity risks also arise in other ways. For example, if you are involved in exotic strategies involving both short and long positions in options, your margin requirement might prevent you from being able to react to a separate investing opportunity. Virtually all investors discover that they live in a world of moderate scarcity, at best, because no matter how well thought out a strategy is before it is entered, opportunities can show up later that might have been better; and there is never enough available capital to respond to all of the opportunities.

EVALUATING YOUR RISK TOLERANCE

Every investor has a specific level of risk tolerance—the ability and willingness to accept risk. This is not a fixed trait, however, but will change over time. Your personal risk tolerance will be affected by your age, income, family status, perceptions of the future, and personality. Your risk tolerance level depends on these factors:

1. *Investment capital*
How much money is available to invest, either in long-term growth stocks or in speculating for short-term income? What portion of your investment capital can you afford to place at risk in options and other speculative investments?

2. *Personal factors*
Your age, income, level of debts, economic status, job (and job security), and potentially unlimited other personal factors will all affect your risk tolerance.

3. *Your experience*
How much investing have you experienced? How comfortable are you in the market, and how long have you been active as an investor? Risks involved in specialized markets such as options are affected by experience, not only in the specific area, but also in the market as a whole. Options are certainly a highly specialized investment product; brokers are required to ascertain your level of competence before even allowing you to trade options.

4. *Type of account*
Risk tolerance depends on how and why you invest. For example, if you use options as part of a self-directed retirement plan, you probably will be limited to only covered call writing. So your risk tolerance is not an issue in one respect; however, the strategy of writing covered calls can vary by risk tolerance as well, so your goals within the retirement investment portfolio have to be defined in terms of risk.

5. *Your personal objectives*
Each investor's individual objectives ultimately determine how much risk can and should be accepted. Your goals may include the desire to conserve capital, hedge

against inflation, maximize short-term income, attain a consistent rate of return, accumulate adequate capital for retirement income, save for a child's college expenses, make a down payment on a house, achieve long-term growth for undetermined future needs, or combinations of these different goals.

Some investors split their portfolios into distinct segments. One part is left in long-term growth investments, while another is dedicated to aggressive income funds, stocks, or speculative products such as options. Most people are willing to use only a small portion of their portfolio for higher-risk speculative strategies.

Whatever profile fits you, any and all investments and their risks should be thoroughly studied before any money is actually invested. You serve yourself poorly when you invest money without taking this step; spending money only on the advice of others, without first making at least a minimum effort at determining risks, is inviting trouble. Never depend only on the advice of a broker; no matter how honest and sincere that broker, he or she operates on a commission basis, and makes a living only when you transact business. That single fact by itself should be enough to inspire all investors to put in research and analysis on their own. Likewise, news or rumors you pick up from the financial media often involve momentary perceptions, but are not really important in larger overall trends and indicators.

Invest with your risk tolerance in mind, and do not act based on immediate reactions to new information that has not been checked out thoroughly. Your personal goals and risk tolerance should be the guiding forces in every investment decision you make. Select the fundamental and technical indicators that you believe provide you with the best information, and apply those forms of information to your personal investment program.

The best investment decisions invariably are made as the result of careful evaluation of factors including risk. By putting down on paper the various types of option trades in which you can engage, and by studying the possible outcomes, you will gain a clear view of how options could fit within your portfolio. Of equal importance, you will discover which strategies are clearly not appropriate for you. The evaluation process will help you to avoid mistakes and focus your attention for your own benefit, given the risk tolerance level you determine is right for you. The risk evaluation worksheet for option investing in Table 9.1 will help you to classify options within categories of risk.

Applying Limits

Awareness of your own personal limits should guide all option investing in your portfolio. Whenever you hold an open position in options, you should know not only your goal and risk tolerance level, but also be aware of the target rate of return you expect or, in the event of loss, the point at which you intend to close the position.

To define these limits, identify option trades you will make defined by rate of return and other features of the option: time until expiration, level of time value, distance between striking price and current market value of the

---

TABLE 9.1   Risk Evaluation Worksheet

Lowest Possible Risk

____ Covered call writing

____ Put purchase for insurance (long position)

____ Call purchase for insurance (short position)

Medium Risk

____ Ratio writing

____ Combined strategies

    ____ long   ____ short

High Risk

____ Uncovered call writing

____ Combined strategies

    ____ long   ____ short

____ Call purchases for income

____ Put purchases for income

underlying stock, option premium, volatility of the stock, overall market conditions, and potential for rolling forward in the event you want to avoid exercise. In the case of selling covered calls, you should also identify—in advance—the potential rates of return if the stock is unchanged versus the rate of return if the option is exercised.

You will improve your chances of succeeding with options if you make your decision based on these points:

1. *Maximum time value*

As a buyer, avoid buying options with too much time value. Time works against you as a buyer, and the more time value, the less chance you will have of profiting from purchasing options. As a seller, the opposite advice applies. Look for options with maximum time value, for the same reasons. Time works *for* you, meaning that the more time value you sell, the better your prospects of future profit.

Example: You are a buyer. You set a limit for yourself that options must never contain more than half their value in time value; accordingly, you will buy only those options that are in the money. If a particular option's premium is currently 4, it must be at least 2 points in the money; the more intrinsic value, the better.

Example: You are a seller. You specifically look for options with maximum time value, and generally will not sell options with less than half their value in time value. You recognize that over time, you have a better chance of profit when time value evaporates from the premium. This allows the option several points of movement opposite the direction you hope for, without loss, merely because time value will diminish.

2. *Time until expiration*

Buyers of very short-term options will be fortunate to realize a profit. If you have only a matter of weeks until expiration, time value will be low, but you will depend on the underlying stock to change in value in the short term as well. Remember that time and time value are directly related and, as obvious as that might seem, investors often fail to act on that information. Sellers may benefit in exact proportion by specializing in short-term writes, but that also increases the risk of expiration and low time value is a disadvantage. It generally takes time for buyers' options to build intrinsic value, and for sellers' options to lose time value. How much time is ideal depends on the exact option, current status of the stock, and relationship between striking price and current market value.

Example: You are a buyer and would like the least amount of time value in the options you buy. You find that, as a general rule, you are attracted to options with less than two months until expiration, this being the range in which time value is minimal. However, it is a long shot when there is less than one month until expiration. The "window" for you is to buy options that will expire in one to two months.

Example: You are a seller who seeks options with maximum time value. However, you also recognize that too long a period until expiration means uncertainty and the risk of exercise. The more time, the more potential for changes in the stock's market value. You have seen that maximum time value in your favorite options seems to occur in the range when expiration is more than three months away; but you are not willing to invest in options more than five months out. The best options to sell in your case will expire in between three and five months.

3. *Number of option contracts*
You need to decide how many options to transact at any one time. You do not have to limit yourself to only a few option contracts. The more you trade at once, the lower your overall trading cost. However, you also increase risks as you increase the number of options you will transact at any one time.

Example: The fee for trading options with one discount broker for trades of $2000 or less is $18 plus 1.8 percent of the premium value. Cost varies depending on the number of options you trade at one time, with an obvious favoring of larger volumes:

- ✔ One option, premium of 3 cost = $23.40
- ✔ Two options, premium of 3 cost = $28.80
- ✔ Three options, premium of 3 cost = $34.20

For three options, transaction cost is $11.40 per option, less than half the fee you would pay to trade only one option. While trading cost is cut in half, risks are three times greater. Every option investor needs to balance these two competing financial realities.

4. *Target rate of return*
Enter each and every option trade with a specific goal in mind for rate of return. Identify this goal in advance, and if two or more outcomes are possible (as in the case of writing covered calls), be aware of both potential outcomes.

Example: You have been buying options with the goal of earning a 50 percent rate of return. You are willing to risk 100 percent losses if you don't achieve your goal, and you do not alter this expectation as expiration approaches. Last month, you bought an option and paid a premium of 4. As of yesterday, premium value was 6. You sold because you reached your 50 percent goal.

5. *Buy and sell levels*
Along with a target rate of return, identify the premium level at which you will close the position. Set the rule and follow it without exception. When premiums rise (for long positions) or fall (for short positions) to your target price level, close the position. And, to minimize losses, also close if you reach a predetermined bail-out point. Buy and sell levels also relate to premium levels at the time positions are opened. For buyers, risks are minimized by setting an upward limit on premiums; for sellers, a minimum sale level justifies the risks.

Example: You usually buy options in groups of three. You avoid options with premiums above 3, so you never spend more than $900 on a single opening transaction (plus trading costs). You also set the standard that you will sell within a specific price/value range. If the value of each option increases to $450 or more (based on cost of $300), you will sell. If the value of each option decreases to $150, you will also sell.

Example: You sell covered calls against a diversified portfolio of stocks. Your standard is that to justify the exposure to risk, you need to receive no less than a premium of $500 per contract sold. Once the position has been opened, you will sell if and when the option's premium value falls to 3 or below. If the premium's value grows because the underlying stock's market value increases, you do nothing; you select options designed to produce acceptable profits in the event of exercise.

By identifying all of the features you consider minimally acceptable and all of the risks you are willing to assume within your range of possibilities, you are then able to select options that fit your limits. If your limits are unrealistic, then you will quickly discover that no options are available.

Example: You have set a policy for yourself that incorporates several features. First, you have decided that options you will buy should never contain more than 25 percent time value in the total premium. Second, they must have four months or more until expiration. Third, they must currently be in the money. However, when you try to apply this combined set of rules, you cannot locate any options that meet all of the tests. You realize that, somewhere in the total configuration, you need to make adjustments.

When considering an option strategy of any nature, first calculate potential profits in the event of expiration or exercise, and then set criteria for other features: maximum time value, time until expiration, the number of contracts involved in the transaction, target rate of return, and the price range in which you will close the position. Obviously, these criteria will be drastically different for buyers than for sellers, and for covered versus uncovered option writing. Use the option limits worksheet in Table 9.2 to set your personal limits. Then always respect the limits you set; if you discover those limits are not realistic, make changes where appropriate (or accept the conclusion that you are not willing to undertake the associated risks). By deciding in advance the characteristics of your option investment, and by knowing when you will close a position, you will avoid the most common problem faced by investors: making decisions in a void. Many have invested well at first, only to fail later by not knowing when or why to close positions at the right time.

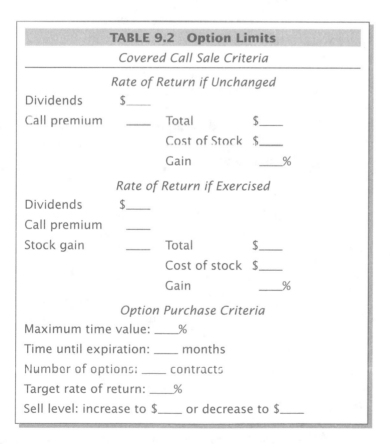

TABLE 9.2 Option Limits

Covered Call Sale Criteria

Rate of Return if Unchanged

Dividends	$____			
Call premium	____	Total	$____	
		Cost of Stock	$____	
		Gain	____%	

Rate of Return if Exercised

Dividends	$____			
Call premium	____			
Stock gain	____	Total	$____	
		Cost of stock	$____	
		Gain	____%	

Option Purchase Criteria

Maximum time value: ____%

Time until expiration: ____ months

Number of options: ____ contracts

Target rate of return: ____%

Sell level: increase to $____ or decrease to $____

LOOKING TO THE FUTURE

Besides setting immediate standards and goals for option strategies in your portfolio, set long-term investing policies. Then fit option strategies into your portfolio as dictated by your policies—if they are appropriate.

It is a mistake to open an option position on the advice of a broker or other adviser without first considering how it fits into your long-term investing policy. Options, like all investments, should always be used in an appropriate context.

Example: You have written out your personal investing goals, and have identified what you would like to achieve in the immediate and long-term future. You are willing to assume risks in a low to moderate range. So you invest all of your capital in shares of blue-chip companies. In order to increase portfolio values over time, you consider one of the following two possible strategies:

Strategy 1: Hold the shares of stock as long-term investments. After many years, the accumulation of well-selected companies will increase the overall value of those investments, and dividends will provide current income.

Strategy 2: Increase the value of your portfolio by purchasing shares and writing covered calls, as long as the rate of return if exercised or if unchanged always will exceed a 35 percent rate of return. Income from profitable turnover through exercise, call premiums, and dividends will all be reinvested in a growing number of shares with blue-chip companies that also have listed options available.

In the above example, the rate of return under the second strategy will be greater due to the consistently high yields you will receive from selling calls. The return can be achieved while also providing a discount from your basis, which also provides some downside protection on your investment. Selling calls also increases your available cash to invest in additional shares.

One interesting point can be made about the covered call strategy described above: The common argument against writing covered calls is that you stand to lose future profits if and when the stock's market value rises. This risk is especially severe when that rise is dramatic. However, given the overall long-term goal, you should assume that the stocks selected here, while excellent long-term growth candidates, will also be less volatile than the average stock. So the risk of losing future profits should also be minimal. It could happen, but it is not as likely as it would be for other issues.

The long-term goal of building up portfolio value can be achieved using options in an appropriate way. For stock investors, selling covered calls is realistic, conservative, and it does produce a consistently high rate of return—as long as you set reasonable policies and follow them faithfully. You risk giving up the occasional spectacular profit when a stock unexpectedly rises in value, since the written call locks in the striking price in the event of exercise; however, giving up that potential profit ensures you a consistent and respectable rate of return which, for most investors, is preferable. If your goal is steady long-term growth, enhanced by current income, selling covered calls against a well selected portfolio of stocks is one sensible way to go.

An impatient investor might be tempted to take the speculative approach, perhaps by buying options instead of stocks. If those options were consistently profitable, you could conceivably reach a long-term goal in months rather than years. Most experienced market watchers will agree, however, that the odds of succeeding in speculation will not be high. A more sensible course, by most people's standards, will involve a portfolio based on stock investments that are considered more or less permanent, enhanced by occasional trades and recurring call writing to vastly improve current income.

All forms of investing contain their own opportunities and a specific set of problems and risks. Options can often be used to help you reach your overall goals, address or reduce risks, and even provide insurance for other positions. You may hedge stock or other option positions, discount prices you pay to buy stock, or simply devote a small portion of your investment capital to pure speculation.

Those investors who do lose consistently in the options market tend to share common characteristics. They do not set goals or select strategies in their own best interests, usually because they have not taken the time to define those best interests. Their intentions and goals are unclear, so they don't know when they should buy or sell. A popular expression in the investment community is, "If you don't know where you're going, any road will get you there." This is as true for option investors as for anyone else.

Those investors who succeed are focused. They take the time to define their goals and risk tolerances and, by doing so, define themselves as investors. They can then select those strategies that make sense. If you would like to be among this group of investors, to profit consistently by using options in appropriate ways that you understand completely, then a rational approach is the first step. Success does not come to those who do not prepare—a cliché to be sure, but one that is true. Success in the options market can be predictable and controllable. If you gain knowledge, learn the playing field, research the stocks as thoroughly as you pick their related options, and apply discipline in your decisions, then you will succeed. To some extent, you also need to experiment, to discover what it really is like to be in a particular situation in the options market and to find out how you will react when the market moves in the opposite direction than how you thought it would (or should) move. Without actually committing funds and being at risk, you cannot really know what it will be like, even if you have worked everything out on paper in advance. There is really no substitute for experience.

Devising a personal, individualized strategy is a rewarding experience. Seeing clearly what you need to do and then executing the strategy successfully gives you a sense of achievement and competence. You can profit from devising and applying a smart options strategy based on calculation and observation. You can also enjoy the satisfaction that comes from mastering a complex investment field and from realizing that you are completely and totally in control.

Glossary

annualized basis a method for comparing rates of return for holdings of varying periods, in which all returns are expressed as though investments had been held over a full year (It involves dividing the holding period by the number of months the positions were open, and multiplying the result by 12.)

assignment the act of exercise against a seller, done on a random basis or in accordance with orderly procedures developed by the Options Clearing Corporation and brokerage firms

at the money the status of an option when the underlying stock's market value is identical to the option's striking price

auction market the public exchanges, in which options, as well as stocks, bonds, and other publicly traded issues, are valued according to supply and demand (Demand drives up prices, while excess of supply softens the market and forces prices down. Those prices are bid upon by buyers and sellers.)

automatic exercise action taken by the Options Clearing Corporation at the time of expiration, when an in-the-money option has not been otherwise exercised or canceled

average down a strategy involving the purchase of stock when its market value is decreasing (The average cost of shares bought in this manner is consistently higher than current market value, so that a portion of the paper loss on declining stock value is absorbed, enabling covered call writers to sell calls and profit even when the stock's market value has declined.)

average up a strategy involving the purchase of stock when its market value is increasing (The average cost of shares buy 100 shares per month:

MONTH	PRICE	AVERAGE
Jan	$40	$40
Feb	38	39
Mar	36	38
Apr	34	37
May	27	35
Jun	29	34

FIGURE G.1   Average down.

buy 100 shares per month:

MONTH	PRICE	AVERAGE
Jan	$40	$40
Feb	44	42
Mar	45	43
Apr	47	44
May	54	46
Jun	52	47

FIGURE G.2   Average up.

bought in this manner is consistently lower than current market value, enabling covered call writers to sell calls in the money when the basis is below the striking price.)

bear spread   a strategy involving the purchase and sale of calls or puts that will produce maximum profits when the value of the underlying stock falls

beta   a measurement of relative volatility of a stock, made by comparing the degree of price movement in comparison to a larger index of stock prices

book value   the actual value of a company, more accurately called book value per share; the value of a company's capital (assets less liabilities), divided by the number of outstanding shares of stock

box spread   the combination of a bull spread and a bear spread, opened at the same time on the same underlying stock

break-even price (also called the **break-even point**) the price of the underlying stock at which the option investor breaks even (For call buyers, this price is the number of points above striking price equal to the call premium cost; for put buyers, this price is the number of points below striking price equal to the put premium cost.)

breakout the movement of a stock's price below support level or above resistance level

bull spread a strategy involving the purchase and sale of calls or puts that will produce maximum profits when the value of the underlying stock rises

butterfly spread a strategy involving open options in one striking price range, offset by transactions at higher and lower ranges at the same time

buyer an investor who purchases a call or a put option; the buyer realizes a profit if the value of the option rises above the purchase price

calendar spread a spread involving the simultaneous purchase or sale of options on the same underlying stock, with different expirations

call an option acquired by a buyer or granted by a seller to buy 100 shares of stock at a fixed price

called away the result of having stock assigned (Upon exercise, 100 shares of the seller's stock are called away at the striking price.)

class all options traded on a single underlying security, including different striking prices and expiration dates

closing purchase transaction a transaction to close a short position, executed by buying an option previously sold, canceling it out

closing sale transaction a transaction to close a long position, executed by selling an option previously bought, closing it out

combination any purchase or sale of options on one underlying stock, with terms that are not identical

contract a single option, the agreement providing a buyer with the rights the option grants (Those rights include identification of the stock, the cost of the option, the date the option will expire, and the fixed price per share of the stock to be bought or sold under the right of the option.)

conversion the process of moving assigned stock from the seller of a call option or to the seller of a put option

cover to protect oneself by owning 100 shares of the underlying stock for each call sold (The risk in the short position in the call is covered by the ownership of 100 shares.)

covered call a call sold to create an open short position, when the seller also owns 100 shares of stock for each call sold

credit spread any spread in which receipts from short positions are higher than premiums paid for long positions, net of transaction fees

current market value the market value of stock at any given time

cycle the pattern of expiration dates of options for a particular underlying stock (The three cycles occur in four-month intervals and are described by month abbreviations. They are (1) January, April, July, and October, or JAJO; (2) February, May, August, and November, or FMAN; and (3) March, June, September, and December, or MJSD.)

debit spread any spread in which receipts from short positions are lower than premiums paid for long positions, net of transaction fees

debt investment an investment in the form of loan made to earn interest, such as the purchase of a bond

deep in condition when the underlying stock's current market value is 5 points or more above the striking price of the call or below the striking price of the put

deep out condition when the underlying stock's current market value is 5 points or more below the striking price of the call or above the striking price of the put

delivery the movement of stock ownership from one owner to another (In the case of exercised stock, shares are registered to the new owner upon payment by the seller.)

delta the degree of change in option premium, in relation to changes in the underlying stock (If the call option's degree of change exceeds the change in the underlying stock, it is called an "up delta"; when the change is less

	CALLS	PUTS
48		
47	deep in	deep out
46		
45	- - - - - - -	- - - - - - -
44	in the	out of the
43	money	money
42		
41		
40	— striking price —	
39		
38	out of the	in the
37	money	money
36		
35	- - - - - - -	- - - - - - -
34		
33	deep out	deep in
32		

(left axis label: PRICE PER SHARE)

FIGURE G.3 Deep in/deep out.

stock price change	OPTION PREMIUM CHANGE			
	1 point	2 points	3 points	4 points
1	1.00	2.00	3.00	4.00
2	0.50	1.00	1.50	2.00
3	0.33	0.67	1.00	1.33
4	0.25	0.50	0.75	1.00
5	0.20	0.40	0.60	0.80

FIGURE G.4 Delta.

than the underlying stock, it is called a "down delta." The reverse terminology is applied to puts.)

diagonal spread a calendar spread in which offsetting long and short positions have both different striking prices and different expiration dates

discount to reduce the true price of the stock by the amount of premium received (A benefit in selling covered calls, the discount provides downside protection and protects long positions.)

dividend yield dividends paid per share of common stock, computed by dividing dividends paid per share by the current market value of the stock

dollar cost averaging a strategy for buying stocks at a fixed price over time (The result is an averaging of price. If the market value of stock increases, average cost is always below current market value; if market value of stock decreases, average cost is always above current market value.)

downside protection a strategy involving the purchase of one put for every 100 shares of the underlying stock that you own (This insures you against losses to some degree. For every in-the-money point the stock falls, the put will increase in value by 1 point. Before exercise, you may sell the put and take a profit offsetting stock losses, or exercise the put and sell the shares at the striking price.)

early exercise the act of exercising an option prior to expiration date

earnings per share a commonly used method for reporting profits, by which net profits for a year or other period are divided by the number of shares of common stock outstanding as of the ending date of the financial report (The result is expressed as a dollar value.)

equity investment an investment in the form of part ownership, such as the purchase of shares of stock in a corporation

exercise the act of buying stock under the terms of the call option or selling stock under the terms of the put option, at the specified price per share in the option contract

expiration date the date on which an option becomes worthless, which is specified in the option contract

expiration time the latest possible time to place an order for cancellation or exercise of an option, which may vary depending on the brokerage firm executing the order and on the option itself

hedge a strategy involving the use of one position to protect another (For example, stock is purchased in the belief it will rise in value, and a put is purchased on the same stock to protect against the risk that market value will decline.)

horizontal spread a calendar spread in which offsetting long and short positions have identical striking prices but different expiration dates

incremental return a technique for avoiding exercise while increasing profits with written calls (When the value of the underlying stock rises, a single call is closed at a loss and replaced with two or more call writes with later expiration dates, producing cash and a profit in the exchange.)

in the money the status of a call option when the underlying stock's market value is higher than the option's striking price, or of a put option when the underlying stock's market value is lower than the option's striking price

intrinsic value that portion of an option's current value equal to the number of points that it is in the money ("Points" equals the number of dollars of value per share; so 35 points equals $35 per share.)

last trading day the Friday preceding the third Saturday of the expiration month of an option

leverage the use of investment capital in a way that a relatively small amount of money enables the investor to control a relatively large value. (This is achieved through borrowing—for example, using borrowed money to purchase stocks or bonds—or through the purchase of options, which exist for only a short period of time but

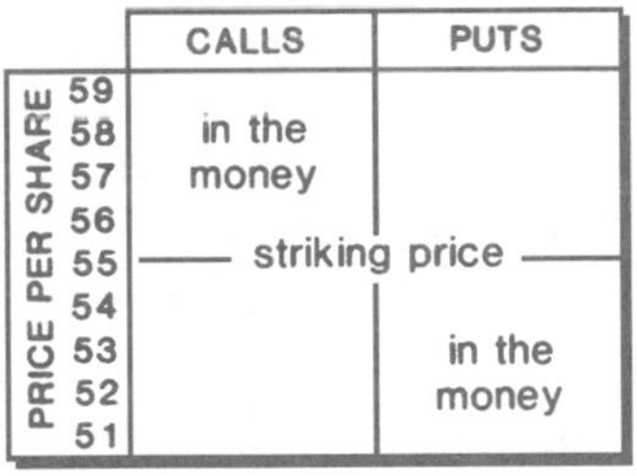

	CALLS	PUTS
PRICE PER SHARE 59 58 57 56 55 54 53 52 51	in the money ——— striking price ———	in the money

FIGURE G.5 In the money.

STOCK VALUE	STRIKING PRICE	INTRINSIC VALUE
$38	$35	$3
43	45	0
41	40	1
65	65	0
21	20	1

FIGURE G.6 Intrinsic value.

enable the option buyer to control 100 shares of stock. As a general rule, the use of leverage increases potential for profit as well as for loss.)

listed option an option traded on a public exchange and listed in the published reports in the financial press

lock in to freeze the price of the underlying stock when the investor owns a corresponding short call (As long as the call position is open, the writer is locked into a striking price, regardless of current market value of the stock. In the event of exercise, the stock is delivered at that locked-in price.)

long hedge the purchase of options as a form of insurance to protect a portfolio position in the event of a price increase, a strategy employed by investors selling stock short and insuring against a rise in the market value of the stock

long position the status assumed by investors when they enter a buy order in advance of entering a sell order (The long position is closed by later entering a sell order, or through expiration.)

long straddle the purchase of an identical number of calls and puts with identical striking prices and expiration dates, designed to produce profits in the event of price movement of the underlying stock in either direction adequate to surpass the cost of opening the position

loss zone the price range of the underlying stock in which the option investor loses. (A limited loss exists for option buyers, since the premium cost is the maximum loss that can be realized.)

margin an account with a brokerage firm containing a minimum level of cash and securities to provide collateral for short positions or for purchases for which payment has not yet been made

market order an order from an investor to a broker to buy or sell at the best available price

market value the value of an investment at any given time or date; the amount a buyer is willing to pay to acquire an investment and what a seller is also willing to receive to transfer the same investment

married put the status of a put used to hedge a long position (Each put owned protects 100 shares of the underlying stock held in the portfolio. If the stock declines in value, the put's value will increase and offset the loss.)

money spread alternate name for the vertical spread

naked option an option sold in an opening sale transaction when the seller (writer) does not own 100 shares of the underlying stock

naked position status for investors when they assume short positions in calls without also owning 100 shares of the underlying stock for each call written

opening purchase transaction an initial transaction to buy, also known as the action of "going long"

opening sale transaction an initial transaction to sell, also known as the action of "going short"

open interest the number of open contracts of a particular option at any given time, which can be used to measure market interest

open position the status of a transaction when a purchase (a long position) or a sale (a short position) has been made, and before cancellation, exercise, or expiration

option the right to buy or to sell 100 shares of stock at a specified, fixed price and by a specified date in the future

out of the money the status of a call option when the underlying stock's market value is lower than the option's striking price, or of a put option when the underlying

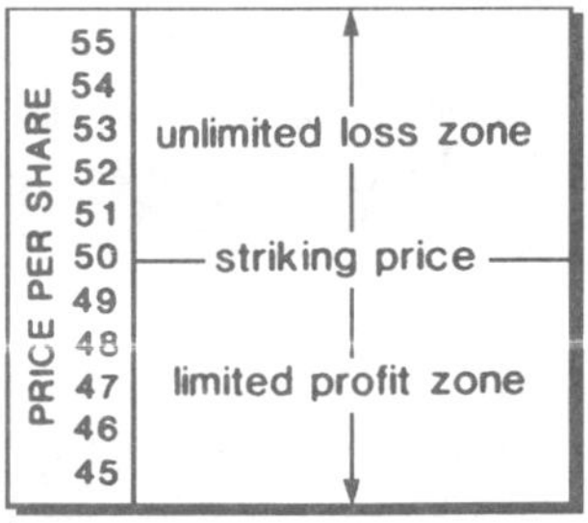

FIGURE G.7 Naked option.

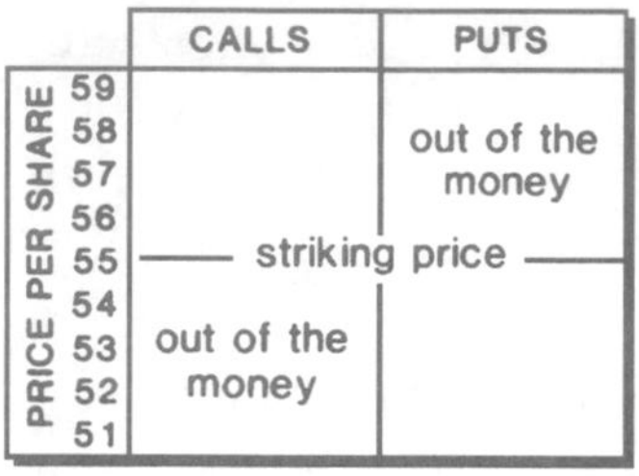

FIGURE G.8 Out of the money.

stock's market value is higher than the option's striking price

paper profits (also called **unrealized profits**) values existing only on paper but not taken at the time; paper profits (or paper losses) become realized only if a closing transaction is executed

parity the condition of an option at expiration, when the total premium consists of intrinsic value and no time value

premium The current price of an option, which a buyer pays and a seller receives at the time of the transaction (The amount of premium is expressed as the price per share, without dollar signs; for example, stating that an option is "at 3" means its current market value is $300.)

price/earnings ratio a popular indicator used by stock market investors to rate and compare stocks, by which the current market value of the stock is divided by the most recent earnings per share to arrive at the P/E ratio

profit margin the most commonly used measurement of corporate operations, computed by dividing net profits by gross sales

profit on invested capital a fundamental test showing the yield to equity investors in the company, computed by dividing net profits by the dollar value of outstanding capital

profit zone the price range of the underlying stock in which the option investor realizes a profit (For the call buyer, the profit zone extends upward from the break-even price. For the put buyer, the profit zone extends downward from the break-even price.)

put an option acquired by a buyer or granted by a seller to sell 100 shares of stock at a fixed price

put to seller action of exercising a put and requiring the seller to purchase 100 shares of stock at the fixed striking price

random walk a theory about market pricing, stating that prices of stocks cannot be predicted because price movement is entirely random

rate of return the yield from investing, calculated by dividing net cash profit upon sale by the amount spent at purchase

ratio calendar combination spread a strategy involving both a ratio between purchases and sales and a box spread (Long and short positions are opened on options with the same underlying stock, in varying numbers of contracts and with expiration dates extending over two or more periods. This strategy is designed to produce profits in the event of price increases or decreases in the market value of the underlying stock.)

ratio calendar spread a strategy involving a different number of options on the long side of a transaction from the number on the short side, when the expiration dates for each side are also different. (This strategy creates two separate profit and loss zone ranges, one of which disappears upon the earlier expiration.)

ratio write a strategy for partially covering one position with another for partial rather than full coverage (A portion of risk is eliminated, so that ratio writes can be used to reduce overall risk levels.)

realized profits profits or losses taken at the time a position is closed

resistance level the price for a stock identifying the highest likely trading price under present conditions, above which the price of the stock is not likely to rise

return if exercised the estimated rate of return option sellers will earn in the event the buyer exercises the option (The calculation includes profit or loss on the underlying stock, dividends earned, and premium received for selling the option.)

```
exercise price 40
purchase price 38
May 40 call sold for 3
dividends earned $80
```

call premium	$300
dividend income	80
capital gain	200
return	$580
	15.3%

FIGURE G.9 Return if exercised.

basis in stock $3800

sold May 40 call	$300
dividends earned	80
total	$380
return	10.0%

FIGURE G.10 Return if unchanged.

return if unchanged the estimated rate of return option sellers will earn in the event the buyer does not exercise the option (The calculation includes dividends earned on the underlying stock, and the premium received for selling the option.)

reverse hedge an extension of a long or short hedge in which more options are opened than the number needed to cover the stock position; this increases profit potential in the event of unfavorable movement in the market value of the underlying stock

roll down the replacement of one written call with another that has a lower striking price

roll forward the replacement of one written call with another with the same striking price, but a later expiration date

roll up the replacement of one written call with another that has a higher striking price

seller an investor who grants the rights in an option to someone else; the seller realizes a profit if the value of the option falls below the sale price

series a group of options sharing identical terms

settlement date the date on which a buyer is required to pay for purchases, or on which a seller is entitled to receive payment (For stocks, settlement date is five business days after the transaction. For options, settlement date is one business day from the date of the transaction.)

share a unit of ownership in the capital of a corporation

short hedge the purchase of options as a form of insurance to protect a portfolio position in the event of a price decrease, a strategy employed by investors in long positions and insuring against a decline in the market value of the stock

short position the status assumed by investors when they enter a sale order in advance of entering a buy order (The short position is closed by later entering a buy order, or through expiration.)

short straddle the sale of an identical number of calls and puts with identical striking prices and expiration dates, designed to produce profits in the event of price movement of the underlying stock only within a limited range

speculation the use of money to assume risks for short-term profit, in the knowledge that substantial or total losses are one possible outcome (Buying calls for leverage is one form of speculation. The buyer may earn a very large profit in a matter of days, or could lose the entire amount invested.)

spread the simultaneous purchase and sale of options on the same underlying stock, with different striking prices or expiration dates, or both (The purpose of the spread is to increase potential profits while also reducing risks in the event that the value of the underlying stock does not move as anticipated, or to take advantage of the timing of the stock's price movement.)

standardized terms same as "terms"

stop-limit order an order from an investor to a broker to buy or sell at a specified price (or within a specified range)

stop order an order from an investor to a broker to buy at or above a specified price, or to sell at or below a specified price level (Once that level has been met or passed, the order becomes a market order.)

straddle the simultaneous purchase and sale of the same number of calls and puts with identical striking prices and expiration dates

striking price the fixed price to be paid for 100 shares of stock specified in the option contract, which will be paid or received by the owner of the option contract upon exercise, regardless of the current market value of the stock

suitability a standard by which a particular investment or market strategy is judged (The investor's knowledge and experience with options represent important suitability standards. Strategies are appropriate only if the investor understands the market and can afford to take the risks involved.)

support level the price for a stock identifying the lowest likely trading price under present conditions, below which the price of the stock is not likely to fall

tax put a strategy combining the sale of stock at a loss—taken for tax purposes—and the sale of a put at the same time (The premium received on the put offsets the stock loss; if the put is exercised, the stock is purchased at the striking price.)

terms the attributes that describe an option, including the striking price, expiration month, type of option (call or put), and the underlying security

time spread alternate term for the calendar spread

time value that portion of an option's current value above intrinsic value

total return the combined return including income from selling a call, capital gain from a profit on selling the stock, and dividends earned and received (Total return

TOTAL PREMIUM	INTRINSIC VALUE	TIME VALUE
$4	$3	$1
2	0	2
4	1	3
1	0	1
3	1	2

FIGURE G.11 Time value.

stock exercised at
$40 (basis $34),
held for 13 months:

option premium	$ 800
dividends	110
capital gain	600
total	$1510
13 months	44.4%
annualized	41.0%

FIGURE G.12 Total return.

may be calculated in two ways: return if the option is exercised, and return if the option expires worthless.)

uncovered option the same as a naked option—the sale of an option not covered, or protected, by the ownership of 100 shares of the underlying stock

underlying stock the stock on which the option grants the right to buy or sell, which is specified in every option contract

variable hedge a hedge involving a long position and a short position in related options, when one side contains a greater number of options than the other (The desired result is reduction of risks or potentially greater profits.)

vertical spread a spread involving different striking prices but identical expiration dates

volatility a measure of the degree of change in a stock's market value, measured over a 12-month period and stated as a percentage (To measure volatility, subtract the lowest 12-month price from the highest 12-month

$$\frac{\text{high} - \text{low}}{\text{low}}$$

ANNUAL HIGH	ANNUAL LOW	PERCENT
$ 65	$ 43	51%
37	34	9
45	41	10
35	25	4
84	62	35
71	68	4
118	101	17
154	112	38

FIGURE G.13 Volatility.

price, and divide the answer by the 12-month lowest price.)

volume the level of trading activity in a stock, an option, or the market as a whole

wasting asset any asset that declines in value over time (An option is an example of a wasting asset because it exists only until expiration, after which it becomes worthless.)

writer the individual who sells (writes) a call (or a put)

Index